THE ENLISTED

THE PRICE OF SERVICE NO ONE TELLS YOU

SKYLA PEARSON

The Enlisted

The Price of Service No One Tells You

First Edition

Published by Tactical 16 Publishing, LLC Colorado Springs, CO

ISBN 978-1-943226-63-4 (paperback)

ACKNOWLEDGMENTS

I owe a sincere thank you to the numerous souls who serve our country.

It gives me great pleasure to render a specific thank you to the service women and men I know personally that I have had the honor of serving with – *especially* those who sat with me throughout this book's journey. All the opinions, reviews, and support that have been gifted to me from my military buddies are kept close to my heart with deep gratitude.

Thank you to my parents for your unyielding belief in my dreams.

Thank you to my brother for being the largest sum of my reasons to stay motivated.

Thank you to my closest family and friends who have supported me in every way possible.

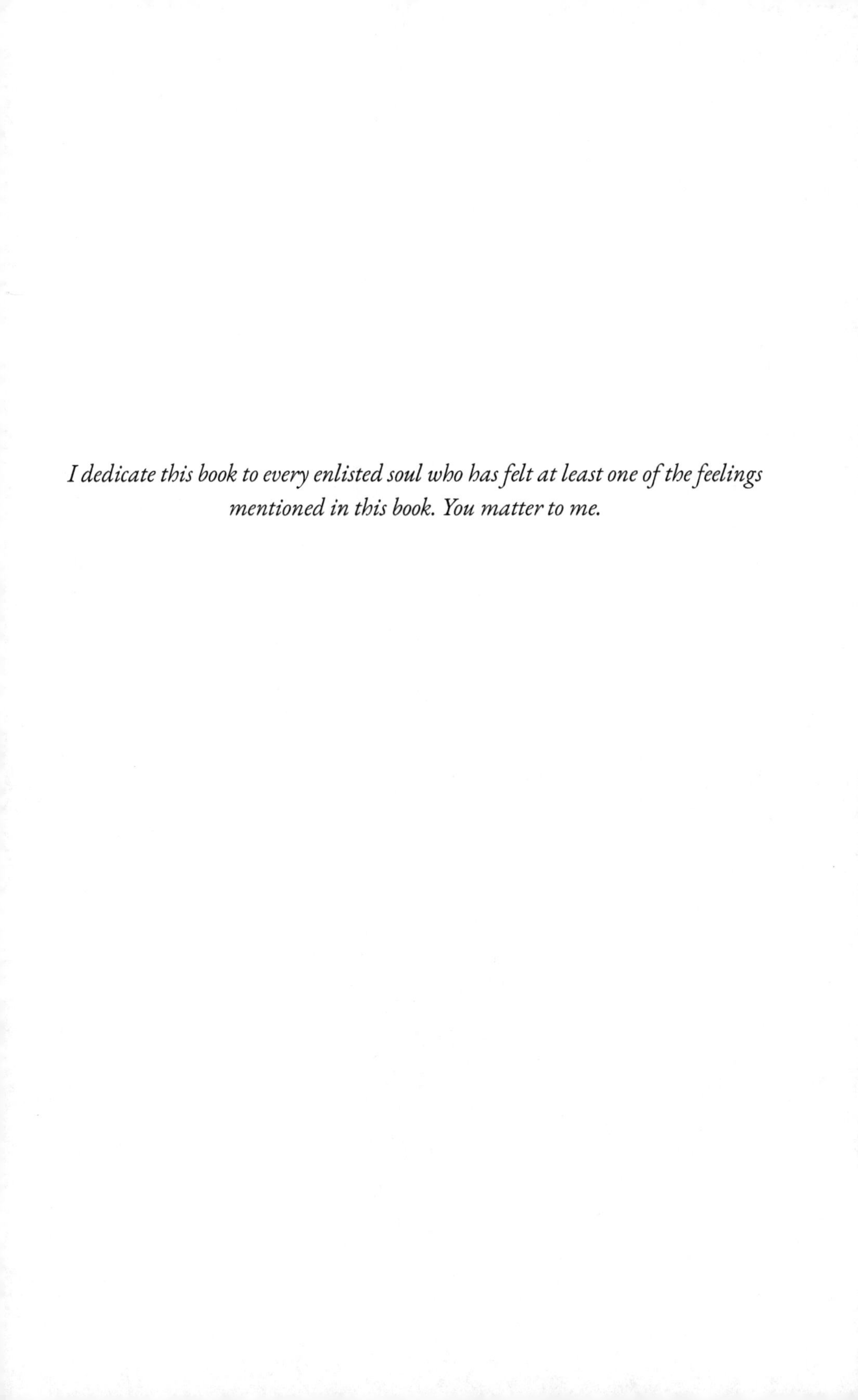

I dedicate this book to every enlisted soul who has felt at least one of the feelings mentioned in this book. You matter to me.

CONTENTS

PART I

HOW IT ALL STARTED

1

WHY DID I JOIN THE NAVY?

T*his is some bullshit*!

Bullshit, bullshit, bullshit!

Harsh, I know, but the sentiment was the only thought echoing loudly in the back of my head on a constant loop. Exhaustion had taken over every fiber of my being as I dragged my sore, sluggish body toward my designated bunk in my floating workplace. It was another brutally long and physically demanding shift, but there would not be an opportunity to wind down and relax because Uncle Sam laughed off the idea of solace by way of an unexpected announcement.

The deployment would be extended *AGAIN*.

It wasn't as if the captain's words were foreign to me because this was the third time I'd heard them on this particular deployment, but this time the gravity of it was far heavier than ever before. It felt like I had the weight of a sumo wrestler juggling elephants on my shoulders, to be exact. And though I'd been strong enough to internalize the words our captain had delivered so callously, they chipped away at my numbed emotions until my dwindling patience was raw and exposed.

The strong, unbreakable Black woman façade that I became accustomed to wearing began to melt at the heat of the announcement. When I'd originally received the news that we were deploying, it was with the promise that I'd be returned to my own queen-sized bed by now, instead of my berthing quarters, and would be able to walk freely around Hanford, the California town in the south-central San Joaquin Valley where I live.

I'd spent weeks marking the days in my mind's calendar, and the ones on the calendar that hung inside my rack. Each big '*X*' that was drawn through the dates served as an emotional anchor and emphasized how close I was to being able to see my parents or be in the arms of my loving guy again. But now, they were nothing more than a mocking reminder of the dashed hopes and deception the military constantly served up on a shiny red, white, and blue platter.

The news was a devastating two-piece blow to my psyche and emotions, threatening to make my knees buckle right then and there as I made my way through the floating vessel navigating through a Middle Eastern sea. To say I was homesick would be the biggest understatement of the century, but when you compounded the swelling disappointment in the pit of my stomach that the extension created with the reason for delay to dry land, it was enough to make anyone physically sick. And a compromised immune system during *this* deployment could cost a sailor their life.

When we first got the orders to ship out, no one could have predicted the outbreak of an airborne coronavirus called SARS-CoV-2, also known as COVID-19, that would cause a global pandemic and change the entire landscape of how the world would operate. There has never been a time in my recent memory that I can recall the same widespread uncertainty and terror that came over everyone when the number of cases began to rise to alarming numbers at breakneck speeds. The number of rumors and stories that spawned from the outbreak became mortifying and hard to keep up with. News outlets around the world presented coverage of the pandemic, and that left every sailor and civilian on my ship with nothing else to talk about.

"The news says the virus began its transmission from a host of exotic bats..."

"I hear the virus originated in Asia..."

"...It seems depression and suicide rates have spiked since the start of Covid-19..."

"Apparently the CDC recommends that you wear protective face coverings in public and maintain a safe social distance of six feet or more..."

"My family makes their own masks to save money..."

Never-ending coverage of this mysterious and rapidly spreading threat left me anxious as virus-related deaths broke record numbers before anyone could even determine its origins or fully understand its symptoms. The sailors on board my ship – nearly 5,000 – were stir-crazy and in limbo with no idea of when we would be able to have person-to-person contact with civilization outside our vessel, let alone with our loved ones.

As I entered my makeshift 'room' with sorrow and frustration playing tug-of-war with my emotions, I was forced to renege what already limited control of my life that I had to quarantine in the dank, lonely, military-commissioned vessel for an undetermined amount of time. Under these conditions, stuck at sea indefinitely while the people dearest to my heart fought a deadly disease nobody knew how to properly combat, I pondered a full array of questions about what led me to this moment.

"Why in the hell did I even join the Navy?" I mumbled bitterly to myself as I stood next to my rack trying to draft up an escape plan.

I'd asked myself that question multiple times during my enlistment, mostly during times when I'd be forced to wake up at the ass crack of dawn for drills or to stand watch – moments when my individuality was watered down to the point that I nearly didn't recognize myself in the mirror once donning my uniform. Before now though, the feelings of confusion would have dissipated, but this wasn't one of those past times.

The news of the extension rocked me to my core and made me reexamine my existence in a career that provided me a cushy life when I was off duty or simply in port. Every civilian who discovered I was active-duty military would high-five my hand and sing me praises. To them, I was living the dream: in my mid-twenties, a homeowner without any children, I had a stable career that not only paid the bills but left money in my pockets afterward.

But the shiny, materialistic glow that came from brand new items had dulled and was no longer worth the ride on the emotional roller coaster I had to endure to receive them. The sense of pride that used to cloak my entire being when I slipped into my service blues was long gone, replaced by a severe case of signer's remorse for agreeing to turn over the reins of my life to a system that had no respect for who I was as an individual – a program where, beneath the government label, I was simply another enlisted sailor who had fallen for the same bait and switch sweet talk that the recruiters used to lure wide-eyed fresh meat into the program. The deceit from a country I'd personally pledged my life to protect made my heart ache.

Had I known it was going to be all of this, I never would have enlisted, I sulked to myself while unlacing the strings of my heavy work boots. Without the strength or will to completely pull them from my feet, I let my recently polished boots hit the floor like two tar-colored bricks. Part of me wanted to erupt into a fit of angry tears while rampaging through the ship like the Tasmanian devil in protest of the extension, snatching up everything in my path and flipping it upside down with no remorse since no one batted an eyelash when the Navy did the same to my life. The other portion of my being longed to feel the strong, warm, and supportive embrace of my man to quell the anxiety that was building in my chest. I wanted off the boat and on land *NOW*!

Surprisingly enough, the deepest realizations can occur at the apex of confusion. Right before you black out into a fit of blind, uncontrollable anger, there's a split second of clarity that unveils an alternate resolution.

It was as if I'd been dipped in cement and left on the boat to eventually dry in place or drown at sea; I was stuck.

Worst of all, I was in this position without ever being given the real information that any sane sailor-to-be would want to be aware of before making the life-altering, fully informed decision to sign a military contract, not just the cushy perks and service rhetoric the recruiters spew at young civilians to make them think the armed forces, specifically the Navy, is the golden ticket they've been waiting for.

While standing next to my designated, rectangular space – that now seemed more like a coffin – recollections of conversations I'd had with other sailors who both shared the same sentiments and looked like me came to mind: female, minority, or both, trying to cope and maneuver in a field that drew us in with alluring promises but only reluctantly welcomed us after we were officially sworn in. If we were in relationships where our significant others whispered all the sweet nothings we wanted to hear and then blindsided us with their true darkness when we least expected it, that would be deemed a toxic relationship, right? But when the culprit that's misleading us is the United States government, it's simply a deeply embedded part of the recruiting process.

Still beside my smaller-than-a-twin-size rack, my stomach twisted in knots, a resolution for my displeasure became clear! *No one* was ever 100 percent honest with me about the intricacies of day-to-day life for sailors at the entry level that we'd have to endure to simply maintain our positions – the real dirt and grime that lurks beneath the national emblem we pledge allegiance to. *I* was going to drop that truth bomb that no one else wanted to drop.

I'm going to do it, I determined, snapping myself out of the trance I'd fallen into after gazing at the untied boots now flopping on my feet after I'd roughly slipped back into them in my inspired scurry. Snatching a pen and notebook from my rack, I rushed the short distance to the berthing's lounge, found a comfortably worn cushion on the same tattered sofa that hundreds of sailors had plopped down on for years, and began to make an account of everything I wish I would have known or been smart enough to ask before signing that dotted line. Focused and determined to help at least one person see the full picture before making a multi-year commitment where the only thing that was truly certain was uncertainty itself, I jotted down each and every topic a civilian should know before they become one of the enlisted.

AND SO IT BEGINS

There is a misconception among most parents of school-aged children that high school is the most formative time in their students' social lives. For me, however, middle school was where the seeds for my future were planted. It was in the halls of Neshoba Central that the idea to join the Navy began.

Without discrimination, I was the girl who associated with everyone in school. It didn't matter if you were in oversized, dark clothes and had pale skin with heavy black eyeliner and lipstick, the prissy girl who was slightly haughty, or the four-eyed bookworm who would rather hang out in the library than at a football game, if you were a part of the Rocket student body, that was all the connection needed for me to strike up a conversation.

Now, thinking back on it, some may have considered me as being odd. While everyone else carefully picked who they associated with based on common ethnic, economic, or religious backgrounds, I was the anomaly who didn't care about the well-defined lines that the cliques had created for each other. I'd jump over them every time to create genuine bonds that would, unbeknownst to me, bode well for me throughout the years.

A result to being an open-minded individual was that it put my name and face in the minds of people who I may have never shared a class with. The ability to freely maneuver through my school's corridors and meet people allowed me the capacity to not only listen but understand different points of view. It taught me how to empathize with issues within the school and world that didn't necessarily affect my own personal life.

The foundation that was laid in middle school began to pay off for me once I moved on to my high school years. A social butterfly who'd been flapping her wings in middle school soared. For under and upper classman alike, I applied the same formula: kindness, honesty, and empathy, and won them all over.

It's funny because there's a stereotype about teenagers that portrays them as selfish and unable to see past their noses. For me, that wasn't the case. Whenever a peer needed help with homework, an assignment, spare change, or anything else within reason, there I was. Extending that olive branch to everyone without prejudice was rewarded in abundance when school election ballots that had my name on them rolled around.

This constant wave of support helped me win nearly every single campaign I threw my name into the hat for, making me eligible for any high school club I desired. Was my record flawless? No, not at all. Even though no one wants to feel the crushing blow of defeat, I am a firm believer that every single thing ain't for everybody.

My campaign victories led me to become the freshman maid, an honor that was bestowed upon the winner during one of the most thrilling times of high school life: homecoming season! It was exhilarating to be honored with the title, draped with a decorative sash, and highlighted at every mention of the celebration. But it was an even more humbling to know that those who chose me were fine with me shining.

As a bona fide people person, I had garnered their support in a *genuine* way. I didn't trick them into putting me into the freshman maid position. My integrity spoke for itself. When I was selected as the student body vice president *on top* of the homecoming honor in my back pocket, I was convinced that this philosophy was the key to success:

There's a way to create and inspire leaders and its definitely not by baiting them with mistruths.

It was in all the campaigning that I'd done through the years that I came to realize I loved working in a team setting. There was something about the well of joy that seeped from my pores whenever I was a part of a collective focused on a common objective.

As a young Black girl growing up, I was thankful that I was able to realize the traits that made me great at such a young age – a true blessing bestowed upon me from a woman who absolutely refused to see me do anything other than succeed: my mother, of course. She is almost solely responsible for the abundant charm that I had at that moment in time, with a double dose of charisma to boot. Learning never was never a challenge since I'd always been a quick and competitive student.

The only thing that God seemed to have forgotten to give me when he was handing out personal attributes was athleticism.

And when I tell you I wanted to be an athlete *so* bad...listen!

I could sit on the far end of the bleachers and watch the female players on the basketball team practice for *hours*. My eyes would widen in amazement at how effortlessly they shot the ball from long distances. I'd scan my brain trying to figure out how they'd become so fast and how they could run so long without passing out in the center of the court!

It was mesmerizing to the say the least. In no way was I able to jump very high or sport a jersey as well as the talented and fit female athletes who seemed to naturally grace my school's teams, but beyond the physicality, there was pure magic to be found in witnessing the discovery of different ways to unite with other individuals for a common goal.

Black, white, yellow, purple, or green, none of that mattered if you had skills and dedication. I was also intrigued by the student-athletes' laser-like focus on maintaining their grades *and* being a contributing factor on their team. Athletes were a tight knit collective that had each other's backs, and I longed to participate in that bond. I wanted to bask in that addictive magic that made crowds flock to games day in and day out.

And then there were the letterman jackets.

Heavy, durable, and ever so cool, the letterman jacket is just one trophy of the golden trio of staple pieces of high school memorabilia that was coveted by *everyone*. You know the trio: the class ring, the diploma, and the infamous letterman jacket. The sleek, leather sleeves and school's insignia on the chest made the jacket a badge of honor. I knew I *had* to get that jacket and be a part of a team, but I had no clue of how I was going to make it happen.

Until it hit me like a school bus.

Back in middle school, I had the honor of watching the color guard from the United States Navy perform at my school during a Friday night football game. The color guard is a group of sailors who participate in highly choreographed and ceremonial presentations of our nation's flag. Like the same athletes I admired, they wowed me from the moment I first saw them. The dark blue uniforms looked like they'd just come from the cleaners with the sharp creases and ornate buttons. Their shoes were shiny enough for me to see the wearer's reflection on the highly polished leather.

Their guns were less than ten feet away from my gated, sideline gaze! There seemed to be a million of them in my pubescent mind. Long, shiny weapons that I'd been taught were only murderous killing machines were being swirled around and tossed through the air in perfect synchronicity like they were measly batons.

The same jolt of astonishment that shot through me that day I saw the color guard was comparable to what I experienced when watching student-athletes take center stage. Sure, there were slight differences; the jocks at school weren't twirling guns in the air or marching around with the American flag. But they worked together toward a common goal: presenting themselves and the colors of our country with pride. If one person was off in timing or out of step, it could mess up everything. It seemed a lofty challenge with worthy rewards.

That's it, I thought.

With the memory of the color guard's performance playing in my mind, I bounced around the idea of joining my high school's NJROTC. The Navy Junior Reserve Officers' Training Corps is a program created in collaboration with the United States military and Department of Education as an offshoot of the National Defense Act of 1916. Its mission, at first, was to teach cadets across the country the importance of citizenship, defending the honor of the country we called home, and completing acts of service.

I didn't see a reason not to join. At the time, NJROTC checked all the boxes that made the decision seem like a no-brainer. The course would count toward my curriculum credits for graduation, I'd get to do athletic-type things to appease that appetite, and I'd learn skills that would help when it was time to step into the 'real' world. Like I did with a majority of the most complicated issues in my life, I called my best friend Janera to seek her guidance in making the right choice.

Janera was that best girlfriend that every teenager needed. Though we were different, we fit together perfectly from the moment we met. She knew me like no other and there was nothing I could hide from her. So, when I explained my uncertainty about joining NJROTC, she absorbed it all in silence.

It wasn't until I'd spilled every concern, probability, and caution in her direction that she finally spoke.

"Skyla, you know you my girl," she started. "I got yo back. So, if you really want to do this...I'll join with you."

My heart nearly exploded out of my chest when that kind offer escaped her mouth and met my ears. Chills went through me. Janera was a lot of things: pretty, funny, quick-witted... but the one thing she never was, was a yes man. Her willingness to go through such great depths to show her support made me feel like joining could have been the best move to make.

Once Janera validated that the thoughts running through my head didn't sound like nonsense or would ruin my high school experience, it was time to speak to my parents. Sorting my thoughts out with Janera made presenting the idea to them a million times easier. This was one of the first major decisions that I was taking to my parents regarding my future.

Not only were my palms sweaty, but every fact that I'd researched and committed to memory added to my rising level of nerves and charged through my mind like a bullet train when I sat in front of them. Don't get me wrong; although I was nervous, I wasn't afraid. My success as both a woman and student were top priority to my parents, and they firmly agreed that joining NJROTC would be nothing short of beneficial.

Armed with the support of everyone I cared about most, I found a new challenge to undertake. Within a week of the conversation, I signed up for NJROTC and hit the ground running like Wile E. Coyote. Little did I know at the time, junior ROTC programs are prime grooming grounds for the armed forces. Had I known that this would be one of the first and last times that I felt a genuine sense of excitement in relation to the military, I wouldn't have even started down that path.

A robust sense of responsibility gripped me from the moment I first put on a cadet uniform. I spent hours ensuring that each piece was perfectly pressed and that there was not a loose thread in sight. I made sure that my relaxed hair was pulled back and slicked down into the neatest bun imaginable. Exhilarated at the possibilities this new endeavor could hold, I was determined to be the most pristine and respectable version of what an NJROTC cadet was supposed to present.

Like everything else I attempted, when I became a NJROTC cadet, I stopped at nothing to excel in every area I possibly could. Though I was now a part of a united team effort like I'd always wanted, there was still a lingering thought in the back of my head: *You're not an athlete, so you're still not good enough.*

The nagging bout with the negative self-talk was one that I'd battle for years, but in the beginning I convinced myself that it was my subconscious way of pushing past my limitations – a way of tricking my mind into believing I was motivating myself. Most of the cadets were stronger, faster, or more agile than I was in some capacity or another, but I had far more grit than anyone could imagine. Even myself.

Every day was harder than the next in the beginning. There was so much information about our country's armed forces to learn that it constantly felt like random military facts and jargon would start spewing out of my ears at any given time. To go from living a 'normal' life to a more regimented one that included uniform care and intense workouts took time to adjust to, but I did.

Determined not to be the weak link in the chain, I buckled down and busted my ass hard enough to earn a spot on nearly every team within our group. Was I trying to be a showoff? No. But was I showing out? Absolutely. Bullheaded since birth, it was in my nature to go as hard as I could to get the results that I wanted. I was dedicated to standing out in NJROTC and there was nothing that could stop me from being the best.

I did extra reps while working out to make myself stronger. I obsessed over the amount of sit ups that I could do, making sure that I didn't start or end a day without completing hundreds. I ran longer distances to boost my endurance and even used weights to strengthen my muscles. And thankfully, my hard work paid off. Because of my borderline obsession with greatness, I was able to excel in the push up, sit-up, and sprint tests and to earn a spot on the unarmed exhibition drill team.

My program chief and commander took notice of me and how hard I worked. And that made them push me harder. Their expectations were high but because I had my own set of insane goals, I blew them out of the water. It only made sense to be the group's gold standard.

Because I was good enough to excel is so many areas, it rocketed my stock in NJROTC. I was allowed to participate in the activities that made us all feel like rock stars. Just like the students on the sporting teams, we were able to travel across the country showing our stuff and building a lofty reputation.

The rush of it all was a thrill in the beginning. As a freshman, I was able to go out of town for competitions without parental supervision. These were the best times, and our team experienced new sights and how different parts of the country operated within each state's lines. Some places were lively while others were more slow-paced and laid back.

We even got to see the beauty of military discounts and perks early on, too. You see, unlike most programs that cut corners when it came to transportation and accommodations, we didn't go on cheap, cross-county field trips. These were overnight and sometimes over-the-weekend adventures. These were fun trips that never found us in cheap, hole-in-the wall motels with goopy, runny food from greasy diners that barely met health code standards.

That was not our testimony.

We got to stay in suites that seemed like the lap of luxury to our teenage standards. Our hotels had sleek furniture that looked like it had never been sat on before – colorful, yet classy paintings hanging on the walls, and some of the plushest beds known to mankind. And if there was a pool or a beach nearby, there was absolutely nothing you could tell our excited group of cadets!

Each time we were away from home we were catered to in a way that made all the hard work that it took to continue through the program worth it.

Another beautiful thing that came from being a cadet was that it expanded my reach far beyond the students who attended our school. At competitions and summer camps, packs of sailors-in-training got together and had a blast when the time allowed it. We worked hard to be at these competitions as often as we could and even made the NJROTC National Drill Competition both my freshman and senior years.

Whenever anyone inquired about why we were able to get such great accommodations it was always credited to our positive behavior and hard work – we were cadets who continuously brought home first place trophies! Whenever we brought these trophies home it not only garnered publicity for our school but for the NJROTC program as well. Of course, this had a trickle up effect that would elicit glowing reviews for the military – making it look even better to the civilian public for creating and maintaining such an enriching program targeted at 'the future of this great nation.'

What no one knew, though, was that as my time continued in the program, it became more and more taxing on me. As I climbed the ranks in NJROTC, it began to require even more of my already limited time. My time in NJROTC made my lifestyle during high school so much different from that of the typical high school student, but back then I was too blinded to be bothered by it.

The social butterfly that I once was had begun flapping away in the distance and I found myself in the constant loop of routine. The other friendships I'd worked hard to garner slowly began to dissipate. Not to say I was alone because, of course, I wasn't. I had a cluster of friends who were in the program with me; however, the friendships and relationships that I had with those outside of NJROTC were fading fast.

While most girls my age were crushing on the popular boy with the fly new shoes or hanging out at the movies, I had the ideals of the United States military seared into my brain. There were only a few people who weren't living my daily reality who sincerely wanted to talk or hear about the inner workings of what we went through in the program. If it wasn't a person who knew the swelling anxiety that came from worrying about being caught out of uniform dress code or memorizing your routine for the next competition, how could a regular student relate?

And there was truly no one to blame for the disconnect, because who really wants to sit around and discuss running laps for hours in the rain in order to build endurance unless you've gone through it? Who can understand waking up before the sun comes up to practice drills? I tried my best to juggle it all and squeeze out as much quality time as possible with family and friends outside of the program, but it was exhausting! My primary focus, along with maintaining good grades in school, was related to NJROTC. Once it drew close to graduation, those other friendships were virtually non-existent.

I spent all four years at Neshoba Central High School in NJROTC. That's right, my whole high school career was dedicated to the program. It was trying, to say the least, but that hard work and dedication did pay off by way of climbing up the ranks as high as the program's ladder went. I earned every single ribbon a cadet was eligible to receive. I was respected by both my peers and superiors in the program, and that felt good. Touted as a true leader, I reached the rank of executive officer (commonly referred to as XO) of my fellow cadets; I was their superior and I didn't take that honor lightly.

The most glorious thing of it all, the thing that truly made all the early mornings, insane workouts, screaming, running, and missing out on functions and normal high school shenanigans worth it by the end was the satisfaction that came from collecting that elusive golden trio of high school trinkets every student longed for. Since I'd maintained my grades, I received my high school diploma with no problem. My parents were thrilled that I hadn't ended up as another statistic and were more than willing to pay for my class ring. And as a result of being in NJROTC all four years, I received that cool ass letterman jacket I had coveted so much as a freshman – the item that led me to sign up for the program in the first place.

Once I marched across the stage, shook hands with the principal, and flung my cap into the air in coordination with the other students in my graduating class, I was done with NJROTC and everything that had anything to do with it. When it was time to take off that uniform for the last time, I shoved it deep, *deep* in the back of my closet behind everything that I knew I'd never wear again to avoid looking at it. I had no desire to research the different branches of the military or any urge to speak with recruiters regarding the next step or how I would be able to have the military fund my postsecondary education.

I was done.

There was no longer *one* morsel of desire for me to continue leading the buttoned-up, repressed lifestyle that I become accustomed to during high school. I wanted to be able to go back to calling all the shots in my life, especially as I entered a new phase. Soon I'd elevate from a young lady to a full-blown young *woman* where I would have to begin to ween myself from relying on my parents and start the process of taking full responsibility of myself. Before that happened, though, I wanted to enjoy my remaining teenage years.

During my tenure in NJROTC I had tunnel vision and was only concerned about my positioning within the program because I thought it would be a career path I'd want to further pursue. Ironically, the program allowed me to see that I did not want to live the rest of my life on someone else's schedule, nor did I want to have to restrict myself to the pressure of being the ultimate example for a bunch of people. So, while other cadets who hadn't reached anywhere near the level I had in NJROTC went on to enlist full-time, I chose not to.

When I was the executive officer over those cadets, I made it my mission, no matter how miserable it made me, to be an example they could look up to without feeling like I was a huge hypocrite. That meant I was required to always be on my best behavior, without fail – no partying, no flirting with boys, and no risks.

I felt as if I were supposed to be a teenager physically yet have the personality of a ninety-eight-year-old. After four years straight, the military was a strong *hell* no for me. I was off of that, and I didn't care who it pissed off. I was heading into the adult years of my life, and I wanted to live them freely.

And boy, did my attempt at emancipation from the service piss off my parents. Though my chief and even a lot of the cadets were absolutely dumbfounded that I no longer wanted to pursue something that I spent so much time doing and was so good at, ultimately, they understood it. I guess that's because at the end of the day, they had no other choice. My parents were an entirely different story though.

They were unable to piece together why I would dedicate so much of my time to something for free but not pursue it full time when the opportunity came to make money from it. For them, they only saw the results as positive attributes that would be beneficial and help me sort through the armed forces if I made the right decision to move forward, although they downplayed how much of my own personal time that I'd lost out on while exceling in the program. They saw the lack of going to parties as less opportunity for me to get myself into trouble whereas I saw it as missing out on chances to make memories and connections during a time that I could never get back.

It was something that we spent the entire summer clashing about. Day in and day out, I heard the grumblings about how I was making a mistake, how much further I could make it in life, or how I was sabotaging myself foolishly. But still, I was not going to be swayed into enlisting.

So, without the financial backing of any scholarships, parents, or the money to pay the insane prices it costs for two small town girls to attend a four-year university, Janera and I enrolled to begin courses at the local community college. I'll admit that growing up I never envisioned myself going to a community college because, in my experience, no one promoted them as viable forms of education and they were sometimes looked at as low-budget education for those with low-budget incomes.

And while considering those insane university prices, one of the most alluring tactics that recruiters use is the potential service member's desire to further their education. To sweeten the pot, recruiters endorse – and I mean really endorse – the tuition assistance program; but recruiters do not always fully explain the limited list of career programs that the military will indeed finance. Looking back, it would have been helpful to know that the tuition assistance program would only pay for schools that fit certain parameters. At the end of the day, I had two choices: dedicate my life to service *or* pay for my education myself. After reflecting on the route that I chose, I am now telling *you* this stuff to encourage your in-depth research that *should* be conducted before simply taking a recruiter's word for it like I did.

But as for me and my friend, if we were paying out of pocket, we were going to community college.

For me, this was okay because, like I said, I wanted some time to breathe. When I found out that Janera was going there during the fall, I immediately enrolled for classes just like she'd done when I wanted to enroll in the NJROTC course. We made an agreement to take the campus and its surrounding areas by storm.

Which we did.

Most teenagers use their high school and college years to discover who they are on a level that's deeper than just looks: what things do you consider fun? What makes you happy? What brings you joy? I asked myself all these questions and shamefully realized that I had no clue what the answers were.

With my lifelong best friend by my side, I was determined to catch up on our 'I'm gonna party' fun that I felt like I'd missed out on while studying and training during high school. We really hit the ground running and had the best time living it up.

There weren't too many parties happening around the campus or the town that we didn't go to. If there wasn't a party to be found on any given weekend, Janera and I would throw one ourselves! With music thumping and the house filled with party-goers dancing shoulder to shoulder, being able to select what I wanted to wear and how I wanted to wear it was like coming up for air after being under water for hours.

My time was freer now that I no longer had to juggle the duties of cadet life. I was able to get back to mingling with a more varied group of people. With new faces, new friends, and a few road trips sprinkled here and there, I felt rejuvenated! I was able to be myself without anyone looking over my shoulder or expecting me to 'do better.'

Freedom is a *powerful* drug and being able to get a taste after being so restricted made me feel bold. If I wanted to wear a face full of make-up or dye my hair bright orange, I could. It was the first time since I hit puberty that I was allowed to act my age and indulge in the reckless abandon that teenagers were expected to luxuriate in.

I bathed in it.

Propelled by the urge to come out of my shell even more, Janera and I joined the school's marching band. Though we were like Thelma and Louise, joined at the hip, we focused on different sections in the band. Janera loved twirling as a part of the color guard while it was still a tad bit too close to my time on the rifle teams in NJROTC. Could we consider that PTSD? I think so. Instead, for me, I got to dip it, pop it, twerk it, and stop it on the dance team.

Unlike the slow, deliberate steps that I marched to when I was a cadet, my college dance team's choreography was straight fire! Never dull and constantly changing, it was a fun challenge. Performing in front of electric crowds that came to life, dancing kept a face-splitting grin spreading across my cheeks.

My dance solos were epic, too. It gave me a chance to let my body lead the way and I thoroughly enjoyed the rush that came along with performing. Dancing let me get out of my own head and gave me the room (or football field, auditorium, and gymnasium) to just *be*.

Since we were free from the watchful eye of parents or anyone with real authority over our lives, the rigid schedule that I had gotten acclimated to following was no longer in existence in college and going to class was *recommended* but not necessary. There was no guarantee that someone would be around to make sure that you woke up on time if you didn't set (and actually wake up to) your alarm. Janera and I learned fast that professors weren't going to beg students to turn in assignments like they did in high school.

Our parents were back at home, and we were the adults in control of our destinies moving forward. Every decision that we made held far more gravitas than before because our parents would not be the ones to receive the blowback from the consequences. It was all fun and games for the first year until one day life made a sharp and unexpected turn that neither I nor Janera saw coming.

After a successful freshman year, I was looking forward to adding more memories to my soul's record book when Janera came into our dorm room one fateful day.

Her energy was off from the moment she crossed the door's threshold. Under normal circumstances, Janera exuded positive, upbeat vibes whenever she entered a room. Her energy was contagious, but this wasn't the case that day.

"Skyla?"

"Hey," I greeted, not looking up from my phone. I'd been lounging around in bed, relaxing and enjoying alone time when she'd come in. Time to myself was another small but much appreciated perk that came along with college.

Instead of the upbeat, goofy response that I'd grown used to, Janera didn't immediately respond. She expelled as a short puff of air from her nostrils before spewing something I never would have expected. "I'm pregnant," she announced when the door shut behind her.

"What?" I jolted upright in bed, setting the phone down beside me on the twin-sized mattress to give the moment the true attention it deserved.

The lackluster color of her normally radiant skin proved that I'd heard her correctly and that she hadn't been joking around or playing a prank on me. She was about to become a *mother* with a child to care for and prioritize. Our entire dynamic was about to change.

"Are you sure?" I wondered aloud, trying to sort through the rolling list of questions going through my mind.

Her wide-eyed expression looked as though she'd watched a train wreck right in front her. Hell, maybe that's what it felt like for all I knew. "I took a test and it said I am."

I hadn't even known that she was late on her period let alone uncertain enough to pee on a stick. We'd talked in passing about having children, along with the husbands and white picket fences that we as women are trained to want from birth, but I'd assumed we both weren't looking for those treasures until we explored a lot more life.

"Damn girl," was the only thing I could think to say in response. Selfish as it may have been, I wasn't ready for a child and in my mind, she wasn't supposed to be ready either. We weren't even twenty years old yet and still had trips and parties we'd talked about enjoying, but in lieu of those arraignments, she had to start thinking about baby names and buying diapers.

When the initial shock of Janera's pregnancy wore off, we tried to continue with our lives as if things weren't changing faster than they truly were. Between her fluctuating hormones, morning sickness, and all the other natural changes that come with carrying another person inside your body, Janera was no longer able to go out with me anymore like she used to. As the months passed and her baby continued to grow, our paths began to diverge.

I kept the emotions within myself, but I felt slightly betrayed by my long-time friend. Once she embraced the new role she'd be taking on in her life, I was just as excited as she was about the coming bundle of joy. Only now I was back to the no party, less fun lifestyle. My go-to since childhood would no longer be available at my beck and call.

Just like that, it was the end of an era.

My attempt at college without Janera by my side was a short-lived run. She went on to become a mother to a gorgeous baby, and I met a man I lost my mind over. But because he was such a huge roadblock to the path that I would eventually end up on, I will speak of him only briefly. We'll call him Shaun.

I met Shaun at a time when I was looking for someone to fill the void in my life that Janera left. Her friendship had been my crutch for so long, I depended on it and her more than I realized. But when I met Shaun, he briefly patched that hole by giving me someone else to share my time with.

And in my eyes, he was fine.

With a new man in my life and a desire to keep experiencing new adventures, I made the decision to drop out of school and move away with who I thought was the man of my dreams. The sweet, humorous man I was willing to turn my world upside down for became someone I didn't recognize at all. His face didn't change but everything else about him became foreign.

The fun we used to have came to an abrupt end, and the trust our relationship had been built on crumbled. What was supposed to be a new start turned into a real-life nightmare that I never thought would happen to me. When the repeated arguments about the smallest of things escalated from verbal to physical abuse, I was backed into a corner that only had two ways out: either end the relationship and start over from ground one or take the gamble that came along with staying in a relationship plagued with domestic violence.

The position his unpredictable change put me in hurt far more than any of the painful blows he ever delivered. I loved him but I refused to allow his toxicity to ruin or take my life.

By the time I'd finally managed to severe my ties with Shaun for good, I'd gone from the good girl who people could always count on to do the right thing to a broken young woman who'd accumulated both simple assault and disturbing the peace charges. Years of being a prime example for others had gone down the drain, and I had nothing show for the time I'd spent in college besides a couple of credits and a failed relationship.

The embarrassment made my stomach churn.

Being forced to move back into your parents' house after getting a taste of living on your own is a special type of hell that I wouldn't wish for any self-respecting adult to endure. There is no way to do so without losing even the slightest morsal of self-dignity. No matter what the circumstances of the child's return are or how old that individual is when they return to the nest, once you go back, everyone starts to resent it shortly thereafter.

It's shear misery.

Phrases like *'it's my house, my rules'* and *'I told you so'* constantly echoed on repeat within my parent's home after I moved back in. You can call it tough love, but it was completely unwanted by a woman who felt foolish for forgoing the band scholarship only to end up back in Mississippi. My parents didn't make the transition any easier for me either.

Aimless, I had no idea what to do next in my life, but the constant nagging of my mother and father put immense pressure on me to figure it out. The only problem was, I'd become so terrified of making another catastrophic misstep in my life that I became too paralyzed to make any decision. Each day that went by, I felt like I was sinking deeper and deeper into the pit of mediocrity, desperately flailing for help with none in sight.

I had no degree, no money to fall back on, and no job. The feeling of having no real allies to help me sort through my thoughts forced me into a silent battle with depression and uncertainty. I needed to do *something* but none of the options I'd come up with worked.

If I'd had a dollar for every time one of my parents brought up how far along in life I'd be if I'd continued to the military after high school, I would have bought a condo in the city within weeks. At my mother's insistence that if I was going to be living back home, I'd need to help with the bills, I applied to what seemed to be a thousand jobs within the town. Twenty-two years old and degreeless, I ended up working as a server at the local Olive Garden.

Olive Garden gave me a first-hand taste of what it must have felt like for the cadets that had been under me during my time as executive officer during NJROTC. Following someone else's orders sucked ass and that's exactly how it felt as a server. Day in and day out I ripped and ran through the Italian restaurant at others' commands.

Every day that I woke up and put on that uniform, my mother's voice echoed in the back of my mind, reminding me of the of the government uniform I could have been wearing had I not thrown my life away being silly over a man – the same government uniform that would have come with the government job and a secure, steady paycheck.

Lost, broke, and humiliated, all my missteps, frustrations, and depression erupted out of me when I knocked over a tray at work and spilled a hearty helping of Zuppa Toscana soup all over myself. It had been my third double shift that week and as soon as the hot broth and sausage combo connected with my body, I broke. *What the fuck am I doing with my life*?

That question, along with the usually delicious-turned-nauseating aroma of the Zuppa Toscana followed me all the way back home that night and refused to give me privacy when I made a beeline for my bedroom and belly flopped onto my bed in dismay. My life was in shambles, and I refused to go another day without having some sort of plan to regain my freedom. No matter what I had to do, I had to put on my big girl panties and get my shit together.

And fast.

That wasn't going to happen if I stayed at Olive Garden. As a matter of fact, I knew that even if I left Olive Garden and got another restaurant gig, it still wouldn't make much difference. I wasn't in need of another quick, minimum wage job. I needed a career that would help me get back on my feet financially so that I could move out on my own again and maintain stability.

What the hell do you want to do? I asked myself once I'd cried my eyes bloodshot red.

The last thing I had thoroughly enjoyed doing was my time on the dance team during my freshman year of college. Being able to move my body freely to good music while connecting with cool people over great music was something I could do for the rest of my life. But the only fast money to be made from dancing came out of strip clubs and that definitely wasn't for me.

You used to do so good in JROTC in high school, the disgruntled baritone of my father rattled between my ears.

There was no denying that just three short years ago I had been the top cadet in NJROTC. Though it was all consuming, the time I spent in that program felt like I was doing something meaningful, *and* I was damn good at it. Reluctant as I was to go back to a regimented lifestyle, I tried to weigh the pros and cons of going into the military.

I grew to love the freedom that came after I left NJROTC, and that was something I would be forfeiting by enlisting. By choosing not to go into the service directly after high school meant that I would start from the very beginning with just the *memories* of what I learned in NJROTC. All the ribbons I'd earned and the title of executive officer would mean nothing to whoever my superiors would be. I'd merely be another enlisted grunt for them to push around.

At least there is camaraderie, I reminded myself while thinking back on all the fast friendships that I had made in the program. As l*ong as I keep my head down and do the work, I should be able to climb the ranks again just as fast.*

The more I thought about it, the more promising the idea became. I was ready to dive headfirst into a change and this was the first test of the waters. In high school I had taken the Armed Services Vocational Aptitude Battery, or ASVAB for short, and passed without a hitch. I was nearly certain that after brushing up on the lingo I'd be good.

Do I really want to go back to wearing those stuffy suits and obsessing about workouts?

No! Was the response my mind immediately returned, but I pushed it aside.

Sitting up in bed, I looked around the bedroom that I'd grown up in and shook my head. I used to love spending time there as a child but now, as an adult, I couldn't wait to leave again. Whether or not I was truly ecstatic about enlisting became irrelevant.

I knew that it would be for the betterment of my life, which was something that I painfully longed for at that juncture in time. In what seemed like a quick a blink, years were flying by, and I refused to die a bitter old lady in the same house I'd grown up in.

That night, with the scent of Zuppa Toscana stuck my nostrils and the fabric of my clothes, I decided that I was going join the United States Navy.

After kicking the idea back and forth in my head for a few more days I began my search for a naval recruiter. I knew I didn't want to go through the lengthy process alone, so I was really hoping for someone who could work with me and look out for my best interest and not just that of the Navy. Thanks to Google, I was able to find a recruiter located in Meridian, Mississippi.

I was nervous during the entire drive up to Meridian. Was this a smart decision or was it rushed? Was this decision to reconnect with the military training that I'd intentionally decided not to pursue years ago going to be worth it or was I making yet another mistake that would eventually lead me right back to the bottom?

The meeting with the recruiter turned out to be not much to write about. He was pleasant and professional and ensured me that I'd made the right choice by making the inquiry *alone* so it could only be upward momentum going forward. Which was nice.

It wasn't slam dunk convincing, but it was nice.

After we gave each other a brief synopsis of our personal stories and what brought us to that moment, I told him about my tenure in the program and my decision to not jump into the service upon graduation. He assured me that he could understand how I felt at the time and that he'd known several sailors who'd taken similar paths and went on to have extraordinary careers. That brought me an inkling of peace, knowing that the door I'd slammed shut upon graduation had never been locked.

My recruiter informed me that because it had been a while since I'd done so, I would need to take and pass the ASVAB again. I felt indifferent about this, but I understood it. The first time I took the test, I passed it with flying colors. On the other hand, that was years ago.

"Do you know what field you want to start in?" he asked.

I felt shame in the fact that I didn't.

"Well, don't worry," he said. "One thing about it, the Navy will give you plenty of time to figure it out. You don't have to figure it out today."

Expelling a sigh that took away some of the disdain that I felt within myself for not having a tighter handle on my life, I was relieved to know that not being sure of a targeted specialty wouldn't ruin or slow down this process. I'd gone out on a limb and let my family know about my plans in hopes that it would get them off my back, so there was no circumstance where I wanted to go back and explain to them why something went wrong.

That was a headache I was happy to avoid.

But then, my mind drifted off to the last time I'd attempted to start my life over. The results of the toxic relationship with Shaun left a permanent blemish on my record that I hoped wouldn't come back to haunt me. "I have a question," I blurted out as my heart began to pump faster than it already had been.

"Hopefully, I have an answer," the recruiter responded.

My neck got tight as the words danced on the tip of my tongue, too afraid to come out in fear that everything would be ruined. *Bitch, suck it up*, I chastised myself. It wasn't like I could go back in the past to change it, so I refused to let it stifle me. All I could do was be up front and hope for the best.

That's precisely what I did.

"If I've been arrested, will that stop me from being able to enlist?"

A soft grin crossed the recruiter's face before he spoke. I'm not sure if he could sense the anxiety I'd battled with because of the question or if he'd heard it that many times before, but he was confident in his reply. "It depends on what the arrests were for but that alone wouldn't be enough to deem you as ineligible," he continued. "That's of course, based on if you pass the ASVAB and everything else in your background comes back clean."

After a few more questions were asked and answered, I shook the recruiter's hand, accepted the printed information that he provided, and began my quest toward enlistment. A new fire had been lit under me knowing that within six months, I'd be in a completely different situation than the one that I'd found myself drowning in. It was just enough motivation for me to push to find the nearest testing facility and schedule my appointment to take the ASVAB test.

I'll admit, going into the test, I was a lot more confident than I should have been. Because I'd taken the test before in high school and passed with flying colors, I took studying this time very lightly. Trying to take the short cut only proved to be pointless when three years after passing on the first try, I failed miserably.

I had been studying old bits of information that I could find laying around my room and through quick searches on Google. There was no way that I would pass if I didn't tighten up and get serious, so that's exactly what I did. Like everything else I set my mind to, the next time that I took the test, I was going to pass.

That's exactly what I did.

After taking the ASVAB for the second time and passing it with a high enough score to qualify for enlistment, the ball was finally rolling, and I could start seeing the bright light at the end of the tunnel that would lead me right out of my parent's home and back into being able to run my own life again.

Or at least that's what I thought.

My excitement began to taper off slightly when the process to enlist took longer than anticipated because of my criminal record. It was like being charged with the crimes all over again as I was forced to explain the events that led up to the incident in detail on multiple occasions. I had to sign excessive paperwork stating that if I were to become a member of the military, I would be an upstanding, law-abiding sailor.

I also had to meet with an advisory board at my recruitment office to persuade them that I'd be a good fit. It felt borderline like I was begging and, under normal circumstances, that's not something that I'd ever do. But for this, I pleaded my case until I finally convinced them that I was a worthy candidate.

In the chaos while I waited for my enlistment waiver, I did all the research I could on what it was like to be an active member of the Navy. Granted, NJROTC gave us an idea of what happened during military life but, let's be honest, it's really just a simulation. No matter how much work we'd put in during the school day, once it was said and done, we were able to go back home and carry on with our own lives.

This wasn't that. I was signing up for life on the high seas and if I could find out any true-to-life information, I wanted to know it. If there was anything that I needed to be careful of or avoid, I wanted to have that information. The more facts I could gather, the more assured I could be in my choice. I desperately needed that.

But everything I saw in the press, on message boards, and by asking others, *raved* about how amazing the Navy was. There were glowing reviews about how joining the Navy transformed lives while protecting the citizens of the United States. According to the internet, the Navy was the best thing since the invention of potato chip, and I'd be a fool to turn down the opportunity to enlist again.

Of all my searching, not one negative review could be found that would deter me from enlisting in the armed forces.

The closest thing I'd gotten that remotely resembled a potential 'con' was that going in enlisted as undesignated could be difficult because it means that you are enlisted in the Navy but have no specific job. It's the equivalent of being undecided in college.

Civilians can sign up to be undesignated firemen, seamen, or airmen, which I thought was an interesting concept. It wasn't common for most sailors to take on this assignment as it required a separate billet from everyone else.

For those who are unaware, a billet is a specific job within a grouping that can be filled by one person. I wanted to enlist as a Logistics Specialist but to my dismay, the billets were full, with no openings in sight. Could this have been a sign? Even so, I persisted on.

When I'd decided that I was serious about enlisting in the Navy, I went through all the information that I could find to get in contact with my chief and commander from my NJROTC program. Now retired, they seemed thrilled to hear my voice when I called which made me feel amazing because I'd truthfully thought they'd forgotten about me.

They ensured that I was incorrect in that assessment. Not only had they not forgotten about me, but they said that they often brought up the impact I'd had on the program in prior years. When I expressed to them how nervous I was about making this move, they assured me that I had what it takes to be successful in the Navy.

Their support meant the world to me, especially when it came to this matter. They'd watched me grow and get stronger nearly every day for four years. If I didn't have what it took to last in the Navy, they would be the ones who would point it out. Instead, they cheered me on and filled me with all the support I needed to keep me from backing away from what I'd started.

It also kept me upbeat that even though there were no current openings for the Logistics Specialist rating, I could still register as undesignated for two years until I'd be eligible for strike. In civilian terms, striking is basically applying for the job once it became available. So, despite how hard I tried, I couldn't find anything...not one single reason, why I shouldn't become enlisted in the Navy.

Because of the charges on my background check, it took a little over six months to process my enlistment waiver. SIX MONTHS. Can you imagine applying for a job and being put through the ringer for more than half a year before finally being told that you're hired?

Nonetheless, I got the waiver and reported to the Military Entrance Processing Station (MEPS) in Jackson, Mississippi where I was sworn in under oath and completed the enlistment process. There were multiple times as I signed my name on the dotted line that my heart skipped a beat. That was the largest contract I'd ever seen!

Before the ink could dry, I was off to spend nine weeks in boot camp. It may have taken more than six months to enlist but it took no time for them to ship my ass off to accession training - or A School - for Boatswain Mates and Undesignated Seaman for an entire month where I would prepare to enter the fleet and my first command upon graduation.

A School is where sailors are sent after bootcamp to get technical training for their military occupational specialty field. The focus in A School is a crash course in what to *expect* when preparing for your first tour of duty. Now, it was time to take what I'd learned during those four weeks and get ready to put it to good use.

The moment I accepted my certificate of graduation from A School, a surge of relief shot through me. I could now clearly see that light at the end of the tunnel that people always talked about. *Finally,* I was getting back on the right track.

I didn't know *half* of what I know now on that day. Had I, I would have conducted a complete U-turn in my life, made some changes in the contract I'd signed, and saved myself a lot of stress that I could have lived without.

CHECKING IN

Once I fully enlisted in the Navy, every day leading up to check-in flew by, all the way up until the night before I was to meet my ship. That night in the heart of Norfolk, Virginia, I lay in my hotel room and thought about all the possibilities that were going to come out of this decision. *This is gonna be big for you*, I kept repeating to myself.

The decision had already begun to show its benefits before I had even left my home in Mississippi for my new duty station and my second attempt at taking on the real world. My parents were starting to loosen up, happy that I would be doing something they approved of for my life. Now that I was set to do something that was more aligned with what they felt was a successful career path, the stern looks and passive-aggressive behavior I received from them began to fade.

It also helped lift my spirits that I didn't have to put on that Olive Garden uniform anymore. Although months had passed, I believed that if I so much as caught a whiff of Zuppa Toscana, my nostrils would flare at the thought of the establishment. Now though, the realization that I wouldn't be stuck in my soup-stained uniform began to ignite a fire in my gut.

First, I'm gonna get a new car...then a house will be next, I'd made up my mind as I started mapping out how I'd spend what I knew would be a hefty paycheck for my service. *Do I want to rent or buy*? For some reason, my mind never dug deep into thoughts of how much pressure and stress I'd be put under during this next chapter of my life and once I beat my alarm clock to wake up the next day, I'd be spring boarded right into the thick of things.

Though I had been reluctant to enlist in the military, I tingled with excitement the entire morning. It was like experiencing the excitement of the first day of school all over again. Curiosity about all of the news things that I would see, the people that I would meet, and how my new day-to-day life would look took over me, making me squeal with excitement on the inside. Unlike high school, I would be rewarded for my stellar duty with monetary gain rather than simply social accolades.

The letterman jacket I longed for in high school during my NJROTC days was cute but the money I knew I was about to make as a sailor in the Navy looked even more promising than that jacket ever had.

As a new sailor in a fleet, just out of boot camp and A School, I made sure that I was fresh as hell. I felt as if I could have been a background dancer in Destiny's Child's *Solider* music video!

Sailors are customarily supposed to wear their dress uniform to check-in; however, I was instructed to wear my Navy working uniform, and so I did. I was wearing a blue camouflage working uniform that was pressed to perfection. There was not a wrinkle or piece of lint in sight. I'd administered a lot of care when shining my boots for the occasion as well and they damn near gleamed bright enough for me to see my reflection. Though I was new, I didn't want it to be obvious by my appearance, so I made sure that everything was up to par. Soon, I would discover that this mindset was an ironic way of thinking.

I'd pulled my hair back into a neat, sleek bun, completely free of fly-a-ways, and my smile was on megawatt. A generous amount of perfume ensured that anybody I got close to or walked past would get a good whiff of my fragrance. All my bases were covered.

Whatever was thrown my way, I was ready for it.

After some brief internal reflection to ensure that everything I needed for my first day was in hand, I was off to check in. *I can't believe I'm really doing this,* I thought to myself during my drive to the base. I was doing this. I was really a part of the United States military.

Soaking in my new city, Norfolk, Virginia, was like stepping into a brand-new world. It was one thing to cross Mississippi state lines but actually arriving in Virginia made everything real. Though I left home during my stint at the community college and stayed on campus, this would be a completely different experience. I wasn't a kid anymore. Now, I was a young, Black woman, *hundreds* of miles away from home, taking on a brand-new life and career on my *own*.

I couldn't just drive an hour or so whenever I needed help with something like I could back in my home state but even that edit in my life couldn't dampen my excitement for this new excursion. Tall mountains or high waters, I was determined to become just as celebrated during this tenure of active military service as I was an executive officer in NJROTC.

I was also looking forward to all the new people and connections that could be made now that I would reside in Virginia. Like college, the Navy is a melting pot of different individuals from all over the country, and Norfolk is a town with a rich military presence since it is the home of the largest naval base in the world. In my mind I'd be able to make connections with fellow sailors as easily as I had with the cadets in NJROTC, which I felt would be beneficial if I ever needed someone to turn to or someone who could relate to the experience first-hand and in real time.

My mind had been racing all day, drawing up a vivid picture of what the naval station would look like once I'd arrived and how I would be welcomed graciously by those who were already actively stationed onboard. According to my vivid imagination, it'd be a homecoming of sorts for all the brave men and women like myself who'd decided to become a part of the efforts to protect our country's freedoms. Now, it seems silly to have expected fanfare but admittedly, that is what I anticipated at the time.

Anticipation aside, my heart nearly stopped when I pulled up to Naval Station Norfolk.

Wow, I thought immediately as I passed the raised security bar at the gated entrance after giving the guard my name, documentation, and reason for wanting entry.

I puffed my chest out proudly as I waited for the naval security man to review my credentials and grant my permission inside. Upon entry, my eyes bulged in wonder as I took in the new surroundings that would become my stomping grounds. The base was bigger than anything that I could have pictured in my overactive imagination.

Taking up nearly four miles of waterfront space on the Hampton Roads peninsula known as Sewell's Point, this was the home port for the Navy's Fleet Forces Command. There were more than seventy ships along fourteen piers and more than 130 aircraft in eleven aircraft hangers. The brochures I'd read and Google searches that I'd done leading up to this day had completely undersold the place.

I was in awe.

Following the directions of my personal sponsor, a boatswain mate and petty officer second class, BM2, who was also stationed at my command, I located the pier on base near where my ship would typically be on days when it was in homeport. It was a beautiful, early morning and while I waited for my sponsor, I seized the opportunity to park my car, get out, and take in everything around me.

I did it, my head bobbed up and down as I inhaled a long, deep breath.

The water in front of me seemed to stretch endlessly for miles, and the way the sun's reflection shimmered off the water motivated a wide grin to make its way across my face. Seagulls squawked overhead, flying just as freely as I felt inside. The number of various ships of different shapes and sizes that were docked at their respective peers was mind blowing! The challenge to remember all of their names quickly became a fun game I made for myself while I waited.

This ship name game only increased my eagerness to climb aboard and explore the one that I would call my own.

For the first time in a long time I felt pride swelling inside of me, confirming that I had done exactly what I was destined to do. After hitting rock bottom, I'd *finally* landed back on my feet. I felt water beginning to swell in the back of eyes now that I'd reached the finish line of what was a long, hard journey but I refused to let the tears of joy fall.

Girl, not here, I chuckled to myself.

When BM2 arrived, he appeared to be was almost as fresh as me. Almost. He pulled up in a brand-new model Challenger that made me swear internally. *I've gotta get one of those.*

Like me, he was donning his blue, camouflage Navy working uniform as well and it looked like he had taken just as much time to put himself together for today's meeting as I had. "Seaman Pearson?" he called out in his husky, hearty voice while removing the dark tinted shades from his eyes.

He exited his car and dropped his keys into his pocket. "That's me," I beamed. I could feel another smile splitting my face as I stretched out my hand. "Nice ride."

He glanced over his shoulder briefly before returning his gaze to me. "You like that?" He returned the firm handshake.

"Yes sir," I nodded.

His smile was warm, welcoming, and filled with optimism. "Well, I'm sure once you get settled in good, you won't have any problem getting one of your own."

It was a promising idea. I had never had my own apartment or paid for a new car on my own before. Honestly, with everything that I'd gone through, I'd never been in the position to do so. Now, thoughts of success didn't seem so far-fetched. Like he'd said, if I worked hard enough, I could have whatever I wanted.

"Welcome to Norfolk," BM2 broke into my thoughts. His eyes scanned over me before landing on the manila folder that was tucked underneath my armpit. It contained every piece of my life that the military required me to present during my check-in day. "May I?" he asked.

Looking at his outstretched hand, I expelled a deep breath and handed the documentation over. My heart rate kicked up in speed as soon as I exchanged the files and he opened it. I stood there, rocking on my heels gently as he scanned over them quickly.

"Everything looks good."

Thank God, I let go of the breath that I had been holding in. "It does?"

He nodded his head up and down before closing the folder. "Hop in," he offered, gesturing his head toward his vehicle again. "We'll grab a bite to eat and then head to the ship."

"It's not here on base?" I yelped, my eyebrows furrowed in confusion.

He shook his head. "It's only about forty-five minutes to an hour, depending on the traffic. Let's go."

I flew around to the passenger side of the Challenger like I was Sha'Carri Richardson burning up a track. BM2 couldn't stop laughing as I practically bounced up and down with excitement. He retrieved the keys from his pockets and unlocked the car. Sliding inside, I buckled my seatbelt and was ready to go.

Witnessing the city I would now call home from the passenger window, my eyes lit up like a tourist. The grass looked three shades brighter than anything I'd ever seen in Mississippi. As one of the most populated cities in the country, the gorgeous skyline could be seen across the Elizabeth River, and I made a mental note to check out the infamous monorail system.

Ten minutes later, BM2 stopped his car in front of a building where the word *Sushi* was written across the front in big, bold letters. "Here we go."

My head jerked back, filled with confusion. I was expecting a five-star restaurant with white tablecloths. I surely wouldn't have considered *this* place if I'd been the person choosing. "Here?"

"Yup," he chirped in an upbeat manner. "It may not look like much, but this is the best sushi in Norfolk, hands down."

I looked out at the restaurant in front of me with a shrug. There was no point in trying to debate the man on something that I knew nothing about, so I had to take his word for it. “Okay,” I conceded.

We got out of the car and made our way to the entrance. Ever the gentleman, BM2 opened the door for me to enter first. The inside of the restaurant was a lot more appealing than the plain Jane look outside. Inside, there was much more of a homely, mom and pop feel to the sushi joint.

“Let’s sit over there,” BM2 nodded his head towards an empty booth on the right side of the restaurant.

I followed his lead in agreement, “Okay.”

Once we were seated, a server came over with menus. I’m not sure if BM2 was as hungry as me but I was starving! It only took a brief minute for us to figure out what we wanted: two orders of California rolls and a couple of waters to wash them down.

“Do you have any questions?” he asked, taking a swig of his water as the waitress came back to the table with our California rolls.

“Thank you,” I responded to the waitress as I pulled the plate of sushi closer to me. I gave our server a kind grin, recalling that I was in her position only a few months ago. “I do actually,” I answered, pulling the paper off the chopsticks. I’d been thinking of several questions since arriving to my hotel and now was the time for me to speak my mind.

“Okay, ask away,” BM2 ordered, popping a piece of his roll into his mouth. He wasn’t uptight and stuffy like most television commercials and movies portrayed, which made me extremely comfortable.

“What does a typical day in the life of seaman look like? What does it consist of?” I asked.

BM2 held up a finger in the air, silently asking for the patience to allow him to finish chewing. Once he’d swallowed the seaweed-wrapped roll, he took a sip of water and cleared his throat. “Well,” he started. “I won’t lie to you

Pearson, it's not a walk in the park by any means. It just depends on the experience that you want to have."

"What do you mean?" I asked, feeling the wrinkles form in my forehead as I tried to figure out exactly what he intended. With my sponsor doubling as one of my bosses, I was looking for an honest and first-hand piece of information, no matter how big or small, that I could use to my advantage. Maybe it was the competitive nature that I had from birth or simply my being too consumed with excitement.

"Well, there are some people who join the military assuming that it's going to be an easy ride and then they find out that they were sadly mistaken," he said. "But if you make up in your mind that you want longevity and success as a sailor, you're gonna have to work hard. Make sure you do all you can to stand out and stay self-motivated. Self-motivation is very important because no one wants to babysit a group of adults."

My head nodded in agreement. "That's understandable," I replied.

"But are you willing to commit to being that type of seaman?" he asked.

I couldn't finish chewing my sushi roll fast enough. Covering my mouth, I spoke in between chews. "Absolutely," I told him empathically. I'd come too far to slack off now and going back home for anything other than a visit was no longer an option. "I'm here to be the best that I can be."

"Long as you keep that mentality, you'll be fine," he promised. "It'll also do you good to get to know the right people."

"Like who?"

At my request, BM2 rattled off a couple names of other undesignated seamen on our ship that I should get to know, and I tried my hardest to dedicate all of them to memory. If he thought these seamen could be beneficial, then I was going to trust that opinion and prove to both my sponsor and myself that I was ready to take on anything.

Little did I know that in the list of undesignated seamen that he'd suggested I befriend, I would find a sailing sister and forever friend in one of them. I didn't know it when BM2 initially mentioned her, but she would go on to fill the void from the friendship with Janera that was now a long distance one.

"So," BM2 continued, "Seaman Stroud is a tough cookie that, on her best days, will outwork everybody," he complimented. "Not only does she bust her ass on a consistent basis, but she hardly ever complains."

"*Really*?" I asked in awe.

My sponsor nodded. "Really," he said. "Matter fact, if Stroud is complaining, it's time for everybody to stop what we're doing so we can evaluate what's going on."

We shared a laugh while finishing up our sushi rolls. I felt at ease and ready. What started as nervous yet excited energy when I woke up had steadily morphed into *sheer* excitement that kept growing with each minute that passed by. *Now* I was charged up enough to race Sha'Carri Richardson herself!

"Alright," BM2 clapped his hands together once both our plates were emptied of everything except a little blob of wasabi on the side. "You ready to go?"

With my stomach satisfied, I was ready to tackle whatever came next on our to-do list.

"Yes. I am," I said as I nodded my head.

Covering the check and taking one last swallow of his water, BM2 slid out of the booth, and I followed to make our way back to the parking lot, back to the Challenger, and along with our day. Our next stop would be the ship I called my own.

I wonder what it looks like.

I wonder how big it is in person.

What does it smell like inside?

My foot tapped on the floor of the car the entire drive. He'd warned me before we started our excursion that the ship was ported far away but it felt like the drive would never end. *Everything is good so far*, I found myself thinking as we continued. *This just might be the best decision I've ever made for myself.*

When we finally did stop, it was because we'd arrived at the heavily guarded ammo handling base where our ship was executing a re-up mission. This is why we were wearing working uniforms rather than me wearing the dress uniform for check-in. The sailors who stood outside and around the gate were armed with rifles, ready for use if necessary. "Identification," demanded the stern voice of the sailor asking for our IDs.

I cheered internally at the opportunity to present my credentials. Though I was bouncing around on the inside like a kid who had just consumed thirty pounds of sugar, I kept poised in my seat. BM2 and I both showed the guards our ID badges and documentation and were granted access without hesitation. It would be the first of many ID check points that we'd encounter throughout the ammo handling base, and I was overjoyed to do so.

"Alright. We're gonna park right here," BM2 stated as he pulled into a parking space and killed the engine to the vehicle. "We've still got a ways to walk before we get to the vessel. That okay with you?"

My shoulders rose towards my ears before falling back down. "Sure!"

"Sure?" BM2 chuckled with a raised eyebrow at how fast I'd chirped. "You sure you're ready?"

"Positive. Let's go."

As soon as he gave a slight nod of agreement, we began our walk toward the pier housing our ship. Each step I took grew bigger and bigger to the point where I almost broke out into a full-on sprint. *Calm down girl*, I had to coach myself silently. But I couldn't. I was walking so fast that my sponsor was eating my dust.

I just wanted to get there.

Jesus Christ, I huffed silently as we were still marching along after ten minutes! He wasn't wrong when he'd said that it was a long distance from the parking lot to the ship. I felt like we'd been walking for *miles* to reach our destination. But after the ten minutes, I could feel myself floating when I got my first, far out look at the beauty we'd trudged that long ass way to see.

She was beautiful.

The ship that I would now call my home was alone at her pier, sitting on the water, daring anyone to approach it. Though she was considered small in comparison to other ships used by the Navy, she was *huge* in comparison to me. Reaching into my pocket I went to grab my cell phone to get a photo but was quickly stopped by the BM2.

"Nah uh," he chortled, pointing towards a sign that was marked *No Cell Phones Past This Point*.

I let out a disappointed groan and put my phone away. My ship was an amazing sight to see and even from the distance, her beauty could be seen from at least a mile away. Since I was not able to get a picture for my phone, I took the time to snap several mental photographs of what it looked like the first time I saw it. This would mark the beginning of a new era. I wanted to immortalize the moment but because of military restrictions, I had to improvise. The vessel ahead was about to become a big part of my life and I could not wait to step on board.

Reporting to my new command made me feel like such a bad ass. *Dammmnnn*, I squealed internally as I approached my vessel, baffled at what they considered small but seemed *massive* in my mind. Yet, I remained cool outwardly. What kind of ship was I assigned to you might ask? Well, of all the ships that were housed at the numerous piers back at homeport, I was assigned to one of the smallest yet most lethal – a destroyer.

Up close, she appeared more bad ass than I could have ever imagined! I folded my arms across my chest and drank it all in. *I work here now,* was all I could think. *I am actually a United States sailor and that is my ship.*

My legs felt like they were turning to jelly, and my hands got sweaty once I finally reached the bridge that would allow me to cross from the pier and onto the ship. Frozen on the brow, I released a short puff of air from my cheeks, said a quick prayer for strength, and made my way to the in-port watch station.

Also referred to as the quarterdeck, it is sort of like the ship's lobby and is the first point of contact for anyone attempting to enter a military vessel. Like the gate out front, it was also guarded by armed sailors trained to take down anyone who was not supposed to be on board. Unlike the gate though, there were far more guards protecting the quarterdeck.

Wowww, I cooed internally. My first time stepping onto a warship, *my* warship, was an intoxicating combination of wrecked nerves and exhilaration. My heart wanted to stop and speed up on multiple occasions. To say this was a surreal experience wouldn't do the feeling justice.

Flashing my ID, the armed sailors stared at me briefly before granting me permission onto the premises. *Here we go*. It was official: this was my first day on my ship.

Once on board the ship, BM2 introduced me to another undesignated, female seaman like myself named Jane. "Seaman Jane Walker, this is Seaman Skyla Pearson," he stated.

"Seaman Pearson," she repeated and extended her hand out to mine.

I took it and gave a firm squeeze. "Pleasure to meet you Seaman Walker."

"Seaman Walker's going to be showing you around and helping you navigate your way throughout the ship," BM2 advised. "She's also going to help make sure that your check-in sheet gets filled out successfully."

"Check-in sheet?"

BM2 nodded and looked over at my escort for the day. "Yes. Walker, please don't forget that every officer within our immediate chain of command needs to sign the sheet. It's important that we verify everyone has been made aware of our newest sailor on board."

That's me, I felt my face getting hot with joy. *I'm the newest sailor on board.*

The excitement of the moment stopped after my sponsor gave Seaman Walker and me our orders. The fanfare that I'd expected at the start of the morning proved to be nothing more than my over-active imagination making my arrival appear more important than everyone else thought it was. For everyone else, it was business as usual and was treated as such.

Any new sailor must go through a checking-in phase because anything that has to do with or is connected to the safety and security of this country requires a thorough instructional process before she or he is allowed to freely roam about any military vessel.

For civilians this is the equivalent to the first day at a new job when the focus isn't necessarily about doing the job at hand but more about the administrative work required to get you into all the systems. And even though I understood the purpose of going through the entire process, it was still a complete buzzkill to repeatedly write out the same information over and over again. It might be a necessary evil, but it felt like *fill out paperwork until your knuckles bleed.*

Once a new sailor arrives with assignment orders, they receive a grand tour of the vessel along with the first introduction to some of the most important people at their new command. This cluster of very important people is commonly referred to as the chain of command, and it is imperative to make a good first impression with these VIPs. I was as nervous as a new student meeting the school principal each time I shook hands with each chief and officer.

To be clear, this process was not something that completely blindsided me. The entire setup had been organized by my sponsor weeks before I made my way to Norfolk. This was a blessing because, fortunately, he'd already given me a brief rundown of what would be going on throughout the day.

People were all over the place, whizzing back and forth, too focused on the task at hand to notice me unless they were specifically stopped along the tour. It truly *was* the stuff that you'd see in big budget military movies. Not only were there nearly 400 people within the vessel but there were unfathomable amounts of weapons and ammunition all around.

"If you have any questions, let me know," was the only thing Seaman Walker said as we maneuvered through the ship.

I agreed. "Okay."

Along the way most of the people I encountered were pretty high on the totem pole and that was a bit intimidating. Even more so, almost everyone that I encountered was moving at breakneck speeds without much time for small talk or other pleasantries. Don't get me wrong, no one was flat out rude when I was being introduced by my escort but hardly anyone had time to do anything other than scribble a barely legible signature on my check-in sheet and say a quick, "Welcome aboard."

The few that did have a little more time on their hands asked a couple of basic, surface-level questions like where I was from and how had my first day in the fleet been thus far. I knew it would be impossible but like I'd done with the ships earlier, I tried to memorize everyone's name and rank. My escort was active in the tour, pointing out everything that she thought would be important for me to learn.

"Thank you," I told her with each tidbit of information that was given. Truly appreciative that she was taking time out of her life to help me get around, I kept saying thank you in spite of her insistence that it wasn't necessary. She described what each section of the ship was, its purpose, and whether or not I would be working in that part of the battleship.

Seaman Walker also helped me increase my naval vocabulary by teaching me the different naval terms and briefing me about meeting the next person on my check-in list.

“Okay, so this is medical,” she stated, pointing at the familiar red cross on the door. “If you’re ever confused, you’ll be able to recognize medical by the insignia on the door.”

“Okay,” I agreed.

“You’re about to meet HM1,” she told me as we stood outside the door. “I don’t talk to her much personally but from what I can tell, she seems nice.”

That was a new term that I hadn’t heard of. “HM1?”

“Yeah, that’s hospital corpsman first class petty officer,” she explained.

“Okay, got it,” I said as I made a mental note of what she’d told me.

She continued to put me up on game. “You can always find her here – she sleeps in here on her duty days and underway just in case of an emergency.” I nodded in response as she turned to knock on the door.

As we waited outside the door for a moment before we got the green light to enter the dedicated medical space, I noticed the numerous ladder wells around us. There were so many! My nerves tried to get the best of me since they seemed so narrow, steep, and dangerous to climb up and down. There were also other narrow passageways that you almost had to turn yourself sideways to walk through and a vast amount of *more* spaces all with specific purposes.

After granted entry to medical by HM1, to my surprise I noticed that it was compact inside to say the least, but I was still in awe. It was filled mainly with a metal interior. The large, heavy door closed behind us. My medical check in was a bit of an extended process as I answered HM1’s numerous questions and sat around while she entered my given medical information into a computer system – completely ignoring that another sailor was listening as well. Nonetheless, once again, a petty officer first class signed my check in sheet, welcomed me aboard, and sent us on our way.

There were so many things to take in that it should have been overwhelming, but my joy and child-like enthusiasm prevented that. As we continued our tour, I was shown several other work centers where the main responsibilities for those sailors were to make sure the basic equipment that was required to repair or save the vessel was fully operational and up to code at all times. I saw the galley and the mess decks where we would eat, the female berthing area where we would sleep, and other miscellaneous equipment rooms that were stocked to the max.

This is crazy, I thought as we passed by a portion of the ship marked TOP SECRET. "What's in there?" I asked.

"Top secret." Seaman Walker pointed to the words. "Only authorized personnel are allowed inside there."

"Oh, okay."

I didn't say anything else about it, figuring that it would be best to drop it and we continued on. Finally, the last place we stopped was the boatswain locker.

"We call this the bos'n locker," Seaman Walker started. "This is where you're gonna be spending most of your time."

Doing somersaults in the back of my mind like Gabby Douglas, I coolly remarked, "Oh really?"

"Yeah," my guide told me. "This is the work center for boatswain mates and undesignated seamen."

Nodding my head, I paid close attention to everything around us since this was going to be my own personal playground. The space was hot, stuffy, and smelly but oddly comfortable. A nautical version of a mechanic shop, the bos'n locker was dirty and congested yet organized. It was filled with life jackets, tools, and several spin reels of large rope and line.

After showing me everything that there was to see, we made our way to what would be my work center. The space wasn't empty as there were several seamen and third classes around the bos'n locker dressed in ragged, paint splattered coveralls, sitting in chairs and on the floor doing maintenance on several life jackets. I was in awe watching them do real-world sailor work. *I can't wait 'til it's my turn.*

"Guys, this is Pearson," Seaman Walker introduced me.

"Nice to meet you all," I smiled politely with a slight waved to everyone in the room.

Nearly everyone in the room continued what they were doing after giving a brief nod in greeting.

Tough room, I raised my eyebrow and gave another polite grin, this one with a closed mouth and lips that went in a straight line.

"Those boots shiny as hell, huh?" laughed a male seaman. "That'll change." He finished.

Thrown off by the left-field comment, I took it personally the moment those words slipped out of his mouth. I didn't know him for the statement to sting as bad as it did, but I immediately took offense to his assumption. He didn't have an idea of what it took to get me here and what I was willing to do to excel.

"No, it won't," I flung the daggerlike words in his direction.

He smirked, sarcastically shaking his head at my definitive proclamation. "Yeah, alright," he didn't bother looking up at me again as he continued his work. "We'll see."

The rest of the day flew by and ended with my entire command preparing to get underway. When the announcement was made, those good vibrations that had filled me up the entire day jumped to an entirely different level. We were going to *actually* set sail and take the ship back to our home port base today! This was a surprise I believed BM2 purposely didn't disclose.

It was set to be short, five-hour sail from where we were but that didn't matter. For all I cared, it could have been five minutes. The only thing that I could think about was hitting the high seas on the massive vessel. *You're about to get underway girl.*

Standing atop the ship as instructed, waiting for it to set sail, all I could do was think about how this very moment was the highlight of my day. I got to witness the hustle and bustle of the crew getting the ship underway on a small boy, a nickname for the destroyer as it is one of the smaller vessels in the fleet, and the number of different tasks and jobs that it required to do so was very apparent. It felt like an out-of-body experience as I watched the other sailors handling the large lines that attached our ship to a pier. The heaving and pulling while simultaneously yelling and motivating each other was all so different yet fascinating to me. It was all quite nautical.

When it was time to pull out of our pier at the ammo handling base, it was my job to man the railings of the ship's foc'sle. The foc'sle is the most forward part of the ship. Though I was thrilled to be doing my first job, it required that I stand terrifyingly close to the edge of the ship as it moved.

Lord, please don't embarrass your girl out here and let me fall off this big ass boat, I sent a prayer up as my eyes looked out at the vast stretch of water out in front of me.

Standing there, with my hands connected, one behind the other, behind my back in a position we call parade rest, I cautiously extended my neck to look down over the railing. The drop looked like it would take forever to hit the hard, cold waters below. I immediately took a few nervous steps back after that.

"Okay," I huffed, pulling myself upright. Looking to my right side, the person beside me was female. Though I knew she wasn't one of the petty officers first class or officers that I'd met during my tour, she seemed familiar. "Hey. I'm Pearson."

"Nice to meet you Pearson."

"You too," I gave a polite grin, pleased to meet another new person. "So, is this shit safe?" I asked her.

While she didn't turn her head, she replied, "You get used to it."

Her answer did nothing to ease my concerns, yet watching the woman handle the task with ease made me want to loosen up enough to be able to do the same. *Why does she seem so familiar*? I couldn't shake the question; however, I didn't want to flat out ask her about the hunch in case I was mistaken.

Glancing down at her nametag, the bells began ringing in my head like I'd hit a million-dollar jackpot: SN STROUD, USN.

Little did I know at the time, I actually had.

The First Glance at Undesignation

The shiny newness of my presence onboard a destroyer wore off within my first few weeks – especially being an undesignated seaman. What BM2 had told me during our lunch about daily life for a sailor had proved right. And then some. It was exhausting.

It was still hot as a hog in heat in Virginia during the months of September and October shortly after I checked in, and I was sweating bullets day in and day out at work. I hated it. Constantly wiping sweat from my forehead and walking around with armpit stains the size of saucers, no matter how much deodorant I piled on daily, was obnoxious.

My ship was preparing to go underway continuously over the next few months to conduct drills and exercises that would allow us to acquire the necessary qualifications for our deployment scheduled for a Middle Eastern ocean in the near future. Thinking about all of the preparations made my heart pound, and it beat faster knowing that my division of undesignated seaman and boatswain mates was undermanned. We'd lost a huge chunk of manpower for personnel issues such as pregnancies, failure to adjust to the Navy, and assignment transfers.

Being short-handed meant that all of the sailors on board had to fill in the gaps and work twice as hard. A heavier workload meant more hours. There was no way around it if we were going to meet our end-of-day goals. Meeting our daily goals was the top priority on our ship.

We worked topside – outside and in the elements – 95 percent of the time. Which, again, was obnoxious. Our work included moving boxes, gear, parts, lines, or equipment throughout our ship. These items were heavy as hell, and the grunt work didn't stop there. We would also scrape, needle gun, and chip paint off of several areas around the ship just to bust down and sand rust.

Somehow, I missed the part in all the paperwork that said it would be a large part of my daily occupation to chip paint off the side of a ship that was umpteen hundred times bigger than me. Yet somehow that's what my talents were used for. If we weren't chipping paint to maintain the ship, there was still the opportunity to prime and *repaint* the big girl.

We also had to perform maintenance on almost every outside inch of the ship or on our gear. It was a routine because if anything happened to the ship at any time, we had to have functioning gear to respond to the situation. If anyone took short cuts or didn't pay close attention to what they were doing, it could yield disastrous results.

The last thing the Navy was interested in was anything disastrous happening to or on their vessels.

With the amount of manual labor that had been thrust upon me daily, I was too busy maintaining the ship to be able to do the same with my own hair and nails. With the amount of grit, oil, dirt, and grime that got on my hands daily it made no sense trying to upkeep an acrylic nailset as trying to keep their appearance fresh would require multiple trips to the salon a week!

With the excruciating heat beaming overhead every day, the cute daily hairstyle I had the nerve to waste my time on was a frizzy mess within an hour of the early morning. This left the only logical hairstyle to be the ol' faithful pulled back bun. It wasn't long before I cancelled even the *idea* of both and was going au natural. But we'll get into that a bit later.

The pristine work uniform I attempted to keep also became a fleeting idea. My coveralls were always dirty or covered in paint, I smelled like a steaming, hot pile of garbage at the end of each workday, and just like the seaman I'd met on my first day predicted, my boots no longer retained the luster and shine they once had. It was rough.

Despite all the impediments and backbreaking work, I was still grateful to be too hurt or upset by anything. Less than a year ago, I was balancing soup and salad and now things had completely turned around. My work was hard but at least I felt fulfilled. At this stage in my career, I was in complete awe every morning when I mustered topside on the foc'sle with my division.

The upswing would come for me with each brand-new morning I opened my eyes. If there was one perk to the tiring labor we constantly did, it was the fact of knowing I was unwaveringly tough. It wore our bodies out. By the time we showered and managed to make it to our quarters at the end of each day, we were exhausted. But I'd survived another day and it was proof I could do it again with the shift ahead of me.

Every single morning, with coffee in a cup I had brought from home waiting for me after our muster, I took full advantage of the natural beauty I woke up to: a gorgeous view of the early morning sunrays sparkling in shades of pink, orange, and gold across the sky and the gleaming reflection of the sun on the shimmering ocean. The silhouette of several warships attached to their piers mirrored on the ocean's surface added to the perfect contrast.

Inhaling the hints of salty fresh air provided me with a comfort that made me forget all about the woes at work. *I am a sailor, and this is what sailors do,* is what I would think to myself as I drank in all the scenery and my coffee.

This is the coolest job I have ever had. My family is so proud of me. I'm proud of me.

There wasn't much more I could ask for. At the time.

The First Glance of Life Underway

Once we'd poured enough blood, sweat, and tears into our big baby, she was ready to start a series of short underway operations. There seemed to be no rhyme or reason for the length of stints at sea, and that took some time getting used to. Sometimes we went underway for a few days and sometimes for a few weeks.

We weren't far from home – just a couple hundred miles away – which was fine for the times when we were working. However, when we had downtime, the distance proved to be far enough that our cell phones no longer received signals. It was an entirely different form of torture. Though it didn't kill me to be detached from technology in bootcamp, I still didn't like it.

One would think that with all the government funding the Navy receives that they would be able to hook up some decent Wi-Fi on these ships, especially during times when we're underway. But no, once we lost signal, we were left to focus solely on our mission and sleep. Our mission trumped the rest.

It seemed that an undesignated seaman and boatswain mate's jobs only increased in responsibility when underway. Not only were we still responsible for our typical day-to-day work, our days underway included standing watches. That's right; not only were we doing work that would fall more along the lines of a nautical janitor than sailor, but now we were acting as watchmen, too.

Having watch was not fun. When this is your role, you are expected to pull quadruple duty as a point of contact, a security guard, look out, and authority in charge for an area. Watch wasn't only reserved for times underway either. We did this standing watch thing while in port too, but on your duty day, with your duty section.

Usually, an individual would only have duty for twenty-four hours, once to a couple times a week. There are people on duty 24/7 on any military base within different duty sections every single day because they are in charge of government property that needs to be protected at all times, so there is no way around it. See, underway the difference is that a sailor stood watches every day, which you could consider having "duty," *every* single day.

It was different for my division though. Being short staffed meant additional watch time for everyone's schedule. Instead of once a day, everyone in my division had to stand up to six hours of watch, twice a day.

Oh yes, that meant you're on your feet every single day between ten to twelve hours a day.

Standing.

And this is *after* you've participated in an array of random drills, along with about four to six additional working hours. PURE HELL! But once again, I pushed forward, still preferring this over what I'd done for work in the past.

I mean c'mon! I got to experience life in the middle of the ocean doing real military drills and exercises. Coolest shit ever, right?

When it was my turn to stand watch underway, I had to do so under special provisions. I was *under instruction.* Sometimes only referred to U/I, I was required to have the naval equivalent of a babysitter making sure that I wasn't sneaking in any extra winks of sleep and conducting watch properly. It was a little annoying because I've never been fond of someone hovering over my shoulder, but it was doable because I was also being mentored and taught the small things I needed to know in order to get better – things like how to stand a proper watch and the protocol on how to report anything that needed to be reported.

There were some watches, such as port, starboard, or aft lookout, that sailors had to qualify in order to stand. This required standing the watch several times while being under instruction, acquiring signatures on the Personnel Qualification Standard (PQS) sheets from the Over Instructor. Once you acquire all the signatures necessary from the O/I, it's possible that you will still be subject to taking a verbal board certification with chiefs and senior petty officers just to ensure your capable of properly standing your watch. It was a lot to go through to have the "privilege" of standing on my feet for hours on end.

Most of the underway watches for undesignated seaman and boatswain mates are stood within or right outside of the pilot house, also known as the bridge. This is the primary area of steering for the ship, so security is paramount. This is also where, underway, you can find the captain, executive officer (XO), and several other officers including the assigned officer of the deck or the boatswain mate of the watch. The pilot house was practically the heart of our ship and where a good bulk of the ship's most valuable officers hung out. Only those who'd gone the extra mile to pass certification were trusted to stand watch there.

Steering and driving our ship was another watch station for my division and was the most advanced watch station for us. My O/I would take me to the ship's steering wheel and teach me the ins and outs of driving an entire warship. I was petrified to be in control of the ship's direction. Otherwise known as the helm, the wheel was housed on a large podium covered with touch screen monitors with varying buttons, moving gauges, moving numbers, calculations, coordinates, and color-coded areas.

The screens were already intimidating just looking at them but trying to learn how to properly read them threatened to make my head explode constantly. Nothing was plainly put, mostly coded, making it necessary to not only know what each code meant but it was something you needed to know for *certain*. And since there wasn't a simulated program to practice with on our ship, it brought with it the terrible anxiety of learning a different, nautical language under the duress of life and death circumstances.

It was overwhelming to say the least.

While trying to understand what you're looking at on the screens, you are actively driving and communicating with your conning officer. The con has the job of instructing you to drive the necessary courses. And to communicate with your con, as I mentioned before, you have to know the lingo. This is imperative as there is very specific verbiage the helmsman or sailor currently driving uses.

You have to know the language in order to be able to communicate effectively.

That was far too much for me. No! Nope! No way! And fortunately, as the newest sailor onboard, my O/I thought as much, too. We both deemed it to be an overwhelming task for someone new who was already carrying such a heavy learning load. This decision allowed me to skip the training altogether for a while.

With the captain and XO always popping up unexpectedly, as if driving the ship wasn't stressful enough, I avoided the helm as much as possible. I was completely fine with standing look out, staring at the sea, and listening to the ocean. It was an *easy* watch.

My Very First Port Visit

The weekend of my first port visit happened in the year of 2017 and to this day I still look back at pictures and videos from that weekend. During my time in the military, I'd experienced a lot, both good and bad, but that trip to Florida will forever stand out in the forefront of my mind as one of the best.

During one of our short underways we were sent to Naval Station Mayport in Florida. I'd been in awe of how beautiful Virginia was once I'd arrived from Mississippi, but I was completely blown away with Florida. The base was right outside of a major city and surrounded by beaches.

We were still getting our big baby ready for her deployment that was right around the corner and, as we prepared, we sailed to Florida for a weekend – free of charge. It was glorious. *Could life get any cooler*?

Once the destroyer was docked, we were back to our "in-port" working schedule that, for my division, started at 0700 and lasted until 1600 to 1800. In civilian terms, that was from 7:00 am until 4:00 or 5:00 pm. Had we ported in a foreign country, only qualified sailors or sailors with the rank of E-5 – petty officer second class – and above would be allowed the privilege of freedom or the ability to be considered off of duty for overnight liberty.

An overnight liberty was hard to come by since sailors had to accrue certain qualifications to be eligible. Since our port visit was within the United States, overnight liberty was granted for *all* sailors of *all* ranks unless, of course, your work section was on duty or you were on restriction for other reasons. Once my division was done with work for the day, my shipmates and I got that golden ticket of freedom. We were allowed to explore the local cities near the base we ported in and enjoy overnight liberty!

The first stop for my new friends and me was Jacksonville Beach, and we tore the strip up on that first night. With the sound of the ocean waves in the distance, we followed the beckoning neon lights to a string of oceanside clubs, bars on top of bars, and plenty of seafood spots.

Food and liquor were all that was on our agenda.

To maximize our night out, my liberty group of five came up with the master plan to split all expenses equally. This way we could all enjoy ourselves without having to return to the ship with empty pockets. As a group of seamen and petty officers, we were far from highly paid. We weren't ballin' out of control at all.

Pooling our funds together allowed us to book a double-bed hotel room for the night. This was great because it guaranteed we wouldn't have to return to the ship anytime soon and we didn't have to rush our night out on the town. Saving a bit of cash in the process was icing on the cake.

After filling up large What-A-Burger cups with juice and liquor, we strolled down the beach, half-drunk, carrying backpacks filled with our cell phone chargers, shoes, and liquor bottles. The sand squished between our toes as we let our hair down and danced to the music booming from the clubs nearby. After a while, we found the perfect place to lounge around and talk until our words were too slurred to understand.

The start of our getaway was also the start of new bonds with Navy acquaintances who would become buddies of mine for a lifetime. It wasn't even anything extreme, but it was a memory I'll forever cherish. Honestly, strolling down the long stretch of Jacksonville beaches with a group of my drunken liberty buddies and exploring for more beachside bars, restaurants, and gift shops was far more fun than anything I'd ever done in Mississippi.

I had so much fun taking in all the sights and sounds around me that I wasn't even upset about losing my debit card *and* military ID somewhere on the beach. "Oh shit," I chuckled, shuffling through my belongings to make sure I hadn't overlooked them in my drunken stupor.

"What's the matter?" one of the petty officers in our group asked.

Like a parrot, a follow seaman repeated, "What's the matter?"

"I can't find my debit card or ID," I looked up from my bag mid-search. "I think I dropped them on the beach."

Before anyone could begin to panic, a solution was offered. "Don't trip girl, I gotchu, just reimburse me through the Navy Federal app when you can."

"Are you sure?" I quizzed as my heartbeat returned to its normal rhythm before it could get out of the blocks to race. "I don't want to inconvenience you."

She waved off the idea. "Girl please," she winked. "Besides, I know where you work."

Everyone in our group laughed.

"Okay, cool," I clapped my hands together victoriously. That was one headache avoided. "What about the ID?"

A different petty officer gave his input. "Long as you have your state ID you're good. All your military information is in the system and when it's time to go back, we can escort you on board."

That night we made plenty of memories to laugh about for years to come! Aside from the dreadful labor that being a deck hand required, I was in love with the Navy at this point and completely in love with my new, nautical lifestyle.

2

MASTER HELMSMAN

Whenever someone asked what exactly it was that I did in the Navy while I was undesignated, there was never one specific answer that I could give them. How could I when we literally did everything?

While I wasn't able to answer that question with certainty, my *favorite* task by far was being a master helmsman. A complex duty to put it mildly, being a master helmsman was challenging, intense, and sometimes scary all at the same time. It was a task that you truly need to be on your Ps and Qs for, and I took it seriously. Not only did I appreciate that it challenged me mentally, being a master helmsman was also my favorite job, qualification, and responsibility.

Because, I mean, how many people can say that they are qualified to drive a warship? After lot of hard work and diligence, I am. It is still an achievement that I am most proud of.

The Day When Enough Was Enough

For a long time, I wasn't bothered by the life and workload of an undesignated sailor, but eventually it finally started to take a toll on me. It all changed for me when my division was instructed to perform tasks in some of the worst working conditions imaginable and I couldn't understand why for the life of me. Our deployment was so close, I could see it coming over the horizon and the pressure to ensure that not only our ship but that our crew was ready to go when the time came was getting more and more intense.

It was shortly after the start of the New Year in 2018 and Norfolk, Virginia was finally feeling the effects of winter. Temperatures had dropped to below freezing numbers and snow had started to fall. And we were still carrying on like it was summer outside.

My crew and I were preparing and practicing anything possible to ensure we would pass our final shipboard, pre-deployment qualifications and inspections, and it was definitely an all-hands job. The pressure and dreary weather made my disdain for the situation worse.

One cold winter morning, my division was scheduled for an inspection of our man overboard procedures. We were visited by some highly respected, very important Navy chiefs and senior chiefs on this particular day. Some of the Navy's crème-de la-crème was coming to inspect us, our performance, and our equipment.

Of course, this put everyone on edge. Not only was it mandatory that we know how to execute the life-saving drill correctly, but we had to do this under their watchful eyes. Whether willing to admit it or not, everybody was jittery in the moment.

The team for the man overboard drill consisted of eight to ten qualified line handlers who would manually lower and lift our search and rescue (SAR) swimmer, who was attached to the end of the line, by a series of slacking down and heaving maneuvers. Dealing with the line alone isn't a cake walk. Picture a thick, heavy rope that is hundreds of feet long...which is exactly why it is impossible to do alone. Because of this, a qualified team is required to properly handle it. This exercise is the epitome of a team sport, and we all needed to be on the exact same page to make it a success.

On the morning of the drill the temperature on our foc'sle was no higher than forty degrees with a drizzling rain – wet, slippery, cold rain that had been going on the entire night, and by morning it was *still* drizzling, so the exposed, pre-staged lines and rope were soaked.

Not only did the unexpected, lingering rain make our lines wet but the water that had settled inside them made the lines even heavier, slightly iced, and harder to handle. These were not ideal conditions to complete the drill under but with a deployment creeping up on us, the higher ups never considered cancelling the inspection and we were forced to perform regardless.

"*Heave*! Heave! Heave! *Heave*!" yelled our petty officer in charge.

We were heaving and it was hurting.

I was wearing long johns under my coveralls along with a raincoat and other necessary gear essentials such as earmuffs, a beanie, and gloves. Despite my efforts to stay as warm as possible while executing my duties, the weather conditions won. After performing the drill numerous times that morning, it took about thirty minutes to regain the feeling of my fingers and my toes.

I felt actual pain in my attempts to make a fist and I was infuriated! Each ache I experienced, sniffle, and drop of rain beating down on me burned my sore body up. *Why wouldn't they reschedule since they had us leave the lines out*? I thought, pulling my raincoat closer to my neck trying to get warm. *Why risk everybody gettin' sick doin' that dumb ass shit*? *It's just a drill!*

While undesignated, I'd done a lot of things I didn't like for the sake of my ship and my job. I risked my life daily practically standing on the edge of the ship, sacrificed time, energy, and sleep because the Navy was unable to retain sailors and our crew had to work double time...but rarely had I complained. Just like my sponsor had suggested, I worked hard and did my job but the incident with the lines was the straw that broke my over stacked shoulders.

For the first time since the start of my career I thought, *Fuck this*!

If we already had to go through all of this while preparing for and during under ways that were a few weeks at a time, I did not want to imagine what kind of crap we'd be forced to do for six months on a deployment. Traumatized by line and rope, a fire burst inside of me, encouraging me to look for other responsibilities to inherit.

By the time my division and I were damn near frozen solid and were excused from the drill to warm ourselves up, we were all disgruntled and embarrassed. A bunch of us dragged our undesignated asses to the bos'n locker, sat around, and complained about the exercise. And our failure to pass it.

"Did anyone even stop to think about what would happen if our fingers went numb? Seriously, I couldn't tell if I was gripping the rope tight enough anymore," Seaman Thomas complained, flexing his fingers in efforts to regain feelings in them.

"We needed to be swapped out! And why are we the only division that does this stuff anyway? If we're saving someone's life, shouldn't half of the damn crew come help us lower and retrieve the SAR swimmer?" Seaman Smith backed.

More seasoned, undesignated seamen and boatswain mates who had been in the division for at least a year found our complaints to be humorous.

"Oh boo-hoo," they whined, mockingly wiping their eyes like kids. "You cryin' over a little rain?"

The unwanted, eavesdropped laughs echoed like they were front row, center at ComicView.

"Y'all might as well get over it because that's just the tip of a big, shitty iceberg."

My friends and I rolled our eyes and outwardly dismissed them and their comments, but I could tell from the looks in their eyes that the suggestions, in combination with the experience, stuck. I immediately stormed off. Determined to not let *this* become my life, I went to look for my sponsor.

"BM2! BM2!" I exclaimed as my wet clothes sloshed with every motion once I caught up to him on our foc'sle.

Surprise coated his face when he turned around and looked at me. "Hey, what's up Pearson?" he responded.

Catching my breath, I huffed. "Yo, BM2, this can't seriously be the type of work that we do underway!?"

His forehead furrowed and pulled his head back like I'd asked for his wallet. "Huh?"

"I *hate* line handling," I blurted out without shame. "Honestly, I don't think I can do it anymore after today. There *has* to be something else. Is there any other job I can do?"

Sarcastically with a chuckle he suggested, "Yeah Pearson. You can become a Master Helmsman. You would never touch another line again."

That's the entire point.

As he attempted to walk away, I hopped right back in front of him, cutting off his footsteps. I respected him as both a superior and man, but I needed him to take my request seriously. Making direct contact and holding the eye contact before restarting, "Well that's what I want to do. I'll do it."

Rolling his eyes, he responded, "Pearson. You barely want to even *look* at the helm on a regular watch. How the hell do you expect to become a *Master* Helmsman?"

Staring at him, I made it clear that I was not joking around. "Boats," I stated firmly, "I said I want to do it."

After a brief pause of nodding his head he replied, "Okay Pearson. Have it your way. I'll get you started."

My First Deployment

I don't care how much a sailor prepares, no one could ever be fully ready for deployment, especially not their first one. However, I did my very best to onload all the snacks I thought my sweet tooth would want. I made sure to stock myself up on several boxes of beef and chicken flavored ramen noodles, bags of assorted chips, and a hefty amount of Ritz crackers with spray cheese. For added variety, I also had several cans of beef stew, chicken noodle soup, and beef-a-roni in my inventory to keep me happy.

To have something to drink, I included twenty-five cans of Red Bull that I guesstimated to last for at least two months. I also made sure I stocked up on bottled water to avoid having to deal with the barely filtered ship water as much as possible. Along with my stuffed sea bag and rack full of snacks, I made sure I had toiletries, professional and civilian clothing for any type of weather, all of my uniforms and uniform items, and just anything else that would make me feel comfortable for the next six months on board my destroyer. My twin-sized, purple and grey sheets together with the numerous pictures of my loved ones that I taped all over my rack helped me feel a sense of ease whenever it was needed.

By now, I had been in the fleet for right under half a year and the painful reality of being an undesignated seaman was starting to truly settle in. The real truth was that there were way more days like the man overboard inspection than our beach getaway in Florida. While boarding my ship on the day we were to leave and deploy to the Middle East, I had one thing on my mind: becoming a master helmsman. Since my BM2 had done as promised and signed me up for the job, I began to learn more about it. The more I learned, the more I wanted the position. I *needed* that qualification.

I discovered that as a master helmsman, I would drive our warship in the most extreme conditions. I would be driving us through bad weather, rough seas, helicopter operations, and any circumstance that required the driving of an extremely trained and skillful sailor. On board my destroyer, this qualification took a minimum of four to six months to acquire underway, and anyone who completed the training was a truly respected individual.

Upon completion, master helmsmen received a Letter of Designation, signed by the captain, officially granting them the title and permission to drive our warship. The hitch was that there were only two qualified master helmsmen on board my ship. We desperately needed more; therefore, whoever signed up to train for the position needed to be dedicated to the work.

"Underway, Shift Colors."

This announcement on the ship-wide speakers – accompanied by blaring horns –indicated that we were pulling out of our pier and headed out to officially start our long-awaited deployment. With the latest responsibility that I'd happily volunteered for, I was stationed in the pilot house observing and standing next to the master helmsman, my O/I, as we departed Norfolk, Virginia. My O/I was a male, quartermaster second class.

Our other qualified master helmsman was a female, yeoman third class who was once undesignated herself. This yeoman was manning another space that would be utilized to steer our ship in case of emergencies, deep down within the aft end of our ship. Her U/I was a familiar shipmate of mine – another undesignated female seaman.

Meanwhile on the foc'sle and on the flight deck, all other undesignated seamen and boatswain mates were doing either line handling or anchor operations in the cold, freezing their butts off. But *I* was chilling in the heat, standing by for some training in the pilot house where you could also find our captain and XO. *Thank goodness I signed up for this.*

When I could feel the rocking of our ship as it was being removed from the pier, I realized that this was the easy part. While we were standing by, allowing the tugboats to do their job of assisting with pushing and directing our ship out of our pier and into the open waters, my O/I minimally had to steer. During this time, QM2 decided to explain in detail what it would take to complete my training and why it takes months to become qualified for master helmsman. He voiced that to receive my qualification, I needed to complete training that would be based on nature and convenience.

I would need to drive at night, during the day and at night throughout a refueling, during the day and at night in the midst of bad weather and rough seas, pull in and out of piers during the day and at night, perform several drills and exercises such as loss of steering and general quarters, and learn how to drive our other modes of steering, especially the ones located in the aft steering. "So, in your case, you need to *pray* and ask whoever you talk to at night for bad weather and rough seas if you want this qual," remarked QM2.

Additionally, I would be performing these evolutions *multiple* times and all while witnessed by the captain on several occasions. Why? Because it wouldn't matter how much training had been done. If the captain did not trust your driving, he wouldn't allow you to qualify.

I was determined to qualify at all costs.

As we pulled away from the pier, I could barely see out of the pilot house windows from the helm when I stood on the steel toe of my boots. I observed the swarm of crew families and loved ones heartily waving us off. Some faces carried wide smiles while others had blood shot eyes from crying. Still others were holding handmade signs with phrases like *See You Soon* and *Thank You for Your Service*, written in bright colors to make sure they were seen. Those who didn't have signs frantically waved their miniature American flags.

It was a beautiful sight that sent a patriotic chill down my spine.

While everyone outside the ship swelled with emotions, the atmosphere in the pilot house was intense. Everyone was on edge and their high-strung emotions were running wild. It was inevitable to have sensitive nerves after kissing loved ones goodbye for the next six months, hoping that we would return home safely.

Mentally, it was a lot.

But we couldn't stay settled in those emotions. It was time to get focused. The pilot house was jam-packed with essential enlisted folk and officers ready to perform their duties as we prepared to take to the seas. I was locked in with the laser focus of an athlete getting ready to compete in a championship game, watching my O/I and his every move, I soaked in every bit of information he had to share.

"It's almost time for the big moment," my O/I warned me once we parted ways with our tugboats and were in the open sea.

Spit bottle in one hand while he drove with the other, there was a tobacco dip in his mouth as he carried on a conversation. Standing to the side of my O/I was the master lee helmsman, the person who controlled the speed or thrust of our ship. Wrinkles in my forehead, I watched as he seemed more carefree than anything. My QM2 didn't seem nervous at all for someone expecting a big moment. And then it happened.

"Come left. Steer course one six zero," commanded the con loudly, catching me by surprise when the speaker blared nearby. The order was directed at my O/I who immediately responded.

Oh shit. What's going on? I thought to myself, my eyes dashed around the interior of the ship.

"Come left, steer course one six zero, aye!" QM2 echoed back at the con, then looked at me and said, "Watch this." He whipped the helm to the left and I felt the ship whip in the same direction immediately! The shift was so fast and unexpected I lost my balance and had to regain my footing.

What the fuck? I swore quietly in a confused daze.

I looked out the windows of the bridge and it was very evident that our ship's bow –

the pointy, very front end of the ship – was flying to the left. "Con, my rudder is . . ." QM2 started.

Cutting across the words, the con ordered, "Come right. Steer course one seven zero."

"Come right, steer course one seven zero, aye," QM2 echoed, as he whipped and played with the helm more. "Con, my rudder is left eight degrees. Coming to course one seven zero."

"Very well," con rogered.

This man was repeating all this verbiage *to* the con and communicating *with* the con while performing the orders given to him *by* the con. It was multi-tasking at its finest. As I watched my O/I work the helm, steering it from left to right in attempt to land directly on his intended course, I could see his absolute focus on the rudder angle indicators that were going bananas. Meanwhile, the ship was *still* in midst of its left turn.

And then, he hit it! The rudder angle indicator landed directly on the course One Seven Zero and the ship stopped turning. The bow of the ship was coasting straight on her new course. Everyone could let go a sigh of relief.

"Con, steady on course one seven zero. Checking, one six five," QM2 reported.

"Very well," rogered the con once again.

QM2 gave me a smug smirk, one that left an unmistakable impression, before he continued his conversation with the master lee helmsman. I took notice of our captain who did not seem to flinch one bit during our first big turn. As a matter of fact, he was kicked back in his chair, eyes on the ocean, while sipping on a *Mountain Dew* carelessly. He didn't seem bothered or worried about QM2, his ability to drive, or if the ship tilted into the sea.

The captain trusted his master helmsman.

Fuck me. This was the only thought echoing in the back of my brain as we continued to sail toward our destination. *What the hell have I signed up for?*

Getting Qualified

In addition to daily working hours, I had to adjust to watch shifts, the training required to earn my Enlisted Surface Warfare Specialist (ESWS) pin, living in a berthing with about fifty women, and hanging out around our ship with my closest shipmates. It took almost the entire deployment to complete all the pre-requisites and training necessary to acquire my master helmsman qualification. But about two months shy of my deployment's completion, I did. By this time, I had surrendered to what it was like living underway.

Despite the questionable food that was served to us, the lack of privacy, mood swings and cattiness that came along with rooming with fifty women, and the constant battle with sea sickness, I forced myself to stay motivated. None of the background noise or drama mattered because I was focused on my goal: becoming a master helmsman.

I had gone through each challenging evolution, trained with both of the qualified master helmsmen on board, and made sure I added extra practice during my regularly scheduled watches. There were times on the helm that I wanted to break down crying or curse every person in the pilot house because of the difficulty. My over instructors never hesitated to yell at me in front of the entire pilot house or point out the most minor mistakes I made while driving – even with our captain on the bridge.

They put heavy pressure on me, expecting nothing less than absolute perfection when I was in training. I didn't like it but there was nothing I could do but respect it. The qualification I was trying to obtain meant that I literally held the lives of the entire crew in my hands. Making a mistake as a master helmsman could be the single-handed reason why sailors get killed, and that wasn't something I wanted on my heart or résumé. Because the duties held real-world consequences, I underwent a litany of stressful, pressure-filled situations. My instructors applied *extra* stress to ensure that I wouldn't fold under the pressure of any occasion, and it worked!

Or at least I thought so.

Although I had successfully gone through my necessary, stressful training, I still hadn't received my certification. At first, I tried to ignore the delay, writing it off as something that was still being processed or coming down the pipeline. But after a while, my nose couldn't help but smell something fishy with the situation.

What's the big hold up with my designation letter?

Upon acquiring the very last signature on my PQS for the master helming qualification, I routed it through the necessary chain of command that needed to be made aware of my completed training. I was expecting nothing less than my Letter of Designation arriving shortly after the routing of my PQS. And with replenishment at sea (RAS) scheduled within the next week, I was hoping it would arrive before then.

A RAS is an evolution that warships go through to receive fuel, food, or parts from a supply ship to continue on with their missions. It's sort of the gas station pit stop of the sea. During this evolution, the two ships must be *extremely* close to each other to exchange their necessities – close enough to easily transfer goods but not so close that the ships actually touch.

It was a complex evolution that required a master helmsman to drive.

We prepared ourselves and our crew for an upcoming RAS by holding a RAS briefing – hosted by our ship's navigator. The nav is an officer in charge of the navigational maps and courses for the ship with the captain's approval. I'd attended several RAS briefs before under instruction, but I hoped the next one I attended would be as a qualified master helmsman.

With the RAS evolution three days away, I was excited to see the watch bill. (The document that identified what duty sailors were to perform during an important evolution.) Head in the clouds, I knew that on *this* watch bill, I would be listed as either U/I or not.

I'd done everything that I could. I'd studied hard and executed my drills and training. Everyone from my BM2 to the captain onboard knew how bad I wanted to be qualified. The watch bill would reveal my fate. It would tell me if the captain had signed off my qualification since I hadn't received my Letter of Designation yet.

The angst that came from waiting was torture. I mean, what was I supposed to do? Rush the captain? I'm sure he had more important things going on than remembering to present a seaman with a sheet of paper. But the *watch bill* was essential.

"The Replenishment at Sea watch bill has been posted in the mess line P-way," I heard the boatswain mate of the watch announce, making me fly directly to the mess line passageway in a hurry. When I arrived, I nudged through the crowd that had gathered around the watch bill searching for their names and specified jobs for the upcoming evolution.

Come on, come on, I gnawed on my bottom lip as my eyes scanned the names on the list until I finally spotted my own.

When I found my name, I noticed that not only was I still under instruction, but that the master helmsmen I had been training with for the last four months had been swapped out. The qualification we'd worked hard to build was forced to an end just to put *me* under the instruction of my fellow female, undesignated seaman in master helmsman training that had somehow qualified before me!?

How and why was I under the instruction of a seaman who had started her training at almost the exact same time as I did threw me into a rabbit hole of confusion! Especially since I was the better driver! Yeah, I said it. I'd witnessed her driving firsthand and I'm pretty sure my O/Is would have told me if they thought I needed more training instead of allowing me to complete it, considering the way Ms. Ma'ams drove!

I immediately bypassed the confusion and skipped straight into a state of fury. I had too many questions and not enough answers. That had to change.

While in my feelings, me and my opinion jumped the entire chain of command and found my division's divisional officer, a male lieutenant.

Okay, calm down before you speak. Remember who you're talking to. Although I was upset, I still approached him respectfully.

"Excuse me, sir, good afternoon," I started.

"Pearson?"

Inhaling and exhaling a deep breath, I removed the emotions that were making my flesh burn with anger. "It appears the RAS watch bill has me placed under the instruction of Seaman Suitor. Would you happen to know why? We finished and routed our PQSs at the same time, but I can't seem to wrap my head around how only hers was approved and I'm now under *her* instruction."

It brought me at least a small piece of validation that he seemed as confused about the placement as I'd been. "Pearson, I don't know what's going on, but I will get to the bottom of it and get back to you," he replied calmly.

Whew. "Thank you," I said, filled with appreciation that I wasn't simply being dismissed.

I did not receive an explanation prior to the RAS briefing the next day, leaving me to simmer and create all kinds of scenarios in my mind. The longer I waited for an answer, the more frustrated I became. The entire situation was leaving a bad taste in my mouth.

As I sat in the briefing for what seemed to be the hundredth time under instruction, I paid close attention to the people surrounding me. With the questionable attitude I'd developed over the past week that come as a result of still being unaware of why I was slighted, I really marinated on the people that I would be dealing with for the next few years regarding this qualification.

Once I removed my black, Navy-issued glasses, I looked around the room of at least fifty people and was shook by a jarring revelation: I couldn't help but notice I was the only African American female there. Not only was I the only Black female, but I was the only Black *enlisted* sailor.

When the hell did I become the speck of pepper in the pile of salt? I thought to myself. *Oh, nope, I'm one of two specks*, I corrected myself when I spotted a Black, male ensign.

I didn't know him from a can of paint or even know what his specific job title was for the evolution but hey, I was just happy to see another face that looked like mine. And as I sat next to Seaman Suitor who had recently qualified and was now my over instructor, I felt like all my questions had been answered. The promotion, or lack thereof, had nothing to do with the knowledge between our ears but more to do with the shade of our skin.

It was a daunting, horrible revelation.

The next day during the RAS evolution, I stood next to Seaman Suitor, under instruction of course, and listened to her go on and on about how she was taught and what she'd learned. It took every minuscule ounce of patience that I had left within the depths of my soul to stand there humiliated, listening to someone give me pointers on something I could do better than her.

She didn't get the hint that I had everything down to a T, though, and kept talking.

"Mmhmm," was the only response I could give, along with a head nod to her mentoring, and not explode in rage on everyone around me. That would probably only spur on the reasoning that I hadn't officially gotten the job. I didn't want to come off as the angry, aggressive Black woman that we're typically stereotyped as.

It was a challenge for my pride to listen to the officers congratulate her on getting qualified while they looked at me in confusion wondering why the designation hadn't been given to me. I couldn't live the situation down when people were constantly questioning *me* about it.

"Pearson, I thought you were already qualified?"

"Pearson, when are you going to be finishing up your qual?"

Once the replenishment at sea was finished and we were all secured from the evolution, I took off. Full speed ahead to find my divisional officer for the last time concerning my master helmsman qualification. Approaching him the second time around for the same issue affected me. After being forced to accept a decision I saw as unjust, I'd lost a lot of respect for him.

"Sir!" I declared, and the word came out twice as sharp as I'd intended. *Calm down*, I thought while catching my breath.

"Pearson I—"

I cut off his words and finished making my statement. "Sir, either you can find out what it is going on with my designation letter and why I'm still standing under the instruction of Seaman Suitor, and quickly, or you can tell the nav that I quit!"

"W – what?" He stammered.

"You heard me," I snapped. "Because frankly, I do not *have* to obtain this qualification. I was doing it voluntarily!"

I received my letter of designation as my ship's newest master helmsman the very next day – hand delivered by the navigator, with only an apology for the delay.

Fishy indeed.

My First Evolution as a Qualified Master Helmsman

My very first evolution after finally, officially qualifying was a replenishment at sea! Replenishments were one of the most nerve-wrecking evolutions to conduct. And as much as I hated being under instruction during my training, this was the *one* day that I damn sure missed my over instructor.

As I stood there in front of my helm without the supervision of an O/I, I could feel my heart viciously beating inside of my chest. I did my best to conceal the fact that I was nervous but as I took a sip of my coffee, I could clearly see my hand shaking. *Breathe*, I coached myself, closing my eyes to regroup. My palms became sweaty and slippery as we were slowly creeping upon the supply ship that was ahead of us inching forward.

Let me go into more detail when describing a RAS for you. Imagine during a RAS, one side of our warship would get within 190–200 feet of the side of a supply ship that was much larger than us and we would attach ourselves to this supply ship in several ways. Although it may sound like a great distance apart, it was not. As I pulled our warship right up next to the side of this giant supply ship, I looked up from my helm, saw the ship directly next to us, and almost shit myself.

I never looked up from my helm again! No ma'am! I looked directly at my screen and my screen *only* with complete focus on my course.

Just focus on your course, I reminded myself, *focus on your numbers.*

I listened to and communicated with my conning officer and executed my ordered courses all while looking directly at my screen. Just the thought of looking up from my helm scared me. I was too worried about getting off course that the fear made my focus as sharp as a machete! Hell, sometimes I'd forget to blink!

What if I turned to the right a little too much?

We could really collide with them!

We would crash, people would die, and I'd go to jail!

When I looked at only my screen, I could assure myself that everything would be fine because I was on course. I forced myself to steer so perfectly that the numbers indicating what course I was on barely made a move. My rudder angle indicator was as steady as a world-renowned surgeon's hands. Even with waves crashing against us causing the ship to rock from side to side, I maintained a steady course and focus for the next five hours or so.

At the end of our evolution, once I was properly relieved from my master helmsman duties by a regular helmsman, I anxiously attempted to walk away from my helm, but I was stopped by our captain.

"Pearson!" he bellowed in attempt to stop me before I was far away.

Surprised at the unexpected stop, I turned to look at him.

He merely walked toward me and held out his hand for a shake. "Good job up there, Seaman Pearson."

I shook his hand. "Thank you."

I spent the rest of my day smiling at my success. The captain had personally taken the time to compliment me. Not only was I officially a master helmsman, but a damn good one at that!

The Day I Realized That I Was the G.O.A.T

One fine day out to sea, about a month after I received my letter of designation, my command was expecting to do some helicopter operations in the Middle Eastern seas with temperatures in the lower 100s. By this time, I was on my way to becoming a seasoned master helmsman considering that I had driven a few special evolutions all on my own, with no mistakes, and a decline in nervousness the more I drove. Boatswain mates and undesignated seamen were essential during helo-ops due to our requirement to man the small boat deck, you know, just in case the helo went down and we had to deploy one of our small boats to rescue people.

But since this was extremely rare, we mainly sat around during this operation that could last up to five hours or more, counting sheep.

It was the hottest part of the day and shortly after I was relieved from my first five-hour watch of the day. I was sitting in the mess decks with some fellow undesignated seamen having lunch. As I munched on some very dry beef tips that I smothered with A1 sauce and sided with some undercooked rice, the One Main Circuit (1MC) blared, "Flight quarters! Flight quarters! Man all flight quarter stations!"

Immediately after the announcement our boatswain mate first class (BM1), walked by.

"Get up! Eat it all now or throw it away but we have to go! Let's go!" he ordered.

Although I was exhausted, I still had to report directly to the boat deck after watch, during my interrupted lunch to participate in helo-ops. After tossing my food, I made it to the boat deck and suited up in my life jacket and hard hat.

So damn aggravating, I complained internally. As I found the nearest shade, positioned the life jacket I was wearing into the perfect pillow-like position, laid down on the deck, and shut my eyes for a nap when the 1MC blared, "Seaman Pearson. Pilot house."

I sat up in anger, looking around for the nearest authority and laying eyes on BM2.

"What the hell could they possibly want right now Boats?"

He shrugged, wiping crust out the corner of his eye. He was as dazed and confused as I was.

In a bit of a rage, I left my comfortable, shaded area and headed up four flights of ladder wells to arrive within the pilot house.

Burning up from the heat and unexpected exercise I'd just performed, I approached the boatswain mate of the watch, a third-class petty officer, and with an attitude, I said, "Yo, what the fuck man? I was asleep."

Since he was the sailor who made the announcement, my aggravation was directed toward him and when I didn't get my answer fast as I wanted, I got even more mad.

"What is it? I literally just got off watch! I'm *not* driving! I know that's what you want because ever since I got qualified, that's all y'all make me do!"

With a surprised expression he responded, "First of all, if I used the 1MC to call you up here, don't you think it's for a good reason? The captain told me to get Pearson up here now! So I used the fastest way. *So* you need to fix yourself, calm down, and take the helm before you get us both yelled at by the captain."

Shaken I asked, "The captain? Why?"

Annoyed, BM3 answered, "*Because* Pearson, he said he needed the best driver up here! He said something about us, about to do some crazy movements with the helicopter. Now go take the fucking helm!"

I looked over to see the captain sitting in his chair looking at both of us. He smiled and nodded at me. *He thinks I'm the best*? I squealed internally as I rushed to take *my* position. Charged up, my exhaustion was gone. From that day forth you couldn't tell me *anything* about my helm skills.

I was the greatest of all time.

INTERLUDE ONE: THE REAL SPILL

I'm going to fast forward my naval career so please don't get confused with the random order of events as you read on.

After a six-month deployment and spending almost two years as an undesignated seaman, I became a pescatarian in my personal life, and in my professional one I finally picked up a rating. Undesignated no more, I chose the rate of logistics specialist. I also picked up the rank of third-class petty officer (LS3).

Soon after, I received new orders to a squadron in California. Before departing from my destroyer in Norfolk, Virginia, I was awarded a Navy and Marine Corp Achievement Medal (NAM) mainly due to my outstanding performance as a master helmsman. That was a bittersweet experience for me. I'd grown so much during my time stationed in Norfolk and I'd met some great people. Leaving would prove to be far more difficult than I'd anticipated.

But when the time came, I parted with the destroyer and its crew to drive across the country to my new squadron in Lemoore, California.

Like Virginia had been a shock to my system when I left Mississippi, California seemed to have the same enchanting effect on me. The clear blue sky and bright sun made me feel revitalized. The beautiful palm trees that seemed to be everywhere pulled a smile from my face. It gave me the feels just being able to call myself a Cali resident and I was determined to make this experience far better than the last.

One month after my arrival, my squadron and I became embarked and deployed upon an aircraft carrier, the largest ship in the Navy. I'd gone from the small destroyer to an aircraft carrier, and it was fascinating. Before my second deployment, when we left port, the world as we knew it was as it had always been. In the midst of the deployment, however, everything changed, and the COVID-19 pandemic started striking nations all over the world. What was supposed to be our four-month deployment turned to seven, leaving me with more free time that I knew what to do with. That was when I decided to write this book.

Enough about me.

We are now about to embark on our own journey together as I talk to you about what the Navy looks like from my perspective and those of other enlisted women and men. Mainly women.

As you read, you'll come across my own experiences that I wrote in my actual journal I mentioned in chapter one, experiences of other women and men, and events witnessed by sailors. You'll read raw opinions and solid advice about the way that things are operated in the US Navy.

Unless you know someone personally who has been or is currently enlisted, you aren't getting the entire story about the Navy. And what I've written is not just the good things and not just the bad things, but every detail.

I'm presenting the real spill to you with stories, quotes, and actual events.

Oh, and beware ...we curse like sailors.

PART II

GOOD ORDER AND DISCIPLINE

3

SAILORS DRINK

I strongly suggest that you listen to the famous US Navy song, *Anchors Aweigh*. Be sure and pay heed to the lyrics in verse two. I suggest this to point out and emphasize the line of the song: "Drink to the foam."

The consumption of alcohol while being a part of this organization is a supported sport. Over the years, there have been restrictions made and programs put in place by the entire military in an attempt to help, support, and control the sailors who abuse alcohol, but drinking is what we do!

Originally written before the 1906 Army-Navy football game, some believe that the foam mentioned in *Anchors Aweigh* symbolizes the sea, and since we are going out to sea, we might as well drink until foam is all that is left in our glasses. With my experience, I believe that after going out to sea several times, we sailors are beyond happy to drink to some damn foam! Just thinking about the foam will make you want to get drunk, or rather, get "drink to the foam" drunk. If you would like to know why sailors drink so much, read this book in its entirety. Bottoms up.

The Liberty Buddy System

Liberty is a favored term in the Navy and music to a sailor's ears. And since many sailors join the Navy to travel the world, liberty is what we look forward to the most while deployed. On deployment, you hope and pray that your ship will have the opportunity to pull into some cool ports. And depending on which side of the world you and your ship are on, it could be an actual possibility!

If you're lucky, maybe your ship will pull into Seychelles, Africa, where you could dine on mouthwatering, authentic Creole cuisine and then later indulge in diving into the clear, azure waters among the many boulder-strewn beaches. Rota, Spain, is not an uncommon port visit either. This fishing town houses a major US naval base. Its medieval atmosphere opens out to the Atlantic Ocean and a stunning coastline!

You and your command could also visit Greece, the cradle of western civilization, Dubai, the home for the Burj Khalifa, the world's tallest building, or Bahrain where its mesmerizing ambience is distinctly known for jewelry shopping. I personally know sailors who have had the rare chance to visit Amsterdam and Australia! I visited Egypt on one of my deployments. Don't worry, I will give you more details on my visit to Egypt later in this book.

Considering the title of this part of our book, I bet most of you are wondering what this has to do with "Good Order and Discipline." Well as we've discussed, sailors are very fond of alcohol. To ensure safety, order, and discipline as we visit foreign or domestic ports, we in the Navy have what we call a liberty buddy system, a subject I touched on earlier.

Depending on rank, sailors have a curfew during a port visit. The lower the rank, the earlier the curfew. We are usually required to explore with buddies as part of our mandatory liberty groups. In any liberty group, there must be at least one designated non-drinker. The entire liberty group will sign out of their command either for the night or until the curfew of the lowest ranking individual in the group, and then sign back in together. Why do we need all this? Because we're a bunch of Americans, most likely very drunk, walking around in foreign countries. We probably shouldn't be alone.

The liberty buddy system only starts to get in the way of your fun and freedom in situations like this: you've been dressed for over an hour and are beyond ready to go out on liberty, but your liberty buddies are not. You've got this one liberty buddy who has changed her outfit 500 times! Then to make matters worse, when you guys are finally out on liberty, you discover that you have signed out with the most boring liberty buddies known to man. All your liberty buddies want to do is sit around on their phones instead of exploring, sightseeing, and trying new foods in a foreign country.

Finally, after much begging, you have gotten your group out and about on the town, ready for some fun and one of your liberty buddies has way too much to drink. Somehow, of course, you end up being the one that takes care of them all night. You end up damn near having to call a marching cadence for them to walk well enough to get across the ship's quarterdeck before curfew. What a night!

When out drinking while your ship is in port, inevitably the end goal is to get across the quarterdeck! That is the goal. Period. Just get across the quarterdeck before your curfew without falling, stumbling, puking, or saying anything stupid and you and your liberty buddies will have had a successful night! Anything other than the exact approach I just described would leave you and possibly your entire liberty group in a world of trouble with some very important people in your chain of command. Why? Well, the quarterdeck is the checkpoint of your vessel. Most importantly, it is the access point to the ship. Your behavior when you step on to the quarterdeck will be heavily examined by the very sober personnel standing there on their duty with the specific orders to defend the ship, detain disorderly sailors or civilians, and report any casualties, shenanigans, or missed curfews.

I totally understand the liberty buddy system. It gets annoying sometimes because we all feel like we are capable of being responsible adults who can consume alcohol without babysitters. And honestly, I wish the liberty buddy system was based more on the age of a person instead of the rank.

Dealing with a group of people after you have all signed out together can surely become a headache. Either way, sometimes your liberty buddy is the one and only reason that your ass doesn't end up going to captain's mast – the ultimate punishment – after a night of drinking.

Alcohol + Sailors = A Questionable Atmosphere

As sailors, we're sworn by oath to abide by our rank system and chain of command. We are to listen to those appointed over us. Incorporating professionalism, obedience, and respect are foundational steppingstones that the Navy is built on. So, one would think that these traits are engrained inside of every sailor, right?

Although this is expected, I always find myself wondering why when sailors hit a port visit, go out on liberty, engage in a command holiday party, or just somehow end up in a gathering filled with several different ranks and some alcohol in a room, all of what's expected of us goes right out of a window. Like a bunch of college kids on spring break, it can be an episode of *sailors gone wild* once some step off base. I'm sure a few of you reading this know exactly what I'm talking about.

I sincerely hate that shit.

As I strolled through the bar of a hotel that I was visiting during the third night of our port visit to Duqm, Oman, I overheard a male, chief petty officer flirting with one of the undesignated, female seamen that I work with.

"C'mon and let chief buy your pretty ass a drink, girl," were his words to be exact.

I paused my stroll and pretended to play on my phone in order to eavesdrop more closely and ensure that she was okay before I let the pair disappear out of my sights.

"Nah chief, I'm okay," she replied politely.

As the chief laughed off the rejection and walked away, so did I. I took a seat at a table that was located close to the dance floor of the bar. My shipmates and I seemed to have taken over this area of the hotel because we had one of four people from my command at the DJ booth, booming unfiltered American rap music. At least twenty of us rushed the dance floor and let loose.

It made my heart smile to see us relaxed and decompressing after being out to sea for almost two months. We deserved this break.

As I took in my surroundings, happy to have a buzz from the alcohol and using hotel Wi-Fi, I noticed a petty officer from the combat systems department on my ship across the room twerking in a split on the dance floor like she was trying to earn tips to pay tuition! To the left of her were two married – and when I say married, I do not mean to each other – petty officers over in the cut making out, with no discretion either. These were simply two spouses too in lust with their sidepieces to give a damn.

Eyes burning from memories I didn't ask to see or have seared into my brain, I decided to step outside for some air. As I exited the hotel and made my way to a bench located across from the hotel's sliding door entrance, I heard a loud argument that was taking place between my very drunk, leading petty officer (LPO), a first class, and three junior petty officers.

"BM1, you need to sit down and wait for the rest of your liberty group! You can't leave without them!" yelled one of the third classes.

BM1 was in a rage and refused to listen to someone with a lower rank. "I'm a first class! You listen to me! I'm leaving! I don't give a damn about no liberty group!" slurred BM1.

I had to squint my eyes and listen really closely to make out what he'd said, which was sad because this was a person who we were supposed to follow – someone who was supposed to lead by example.

Instead, he was publicly being a loud and disorderly representation of the Navy.

As the third classes attempted to grab him, BM1 snatched himself away from their grips, stumbled with a loss of balance, and fell forward. His face slammed into the pavement, and the sound of his skin slapping the street echoed in the air. Once he face-planted on the concrete, the third classes struggled to lift him off of the ground.

"I'm fine! I'm fine!" BM1 assured. Shaking my head in disgust, I decided to locate my own liberty group on the dance floor so that I could ask them if we could just head back to the ship.

I'd seen enough for the night.

The next day, my crew and I were preparing to pull out of Duqm, Oman, and head back out to sea. With the entire crew in their respective work centers and areas of operation, there were hundreds of conversations happening throughout the ship, discussing the night before. Many eyewitnesses shared their accounts of what happened while those who hadn't seen the events passed on the gossip at the first opportunity possible.

What stood out to me the most was the rumor in circulation among the lower ranking officers who were on the bridge. They talked of a certain officer, an ensign, who was so drunk that he allegedly urinated on himself, passed out, and had to be carried back to the ship by some chief petty officers.

Now, answer this: if you were in my position, would *you* be able to take orders from your leadership seriously ever again?

Fear
Gunners Mate Second Class Beverly Stroud
Twenty-five years old. White. Leo.

"My biggest mental challenge since joining has been answering to people that I don't respect simply because of what is on their collar and having to respect someone or show respect to someone that I do not believe is a good person. People who have a higher collar device than you hold power over you in the Navy and normally in real life, you're nice to someone because it is the right thing to do but if you don't respect someone, you're free of having to show them respect. You can still show respect, but you don't *have* to hold yourself back because of fear for what they could do to you."

The Result of Not Taking Your Leadership Seriously

When I was deployed as petty officer third class on the carrier, I worked with a petty officer second class who was four years my junior. I tried my best to be patient with him, but he was the type to freak out if a master chief petty officer walked into our work center unannounced. His reaction was always so annoying to me.

"LS3 stand up, stand up! Start cleaning or doing *something* guys! Quick, quick," he'd say. One day he even ordered me and a few other junior sailors to do sweepers in our master chief petty officer's personal office and p-way. This order was to include taking out the master chief's trash as well. I couldn't help but wonder why the master chief, a grown man, couldn't clean up his own office and p-way. Or why couldn't this man take out his trash himself?

"I ain't no damn maid," I grumbled under my breath. We cleaned up after *our*selves, so, I just couldn't wrap my head around it. Was it because he's a master chief? Just because of his fancy title, he didn't have to clean up after himself?

Tuh! Please!

To be completely honest, what aggravated me wasn't the difference in my superior's age and rank, nor was it taking out the trash necessarily. My aggravation solely resided in the opinion that our master chief was a scum ball. After what I'd seen with my own two eyes – our master chief, flirting with our female chief in port last week when they were intoxicated – my tolerance for him was as low as his tolerance for liquor.

I saw it!

They were in an area where the chiefs were hanging out and as I walked by, I saw his hand rubbing on her upper thigh as they sat so close that they were nearly sitting on top of each other. They, too, were married to other people and both had the nerve to wear their wedding bands to work every day despite desecrating their vows.

Knowing far too much of the master chief's personal business made it ten times easier for me to tell my second class, "No."

I had no respect for either of them. Not the master chief and especially not my second class who only made it to his rack safely and without getting into trouble on the first night in port because of the good people in his liberty group.

In my head, my immediate response was, *Fuck that, you, and that master chief's inability to do his own sweepers. Learn how to handle your alcohol first, kid, before you attempt to boss me around. And tell that master chief to take himself out! He's trash.*

"Excuse me, Pearson?" asked my second class with an arched eyebrow, pulling me out of my thoughts and back into the room. He looked at me with wide, confused eyes and a narrow gaze.

You think that made me back down? Absolutely not. "I said no, LS2. I'm not taking out another grown man's trash for him." Because honestly, what would happen to me for my defiance? Would I receive a counseling chit?

Oh no, what ever shall I do if I receive a counseling chit because I wouldn't do sweepers in another grown man's office and take out his trash?

Get outta here! I could care less about that. The master chief is younger than my actual father who cleans up after himself without a problem. If I didn't have to pick up behind the man who was instrumental in my existence, I damn sure didn't have to do it for some sleazy cheater just because he ranked higher than me.

I didn't move that trash can an inch.

There was a seaman, a logistics specialist (LSSN), who took the initiative to do it despite my example of defiance. And later that day, after our master chief's surprise when he walked in his office and noticed that it was clean and his trash had been emptied, he came to our work center and presented that LSSN with a coin – a reward common in the military – and in front of everyone, thanked her for her initiative.

Meanwhile, my second class sent me to do inventory in one of our largest storerooms. The master chief could get away with being a lying, cheating creep without consequence but because I wouldn't empty his trash I had to be "punished." It was all laughable.

What are morals? Because apparently, I seemed to have them mixed up.

In Attempt to Gain the Respect of this Generation's Sailors, Try This:
Culinary Specialist First Class Skyler Gregory
Twenty-eight years old. African American. Taurus.

"The new Junior Sailors are only going to *mimic* what you do as a leader. They're going to mimic what I do. See, the Junior Sailors today don't need a boss. Some of them *do* need a supervisor but that's not what they want. They just want to be respected. You've got some supervisors that operate like: 'I'm your supervisor so it has to be my way!' This generation doesn't operate like that. They want somebody next to them. A lot of them are misled, from different environments, and didn't grow up the same way. So, in order for me to bring them together, I'm going to work right beside them. At the end of the day, in order for them to respect *you*, you have to work beside *them*. Try talking to them on a friendly level or even a brother-sister level. They just want to be treated like they are human. That's all they're asking for."

4

SHIPBOARD LIVING AREAS

On my second deployment out in the Middle Eastern seas, my job as a logistics specialist granted me the privilege of having my own desk, a snack drawer, and two other drawers for my personal belongings within my division's office. The air conditioning in our office was so cold that I'd have to wear a jacket, gloves, and sometimes my beanie to work comfortably. My office also contained a plain old telephone system (POTS) line that had the ability to make official or emergency outside line phone calls from the middle of the ocean.

I would use this line to call my family every Sunday. Getting the chance to hear their voices gave me a nice touch of home to look forward to each week. It made my heart swell to hear my parents going back and forth about how proud they were or to crack jokes with my brother.

Talk about an enormous upgrade from being undesignated.

But even with the upgraded working environment because of a new rate and rank, I would soon learn about one of the differences between the enlisted and officer ranks: the enlisted berthing versus an officer's state room.

One slow day in my floating office, my co-worker and I were having a relaxed day. My co-worker was scrolling through pictures on our ship's shared drive to pass the time and keep ourselves busy. These pictures consisted of events, award ceremonies, or just everyday operations that could be found on the ship's Facebook page. Bored and leaning over my chair to observe the pictures as she clicked through them, she ran across a picture of a space on board that I had never seen before. The picture was of our aircraft carrier's captain who was with other officials standing in an unfamiliar room that looked a million times more lavish than anything I'd seen in the ship.

"Where's that at?" I asked.

"That's the captain's cabin. You've never been there?" she asked.

I shook my head in response.

"Well yeah, it's super nice. He has his own mini kitchen, a dining room, and living room," she proceeded to explain.

It sounded like a mansion in comparison to the cubby holes that we'd been stuffed in. "So, it's like a whole ass little floating apartment?" I asked in shock.

She nodded her head yes and continued "Girl, that's not even all of it," she insisted. "It's got two bedrooms and usually when a new sailor checks in on board, they take you on a tour and allow you to visit his cabin. I saw it myself. He even uses a personal chef that's probably a culinary specialist second class or above."

Baffled at the discovery of this gorgeous apartment we had on board to house our captain, I no longer wanted to look at the picture. It was a total buzzkill to see the drastic differences between his luxurious space considering my own living conditions of a berthing. Thinking of the metal, rectangular area we slept in called a rack – where I couldn't even sit upright in due to all of the top racks being taken – I thought how middle bunk living sucked. The captain's cabin really upset me.

She asked, "Isn't that cool? His kids are probably so proud of him. He's a captain! That's a high ass position to have in the military. Cool right?"

Looking at my own computer screen, I shrugged my shoulders lazily. "This is some fuckin' bullshit," I complained silently. My foot tapped against the floor as I attempted to contain my anger.

"You don't think it's cool?" she persisted, clearly unable to read the stoned expression on my face to take the hint. "I bet it smells so good in there."

What? I turned to look at her, rolling my eyes to the top of my head. It wasn't my intention to be rude to her but the fact that she didn't see anything wrong with it only made my frustration climb.

"Girl, it's cool and all but I can't sit here and pretend like I'm impressed. All I can think about is where we sleep and what we sleep in. Do you think it is cool to sleep in a cold, metal coffin? Is it cool to smell random farting, listen to random snoring, and be woken up every time someone cuts on their rack light in the middle of the night?" I snapped.

"No, I wouldn't say it's cool but it's the job you know?" she said.

I rebuked her attempt to play devil's advocate. "Sorry not sorry, I don't consider living with fifty women in a space smaller than my own home cool." I ranted. "Shit, I live in a house that is 1,300 square feet. My house is bigger than our berthing and I wouldn't dare allow five people to try and live with me! Let alone fifty. But he gets to enjoy all that space and privacy to himself. He has a two bedroom for Christ's sake. He's only one person, what does he need an extra room for?"

The colleague beside me looked like I had three heads sprouting out of my neck.

"I don't know why you're so mad," she said limply.

There were a million reasons for me to be mad and since she didn't understand, I continued to lay them out. "That shower that we use is not cool! Its dirty, dank, and the water barely gets hot. Less than ten percent of the people that live in my berthing can shower at a time. Do you know how cool it is to ensure that everyone is able to do something as basic as washing their ass every day?"

"You're taking your anger about our berthing out on the captain's cabin, though?"

I continued, "No, I'm mad because it's what we have to deal with while he's comfortable in his plush bed. Think about it! He can privately take a shit but there's a brown paper bag on the floor next to our toilets for everyone's fucking tampons! He has a private phone line! I didn't get to use the phone last Sunday because the line was busy all day and all night."

"I—."

In a complete tailspin, I continued to run off my list of complaints. Before we'd pulled the pictures up, everything had been fine that day. I was calm, cool, and collected. Now though, after the fact, all the disdain I'd forced down and never spoke of came rushing out of me relentlessly.

"My mom was looking forward to a call that she's going to have to wait another week for," I continued. "The food here is trash and to be honest, I've considered breaking my diet as a pescatarian a few times just so I can get full! They don't serve us fish every day you know, and I ran out of tuna packets last week. I ate whole kernel corn and rice as an entrée three times last week," I smacked my teeth. "All while he is living like the king of the world. Now let's compare all of that to his living situation on board. I damn near live in jail because I chose to enlist. Inmates have more space to sleep in than us! No wonder he's okay with his position in the Navy! I would be more impressed to see him come and live in our berthing for a day."

"Pearson, I am so sorry. I didn't mean to upset you," sympathized my co-worker.

Her apology proved to the be tranquilizer dart that I needed to calm my nerves. "No, I'm sorry that I am being so negative," I sighed rubbing the back of my neck. "And I am sorry that I went off like that, but I really need you to understand something: Yes, I think it's cool. But I also wonder why it's only cool enough for him."

I don't think you guys hear me though. No, no, I don't think that you do. I need you to really hear me; so, allow me to explain further.

It wasn't just the captain's cabin that upset me. I'd expect the captain of an aircraft carrier to have a better living situation than his crew of almost 5,000 people. But just considering the living situation of other officers underway upset me too. Officers sleep in areas considered state rooms and only have to share it with one roommate. It wasn't rare for officers to conduct business and work out of their state rooms either, which allowed them their own computers and phones.

Officers do, however, share their head – or toilet – with other officers. But that's nothing compared to the enlisted folk that share a berthing, lounge, and head where in some situations, thirty to one hundred people use during the day like a group of cows huddled together. I went off on my co-worker out of frustration.

It frustrated me to witness myself and thousands of others accept these cruel and unusual situations that we have dealt with for years. This was what they deemed an appropriate setup for those who decided to serve the country. It is not cool to sleep in a metal box for eight hours – if that – only to wake up with several others around you attempting to get their twelve-to-sixteen-hour day started as well. Always having to make the effort to not be too loud or move too much out of respect for those still sleeping.

I hated trying to put on socks and shower shoes inside of my rack before I hopped down out of it. But it was a necessary evil since I didn't want my bare feet to touch that disgusting floor.

Yes, we sweep and swab it every day in an evolution we call berthing cleaners but let's keep it all the way real here: our toilets weren't constructed with five-star plumbing. While we are out to sea, the smallest accident, like tossing too much of our one-ply toilet paper into the toilet, could clog it up.

And when that happens, everything that has been flushed down comes right back up because the pipes are too backed-up to allow the waste to exit.

That is thousands of pounds of bowels and waste covering the floors. It's disgusting to say the least and, even worse, this isn't uncommon. Toilets flood and overflow often! With that in mind, consider the countless amount of people who wear their shower shoes into the head and back into the berthing at all times of the day, tracking nasty shit onto the deck.

I try not to cry and puke when my arm touches a wall in our showers as I lift and maneuver in it to thoroughly clean myself. I will go as long as I possibly can without shaving my legs simply to avoid having to bend over in the shower. The idea of my bare butt touching the walls makes my skin crawl.

Even looking down the drains is gross because they are never clear. There's always strands of hair all over the showers of different textures, colors, and lengths and the last thing I want is some stranger's hair sticking to my wet ass. Sometimes I get sick to my stomach having to squat above the toilet, hovering above the seat to pee, inhaling the smell of God knows how many tampons in the brown paper bags on the floor next to me.

Reminiscent of the smell of tainted copper, it singes my nose.

Now that you understand, I would really appreciate it if someone, anyone, could tell me where in the hell is good order and/or discipline here?

Berthing Thieves

"I'm so sick of this shit. I hope that all berthing thieves rot in a special place in hell," I growled to myself as yet another one of my personal belongings turned up missing.

Though we all worked for the same people, for some reason there are people who will steal anything just for the sake of doing it. Maybe they get a rush out of taking from other people or get high off of seeing others squirm, but I couldn't figure berthing thieves out for nothing. Especially those who steal shit that doesn't make sense to take.

Of course, the occasional Apple watch or AirPods go missing, but people's laundry randomly goes missing as well. Yes, there are people who will steal your underwear and socks, dirty or clean! Now I can rationalize taking someone's headphones but their dirty drawers?

One night on board my aircraft carrier during our deployment, I woke up around 0200 when suddenly all the lights came on simultaneously. *What the fuck*, I groaned, throwing my hands over my eyes in an attempt to adjust to the bright light. Upset, I opened my rack curtains to see what the heck was going on. To my surprise, I saw a close friend of mine – a petty officer third class – rummaging through other people's things.

"Are you okay?" I whispered, trying to be courteous of the other resting sailors around us.

She, on the other hand, was too livid to care about being polite. Sista girl was straight up pissed off and she didn't care if she let the entire ship know it. Loudly, she responded, "No! Everybody in here is about to wake the fuck up! Someone took my shit!"

"What? You sure?" I asked, wiping my eyes.

If looks could kill, I would have been a goner when she threw her piercing eyes in my direction. "Yes, I'm sure," she spewed. "I'm not an idiot."

Because I knew the smart attitude wasn't her typical character, I let the remark pass without getting offended. Immediately hopping out my rack, I threw on my hoodie and sweatpants, and began to help her search for her belongings.

"What are we looking for?" I asked, trying to speed up the search. I was tired and wanted to get back to resting.

Apparently, she was getting prepared to call it a night and thoughtlessly set her toiletry bag on our berthing's lounge table to quickly run to the head and grab something she forgot. As she came back down from our head – which was one ladder well up from our berthing – she discovered that in less than two minutes, her toiletry bag was no longer where she had left it.

A woman's toiletry bag is the Holy Grail for a female sailor. It is stocked full with hair products, toothbrush, toothpaste, and perfumes, and hers had vanished. Her frustration was understandable considering that we were underway, and it was highly unlikely that she could go a nearby Walmart to restock her stolen items. With her angry rummaging, she made sure to wake up the entire berthing by throwing things around and banging against the walls.

After waking up a petty officer first class, who seemed to be the only first class in the berthing at the time, she began to question my friend about what was going on and why she was so upset.

"Okay, okay. Someone stole your bag. I get it, but you need to calm down!" yelled the first class.

Obviously as upset as my friend was, she did not respond kindly to the first class's orders and continued to shout and throw things around. "Don't tell me to calm down, bitch!" yelled my friend.

"Okay, that's it. I'm calling security!" responded the first class as she made her way to our berthing's phone.

Not only did she call our ship's security down to the berthing to assist in either calming down or restraining my upset friend, but she also called a female chief petty officer. Once our berthing was filled with 5-0, a chief, and other confused, half-asleep residents of the berthing, security assessed the situation by asking questions and trying to keep my friend calm.

It all went from zero to one hundred...real quick.

Meanwhile, the first class was over in a corner singing like a bird to the head of security. "Yes, she called me names when I tried to calm her down and started throwing chairs! I didn't know what else to do."

Fortunately, security was not as upset as I thought they were going to be and showed sincere understanding as to why she reacted that way. They advised her to make a statement regarding what happened and asked her to describe every stolen item. After the smoke cleared, I went to the head where I talked to another lower ranking friend of mine.

"She did not have to call security! We could have handled that situation in house!" I stated with my friend's nodding in agreement. As we continued our venting session, stating our disagreement with the first class's actions, we were interrupted by another petty officer first class who seemed to have been listening from afar.

"Hey! First of all, she's a whole first class that had a damn third class in the berthing freaking the hell out at two o'clock in the morning! She tried to calm her down, and the girl started calling her names. What was she supposed to do? Tackle her? No! There are people that get paid for that and those people are security. You guys will learn in your careers that every action has a reaction." Then, she walked out of the head.

My friend and I were left speechless and walked out soon after.

After finally climbing back into my rack and getting into a comfortable position, I lay there wide awake, unable to sleep because of the chaos that had just occurred. I was bothered by the petty officer's words in the head earlier.

Every action has a reaction.

So, who was wrong? Feeling like making another entry into my journal, I hoped that writing it out would help me make sense of it all.

Pearson's Journal

Here are the facts:

- *The third class petty officer's personal belongings were stolen in her berthing. The thief was probably someone that was currently in the berthing, which I am sure is what really drove her anger to its extent. For all she knew, it could have been the first class who was trying to calm her down that stole her things. My friend, who is African*

American, was now missing hair products that our ship's store does not contain. She feels like these certain hair products are essential for her to comfortably conform her hair to the Navy's regulations daily. Would you have thrown a fit as well or have been calm about the situation?

- *The first class petty officer was the highest rank in the berthing at the time of my friend's loss of temper. It was literally her job to gauge the situation and attempt to deescalate it. Although she wasn't very compassionate, she did try and calm down my friend but, when she refused, she called security. To her, it did not matter if my friend had the right to be upset or not. What mattered to the first class petty officer was that a sailor who was told to calm down, did not. When the sailor continued to throw things around, the first class considered her dangerous and called security. She did her job. Would you have gone about this situation the same way as the first class or would you have taken it upon yourself to figure out who the berthing thief living amongst you was?*

Good Order and Discipline at its finest.

5

OUR BEHAVIOR TOWARD OFFICERS

An Opinion on Power and Authority
Aviation Structural Mechanic Safety Equipment Third Class Karissa McCormick
Twenty-seven years old. White. Scorpio.

"Although the Navy is trying to clean its ways, there are still things that stand out. There is still sexism, racism, ageist, and rankism. Speaking of rank, I understand the aspect of respecting rank; however, you are no better of a person just because you have an extra chevron, an anchor, or a star. You are still a human that makes mistakes. I feel like the Big Navy looks at higher ranks and believe 'Oh, they're definitely not at fault. It's fine. Pat them on the back. We'll have a fall guy that's probably lower ranking'."

The Salute

Upon enlisting in the Navy, you will notice that the way the enlisted folk act toward officers within any military organization is with the utmost respect, to say the least. They are treated much differently than us. Officers are looked upon like they are the upper echelon while the enlisted only got treated in high regard by civilians.

The first clear distinction is the way they are to be addressed.

For example, when any enlisted personnel approach an officer outside or within a building or hangered area that is extremely vast in height, we are to initiate a salute and hold that salute until either the officer returns the salute or we have completely passed by the officer. There are instructions detailing distinctly how to salute under any circumstance, but the point is that enlisted personnel must salute officers to show respect. Officers are supposed to salute higher-ranking officers as well.

But if you are enlisted, you will be saluting every single damn officer no matter your rank. Not only was it mandatory to salute, but you're also to address them as sir or ma'am. No exceptions. Period.

While deployed upon our aircraft carrier in the Middle East one regular military day, a seaman by the name of LSSN Leaman and I were ducking and dodging the many aircraft in our hangar bay as we headed back to our work centers after retrieving parts.

"LS3 Pearson, are we supposed to salute officers while in the hangar bay?" asked one of the newest LSSNs in my division.

"Yes, we do while in port but not while we are underway," I responded.

"So why don't we salute senior chiefs or master chiefs? I always wanted to know that, but I was too afraid to ask in boot camp," she questioned.

As we pulled our pallets and pallet jacks topped with boxes of aircraft parts throughout the hangar bay, I sighed sadly under my breath as I thought of the best way that I could explain this to a new, motivated sailor without sounding too negative. "I'm not exactly sure Leaman, but I do know that it is a tradition that has been followed for decades. The enlisted salute officers as a sign of respect."

As I anticipated her response, she answered, "But I just don't get it! All of these master chiefs and senior chiefs have been in the Navy for so long and are so much older than the Ensigns and Lieutenant JGs. I think that we should salute chiefs and above."

As much as I wanted to revamp her opinion about what we are taught to do regarding saluting, I couldn't. I agreed with her too much to go against the sentiments she'd expressed.

"Well, I guess it depends on the way you look at things, Leaman. Personally, I don't believe a twenty-year master chief in the Navy should salute or address an ensign that has barely gained his or her sea legs by sir or ma'am, but hey, we're all entitled to our own opinions. Just like you, and any other person in the military, has the right to feel patriotic as hell when saluting officers if you like," I told her. "With my experience though, it gets old to most enlisted people – *especially* the ones above the rank E-6 and above. It makes me wonder *why* officers are treated as royalty and *we're* the peasant. Most sailors overlook this tradition because it has been around for decades. But as for me, I believe that new traditions have the right to replace old traditions at some point. So, I agree with you, Leaman. I agree."

"Why can't somebody change it? It doesn't make any sense," she pondered.

Again, I agreed with every word she'd said.

A Different Case
Personnel Specialist Second Class Dominique Lucas
Twenty-four years old. African American. Gemini.

"These officers are a different case. They come in not knowing a thing about the fleet. Especially when they come in new to a ship, they are bred to think that they are high and mighty, and most have the *audacity* to look down on junior enlisted sailors just because they went to school for the Navy, because they are commissioned. School doesn't teach you shit about the fleet and some of these seamen are thirty years old! We are *all* adults . . . show some common decency Sir or Ma'am."

Cranking

In the Navy, the word *cranking* is used to describe the endeavors of our food service attendants, also known as cranks or crankers. Enlisted sailors who are not culinary specialists (CSs) or cooks by training are sent by their divisions, usually when lower ranking and new to a command or ship, to go cranking to augment the normal number of culinary specialists available and provide extra assistance to serve the crew, to simply give back to the crew, and/or for a humbling experience.

Cranks are to assist culinary specialists with whatever they may need. This means everything from dishwashing and sweeping, to swabbing or wiping down the galley. You could also end up serving food on the mess line or transiting boxes of food and food supplies throughout the ship.

When I was an undesignated seaman on my destroyer, I was sent cranking by my division while my ship was in home port, and although most junior sailors do not look forward to this assigned task at all, I couldn't have been more excited! It gave me something to do outside of my customary routine.

You guys are telling me that instead of doing manual labor, I am being sent on Temporary Assigned Duty (TAD) to help out in the galley? I thought to myself. Inside I was jumping up and down like a kid on the way to a candy store. *So, you want me to work inside all day, serve food, and wipe down some tables? When do I leave again?*

I was ecstatic!

While cranking, I discovered that there are numerous jobs that a crank can do. You can be assigned to do dishes in the deep sink, serve food on the enlisted mess line, work within the chief's mess, or work within the wardroom where the officers eat. The hardest working and most spot-on cranks are designated to either the chief's mess or wardroom, which are the best positions to obtain under most circumstances.

When I started my cranking duties, however, both of those positions were taken already, so I was sent to the general mess decks for enlisted personnel, which I was still completely okay with. Up to this point, I found cranking to be a decent task. Until all that changed one unfortunate day.

A shipmate of mine who usually worked the wardroom became ill and was sent to be sick in quarters (SIQ) to recover and ensure she didn't spread whatever sickness she had to others on the ship. In her absence, I was instructed to cover her shift within the wardroom. Operations in there were a lot different than taking care of my fellow shipmates on the enlisted mess decks. Immediately, I was briefed by the wardroom's culinary specialist on the etiquette of the space.

When setting up the wardroom tables, I was to use a specific set of fancy dishes in which I placed the fruit, desserts, and other condiments. I also had to set places for the captain and executive officer with specific silverware in a certain order. It was also my responsibility to fill up a pitcher of water, half-way with ice, along with two empty glasses, and set it at the reaching convenience of the captain and the XO's seating.

Every other officer grabbed their own silverware and beverages.

As officers trickled into wardroom, I stood by and awaited their observance of the written menu until they placed their orders. I would then deliver their order, usually written, to the wardroom culinary specialist and stand by for either more orders or until an order was prepared. Once an order was prepared, I would retrieve it from the CS and stand by with the plate in hand until the officer was seated, and then place the plate with the officer.

Honestly, most officers weren't assholes and would just take their plates from me if they noticed it was theirs, but then some would sit and wait for it to be presented. I would do this continuously until all officers were taken care of. I also had to stand by in case an officer needed anything. Sometimes, depending on the topic of conversation at the table, the officers would dismiss me until after chow.

Once all the officers were finished eating, disposed of their own plates, and the wardroom was clear, I could then begin to clean up the wardroom. Honestly, I loved cranking and all, but I wanted to be back on the mess decks with the other enlisted people. The evening had struck a chord with me, reminding me of the dreaded time I'd spent at Olive Garden. I hated it and couldn't wait for my shipmate to return.

I felt so belittled and unwelcomed. I couldn't understand how it was okay for me to treat people this way after coming from the line of grunt work that I did for the Navy. The fumes shooting out of my ears could be seen from at least one hundred yards.

At least on the enlisted mess decks I could joke around with my shipmates who retrieved their own food, beverages, and silverware, disposed of their own trash, and had most likely cranked themselves! It didn't belittle my self-esteem to serve them. I felt appreciated, welcomed, and more at home.

They really got my ass, I thought to myself.

Fortunately for me, as I've mentioned, I went cranking while my ship was in port. There were sailors that cranked underway and honestly, being instructed to crank in the wardroom was a nightmare come true for most junior sailors under way. If you were a wardroom crank on a small boy, you could basically consider yourself attached to the hips of the officers in the wardroom as a maid, since you had the added responsibilities of taking care of their laundry and cleaning or restocking their heads.

I keep askin' y'all, whose idea of Good Order and Discipline is this?

Speak Up and You Will Be "The Problem"
Personnel Specialist Second Class Dominique Lucas
Twenty-four years old. African American. Gemini.

"It's hard to be quiet when things are not fair; I tend to speak on it and that brings me many problems. After I was done with being a deck seaman and I had finally picked up my rate as a personnel specialist, I merged into the work center with the other PSs at my command. I understood that I was new, and that new, lower ranking people usually got the bitch work, but I wasn't tolerating being treated like shit. I spoke up about it. I'm trying to understand and learn. Do not treat me like shit . . . and since I didn't hold my tongue about mistreatment, it almost never worked out in my favor. I looked like the problem because I spoke up."

Sea Story
By: Aviation Ordnanceman Airman Labria Lowe
Twenty years old. African-American. Libra.

I'm really big on respect. I give it to everyone freely until they give me a reason to feel otherwise.

It seems that everybody with rank feels entitled from what I've experienced, especially officers. It kills me when an officer who just came into the Navy, is damn near my age, and thinks that they know everything under the sun simply because of a rank or tenure. So annoying.

Ever notice how cool and coo-coo-ca-choo you are with a chief but then you're made to be scared or feel some type of way when an officer is around? For example, I can call my chief whatever the fuck I want within reason and respect, and we can be cool and joke around, but I have to monitor so much to the point where I'm being fake with an officer because I'm scared. And it shouldn't be like that.

Onward with more ridiculousness.

We'd been out to sea for sixty something days without a port visit. I was on the flight deck sitting on the tire of an aircraft. I was tired. I'd been locked in for two months straight, no break, seven days a week, twelve-plus hours a day. I was *so* tired. I had just carried six tie-down chains on my back so after I put them down, I sat there on that tire with a fellow third class, chilling and talking. We were already prepped and ready to go for a flight schedule. The carrier air wing maintenance officer (CAG MO), a lieutenant commander, saw us and came over angrily – charging! I could just tell that he was about to get in my ass.

So, I prepped myself. Not in a way that I was looking for a fight but more bracing myself for whatever ignorance spilled out of his mouth next. *Alright, let's see where this is going.*

He started yelling and screaming, "Get the fuck up!" pointing his big, chubby ass finger in my face. He continued to shout like an insane lunatic who was off his meds. "Why are y'all sitting on this motherfucking tire? Y'all are lazy! What the fuck are y'all supposed to be doing right now?"

Just on and on, and he hadn't even had the decency to introduce himself. It was clear he only wanted to hear himself talk since he wouldn't let anyone else get a word in edgewise. To speak, someone else had to talk over him.

That didn't slow him down though.

What a narcissist, I thought, shaking my head from left to right.

He then told us to go to the flight deck control office so that he could report us to the other officers and chiefs. Although it was just me and the shipmate I was sitting with, he wasn't pointing his finger at the third class – just me.

"Sir, can you please stop yelling? I'm not saying this to be rude. I'm saying this because you are yelling, and I truly cannot understand you," I said, trying to keep cool. "And I'm not going to receive the information any better from you yelling at me than if you were to talk to me like I'm a human being. I feel like you're being disrespectful right now. All of this is not necessary."

"Asshole," he shouted in retort. "You don't know what disrespect looks like."

As a young Black woman in the military, a young Black woman, period, I didn't know what disrespect looked like? No, that wasn't going to fly with me. Especially not as a member of an entire class that society disrespected for sport.

"Well sir, you're doing it right now!" I let him know since he clearly had no idea what disrespect was. It took everything in my soul not to lose my shit at this crazy man screaming at me.

He didn't slow up, his little fragile ego too broken to simply walk away. Instead, he continued to yell. "*Go* to flight deck control!"

"Okay I'm going but, sir, I'm letting you know right now that you're being disrespectful as fuck! Straight up! And I'm not with that shit!" I stated.

We got to flight deck control, and he put me on blast in front of everybody. "This one right here is trying to make me seem like *I'm* the bad guy."

He had completely changed his demeanor and even banned me off the flight deck for the entire day because I spoke up! He brought in my maintenance master chief, my LCPO, and LPO. He even tried to bring my lieutenant in it to get me into as much trouble as possible. While his actions were A-okay.

Eventually my master chief organized a meeting with all of us, including the CAG MO, so that we could discuss what had happened. The way the CAG MO talked in front of them was not the way he talked to me.

He watered down both his aggression and the facts of the story. "I just need these guys to understand that we always need to be on the ready and that we always have to be on the go. We need to always be on alert, so with the way it looks, sailors sitting down on tires, perception is reality...." Blah, blah, blah.

It was bullshit.

But the same crap you just said calmly in front of all of these other authorities is the same crap you could have said when I was sitting on that tire outside, I thought.

After the meeting, my LPO, an enlisted person of course, said, "I know that was some bullshit and I know that's not at all how it went on the flight deck." He also told me not to worry about it. "I guess we just can't sit on tires anymore. Enjoy your day off," he finished.

Shortly after our orchestrated talk, I was going through the admiral's p-way, headed to enjoy my day off, when the CAG MO stopped me, "Hey ship mate."

He approached me in a calm manner and proceeded to talk to me about the situation some more. "I apologize. I think I overreacted." He admitted in a low tone.

I was okay with the apology, but I still couldn't understand why I had to go through all of that to receive it! This man stressed me out simply because he was being an asshole for no reason and couldn't accept me calling him out for it.

This was my first cruise on the boat, so when that incident happened, I was trying to figure out who the hell was yelling at me! And was I supposed to automatically salute him and give him whatever he needed just because he was an officer?

After he approached me like that? Hell no!

Look, I get it. Everyone was stressing on deployment, and we hadn't hit a port or nothing yet, so I was going through it, too. But I shouldn't have been attacked like that solely because someone who outranked me felt entitled.

And do you really think my Black ass *isn't* going to say something when I feel threatened?

No!

Because, if you get a pass, all of you get a pass, and I'm not with that shit!

Advice About Having Power and Authority
Airframer Third Class Tyler Vickers
Twenty-five years old. African American. Aries.

"The Navy is full of narcissistic, sociopaths that get off on power. They like to see other people beneath them, hurt, or humiliated. It literally makes them happy. It's the *people* and not what we do. It's the culture of the Navy. It doesn't have to be this way. If you all hate each other and you all despise your lower ranking, what if shit really hits the fan? Negligence is a thing. You expect me to save your life if you just humiliated me in front of thousands of people or whatever the case may be? You expect me to help you if I see that something fell on you and your leg is broken or stuck underneath it? Or what if there was a serious casualty and the day before or the hour prior, you just disrespected me for no reason? Do you really think I'm going to help you? I'm sorry. That sounds so messed up. But that's what I want to get through people's heads. You've got to be kind to everybody because you never know."

6

THE STRUCTURE OF RANK

An Opinion on the Ranking Structure
Navy Counselor (Career) First Class Elon McDuell-Briscoe
Thirty-six years old. African American. Taurus

"I've met some of the *best* people that did not or could not advance in rank and have gotten involuntarily separated from the Navy for people that were complete dumb asses. The way the system is set up, there is no equal opportunity like they try to make it seem. It's a '*who's my favorite*' Navy still, which is incredibly sad."

Let's be realistic: we need structure in life and within the Navy. How else would we get things done? In life, this is why we have CEOs, managers, assistant managers, council, court officials, police chiefs, deputies, etc. However, it's the process of how rank is acquired that makes me raise an eyebrow. Navy enlisted personnel, E-1 through E-6, take tests based on their rates to increase in rank.

Once enlisted personnel make the paygrade of E-7 based off the test, they are considered "chief selects." They then submit a package to be considered and/or accepted for the rank of chief petty officer. Officers, O-1 through O-

3, automatically increase in rank after serving a certain amount of time in the Navy until the level of O-3. When they want to advance to a higher rank after that, they submit packages and attend boards to be considered and/or accepted for the next rank.

For enlisted personnel, advancing in rank depends on the quotas available for the next rank and that determines how many sailors will be able to advance. It is the sailors who scored the highest on the exams who will be the ones to advance. Sailors can pass their exams and still be unable to advance due to quotas needed or not needed. I believe that basing leadership off how well a person can take a test is a set up for disaster.

I personally know sailors who would make amazing leaders, but they do not test well. I understand that the test determines how well sailors know their rates, but there is more to the quality of a leader, a person in charge of people, or decision makers, than solely knowing the ins and outs of your rate.

I have several theories that I believe would increase the quality of the ranking structure. Here are a few of my own ideas:

Tests for enlisted personnel should be the basis for increases in pay and pay only. Becoming a higher ranking commissioned or enlisted leader should be based on a command vote and based off the voting's results and require a board thereafter. Once sailors have passed their boards, there should be a training of indoctrination lasting for at least a week to properly train a command's newest leaders within their rate or expertise. Once all these steps have been completed, a command should host its pinning ceremony, officially welcoming its newest leaders. I also believe that for a commissioned officer to rank up, he or she must first spend a certain amount of time as a lower ranking, enlisted sailor to qualify for commissioned advancement. The thought of having all ranks and rates enduring an advancement process similar in structure or exactly the same has crossed my mind a few times. Because, if we were to leave things as they are, what is so wrong with having officers test the same way that we do or having enlisted advance after spending a certain amount of time in their rate?

Annual Evaluations

Evaluations in the Navy happen for every rate and every rank once a year to assess a sailor's performance over the course of the past fiscal year. I even received evaluations when I was undesignated. The scores of an evaluation are generated through the categories of professional knowledge, quality of work, command or organizational climate/equal opportunity, military bearing/character, and personal job accomplishment/initiative. Each category can be scored from a low 1.0 to an excellent 5.0.

The overall determination – in order from worst to best – are: significant problems (SP), progressing (P), promotable (P), must promote (MP), and early promote (EP). Getting the EP grants an enlisted sailor two free extra points toward their advancement exams. Most sailors are even okay with receiving the MP because the MP grants one free extra point on advancement exams. Unfortunately, there is a specific number of EPs that each command's working departments can hand out among each division – which is not many at all. For example, at my squadron, there were three third classes within my rate and in my division. Only one of us received an EP.

Another unfortunate fact about an evaluation is that they are left solely to the discretion of your immediate chain of command. Your acquired qualifications and accomplishments come together to create the eval, yes, but then it is your first class, chief, or divisional officer that determines who gets what. Sadly, for some, evaluations can end up being a favoritism game. And even if that's not the case, chains of command often determine evaluation results by the longevity of a sailor's time at their command.

For example, I received my first MP eval shortly after arriving to my squadron. Although I had acquired more qualifications faster than any of my divisional peers and hadn't been in any trouble at all, that meant nothing. Since my peers had been there longer than me, the EP was given to the senior third class who had not been in any trouble during his term as well.

And I'll keep it 100 percent real with you guys: I got qualifications as fast as I possibly could and not because of my naturally competitive spirit. I plowed through quals *solely* to look better than my peers. My appetite for these qualifications was not natural. I had tunnel vision with my sights set on an EP. I am confessing this to make a point: I've seen many occasions where sailors will race to get to the top, step on toes, sell fellow sailors out, and only become an outstanding sailor when someone important is looking just to make sure they are in the lead for the EP on their upcoming evaluation.

This in turn leads to sailors being put up against each other and despising one another – which is terrible considering that we are all supposed to be on the same team. It is very toxic and can sometimes land the wrong people with an EP. But in this world, it is hard to not get caught up in the EP hype. Because if you're not one of the sailors fighting for the EP, you're probably a dirtbag in most eyes of many command leaders.

But don't worry because there are options!

If sailors feel as if their evaluation results were not graded fairly, they are able to submit a statement about their disagreement with their results. And here's what I have to say about that: good luck! Fighting a battle against your entire immediate chain of command that is higher ranking than you, including your divisional officer, is almost always a loss. I'm not saying it's impossible, but you better be damn sure you can win. Other times, evaluations are recorded fairly if you have a chain of command with great moral standings and an emphasis on fairness. Hopefully, this is the case.

As I sat at my desk checking my work email on a regular early morning at my squadron, I overheard my LS1 asking a fellow LS3 of mine how their junior sailor of the quarter board went. Several of the most outstanding sailors are chosen to compete for this title and if chosen, this is a brag-worthy achievement. "So, what kind of questions did they ask you in there?" asked LS1 excitedly.

"Well, they asked me about a few current events and then asked me if there is one thing that I could change in the Navy, what would it be," responded the LS3.

"Okay and?" pondered LS1.

"I told them that I would like for evaluations to be scored digitally," LS3 said. "I would rather have my evals scored by a computer where we could input all that is necessary for each category and have a system digest the given information and then spit out our result. At least then we could eliminate not only the bias in scores, but the unsafe likelihood that sailors do not know their new jobs, roles, or positions they acquired very well while competing for that annual EP. I also explained that I believe that sailors who obtain qualifications in competition acquire so many qualifications so quickly that they never slow down to let their new responsibilities sink in. They are most likely only in it for the EP; not to actually do the job and that needs to change."

A week later, we were informed that LS3 was chosen for junior sailor of the quarter.

Living up to the Expectations
Logistics Specialist Third Class Laura Baxley
Twenty-eight years old. African American. Aries.

"I have dealt with a lot of depression while being in the Navy. Being the person I am, I'm afraid to fail. Dealing with everything that comes with the Navy, mentally or physically, really aggravates my triggers. It's the expectations from people, and they're not always bad either. People can expect good things from you that you feel you have to live up to all the time in the Navy."

The Meritorious Advancement Program (MAP)

It can really hurt your pride when a friend or fellow shipmate advances in rank before you do. Don't get me wrong; you're happy for them, but it still hurts. Here's an example from a sailor I worked with whose name has been changed for privacy.

Seaman Tyrone had been a Retail Specialist Seaman (RSSN) for almost four years because, unfortunately, the quotas to rank up to a petty officer third class in his rate were less than 5 percent since he joined. But these obstacles did not harm RSSN Tyrone's optimism. RSSN Tyrone was also a married man, a new father, and a hard worker who had never been in trouble in the Navy. He was truly looking forward to advancing in his career.

Every night for two months, prior to his exam, Seaman Tyrone stayed up late, well after his family had gone to bed, and studied. He also made sure he remembered to take his flash cards with him to work, especially on the days he had watch so that he could study more. Sometimes after work and on the weekends, he even had his wife quiz him. He spent twenty dollars on a cool little app that the Navy offers for sailors to study for their upcoming exams, too.

He eventually took the exam and then a few months later, the advancement exam results came out only to reveal that Seaman Tyrone missed his chance to advance by 0.5 points. It was a tough break to say the least. Maybe he'll get it the next time he is eligible to take the exam again in six months.

As Seaman Tyrone sat on his couch at home that night after exam results came out, he had just finished a stiff glass of whiskey when his wife wanted to discuss his disappointment. "I just don't understand babe. You studied *so hard!* Do you think it could have been an error?" she asked with compassion.

"I wish it were honey, I do. But that's just how shit goes in the Navy. And it's not even that I didn't make it this time; I'm more upset about GM3 Sally. *She* made it on her first try," responded Seaman Tyrone.

"That lazy girl you're always complaining about?" gasped his wife. He nodded.

"Yeah, her! She's only been in for two years and made it! She is single, lives in the barracks for free, and is, as you know, lazy as hell! And for someone that doesn't even like their job in the Navy, she sure is happy about making third class!" expressed Seaman Tyrone. "I overheard her say that she guessed on almost every question on her exam and didn't even study, but I guess you can do that when your rate's quotas for third class are 100 fucking percent!"

Guys, I know exactly how Seaman Tyrone feels. My only argument is that at least he could take an exam! When I was an undesignated seaman, it hurt to watch new sailors with rates check in to our command after me and rank up before me. I could not take an exam because I did not have a specific rate. There is no such thing as an undesignated third-class petty officer. So, for two years, I watched my shipmates pass me by. I watched seamen that I trained myself become my bosses, so I completely understand how Seaman Tyrone feels.

There is, however, a program in place for sailors who have these unfortunate circumstances like Seaman Tyrone. It is the Navy's infamous Meritorious Advancement Program (MAP), also known as mapping program or getting mapped. The MAP program helps commands promote overqualified sailors – who can't pass the exam – to the next rank.

The chain of command will put together a MAP package for you, route it to all the necessary, highest ranking deciding factors, and based on your track record of awards, evaluations, collateral duties, qualifications, and overall participation and work ethic . . . may the best sailor win. It is not guaranteed that you will get mapped just because you didn't make it on your exam. It's honestly more in your control to take the exam in hopes of making rank than it is to hope for the approval of your MAP package.

There are a certain number of sailors who can get mapped in the Navy per command and a certain number of sailors who can get mapped within your command per rate. I actually like the MAP. I think it is a great way for the

Navy to acknowledge that their ranking system may be a tad bit screwed up. It sounds like, “Here you go guys. We know that we don’t have the fairest system of acquiring rank in place so here’s a program that will give you more hope and another chance.”

I’ve seen sailors get mapped based on pure favoritism within chains of commands. I have witnessed sailors – who are complete assholes – make rank off the MAP due to their talented ability of sucking up to the bosses. These people usually treat their junior sailors like crap once the important eyes have stopped looking. But fortunately, I have also seen the MAP come through on its purpose for deserving, hardworking sailors as well. It’s bizarre, but sometimes it’s right.

Good luck out there.

Receiving a Coin

Sometimes when a sailor does something well or has been working very hard, an E-7 or above will award them a coin. These coins are usually customized for the person who gives them out. They have the potential to be very fancy with cool designs, emblems, or aphorisms. You could really consider receiving a coin as a gift of appreciation – something that says *atta boy* or *good job*.

I received a coin from the captain of my first command shortly before I departed for my new assignment. Giving and receiving a coin is a traditional gesture in the military. Some sailors collect coins from each command or port that they visit even if they must purchase the coin themselves. Some may think that receiving a coin is cool and some think that it is unnecessary. So, in conclusion, you’ll either end up with a cool story and a coin to show for it or a salty attitude wishing that you could receive more than a fake coin for your hard work.

Restriction

During the first month of my second deployment after a long twelve-hour shift on the carrier, I was headed to my berthing when I saw the weirdest thing. A young man walked by and had an extremely noticeable red letter "R" attached to the front chest pocket of his coveralls. Curious, I stopped him. "Excuse me. What does the R symbolize?" I asked.

A bit baffled he answered, "Oh, uh, this means that I am on restriction."

Immediately I was infuriated. *What the hell?* I thought. *This is a thing? Big "R," Boom! I'm on restriction! Acknowledge that I'm a troublemaker! Seriously? I don't want to immediately judge someone and assume bad things when I look at them!*

"I am so sorry! I didn't mean to pry. I just didn't know. . ." I explained.

He nodded.

"Why on earth would you need to wear that? And how do you feel about it?" I questioned.

"I'm not sure why we have to wear it. I was instructed to keep my ID in it and *believe* it's just another form of the punishment; you know, like a scarlet letter. I feel embarrassed having to wear it honestly," he replied.

I can't express enough how disappointed and angry I was to discover this! This was *not* a thing on the destroyer. Maybe because a destroyer is such a small command where everybody knows everybody, *especially* the sailors on restriction, so having them wear a scarlet letter would probably be deemed unnecessary for that type of ship but after this discovery while I served upon the carrier, I immediately hated it!

Being on restriction already comes with taking so many L's. For example: some sailors may become demoted in rank, take a cut in their pay for thirty to ninety days, are not allowed to go anywhere outside of their actual command during the time of their restriction, *and* may have extra duties assigned to them on top of their normal work schedule. This means that as a restricted sailor, you will be performing extra work with less pay. So, on top of all of that, you're telling me that restricted sailors must walk around with a scarlet letter, too? Are we just telling them to go ahead and kill themselves?

"May I ask, what did you do?" I inquired. Assuming the worst and expecting it to be along the lines of drug use, disrespecting authority, or something even worse, I was nervous about the answer. To my surprise, he elaborated on the fact that he took a pay cut for fifteen days, lost his rank of third-class petty officer, and was demoted to seaman, while also having extra duty and the burden of wearing the scarlet letter all because he got caught utilizing a vape on board the ship during our deployment.

Yes guys, vaping on board is strictly prohibited. Just having a vape on board an American warship is considered having paraphernalia and that can, obviously, get you in a lot of trouble. Why? Well, vapes have the tendency to blow up or catch on fire, so on board, they are a big no-no.

"And I get that I'm not supposed to have a vape; I was wrong," he continued. "But *shit*! I don't want to smoke cigarettes all the time and to be honest, when I'm lying in my rack at night, I like to vape and decompress. It was a good way to relieve some stress while I watched movies on my phone or thought about my day."

And he is right. The rules were made, and they should be followed. But this was also his first offense; a man who is married with a mortgage to pay. I just do not see, especially with this type of offense, what would have been so wrong with maybe a one-time fine and a bigger fine if a second offense was committed. Then, if sailors receive third offenses, the ultimate punishment. Because honestly, if I leave my phone on its approved and safety checked charger for too long, it has the tendency to get too hot. So, what now? Are we going to prohibit having cell phones on board as well? And what about lighters? Because I have seen some sketchy ones on the smoke pit! Laptops, chargers, flammable perfumes? The list goes on of what could have the potential to be considered a crime on board.

At the end of the day, since the Navy does not allow them, vapes low-key became a "don't get caught" type of deal. Sailors are trusted to work with dangerous, multimillion-dollar equipment every single day – even equipment with the potential to kill us. Yet, trusting us with one hundred dollars' worth of vape equipment is too much for us to handle I suppose – although, most people learn how to maintain their own vapes by changing their coils in a timely manner and such. Kind of like how we learn to maintain the Navy's equipment to prevent mishaps, right?

Good Order and Discipline.

7

CHAPTER 7

Operations Specialist Second Class, Mya Davis
Twenty-four years old. African American. Aquarius.

"My biggest mental challenge since enlisting has been not getting justice when I felt I should have. Going through a court martial has been my *biggest* challenge. During and after that process I felt hopeless, betrayed, and let down by the military justice system. I feel like if I were a different race, the verdict would have been different. But because I am an African American woman and I stand strong and hold my head up high, they see me as this embodiment of someone that would be okay, and I know that is simply because of the way that I look."

Sea Story
By: Operations Specialist Second Class, Mya Davis
Twenty-four years old. African American. Aquarius.

What happens when the people who signed over their lives to protect and serve the citizens of the United States need to be served and protected?

It's a question that I'd never thought I'd have to ask myself when I signed my name on the dotted line to enlist. I never considered myself naïve before joining the Navy but my time enlisted has proven otherwise.

I was lured into the military the same way most young African Americans are: the promise of a paid education and global travel. I've always loved seeing new places and meeting new people. The pitch I got sold me on the promise that the Navy was made up of the best-of-the-best men and women in the country.

Right out of the gate I took my career in the military seriously. I wanted to give as much to the Navy as they'd promised to give me. I found out fast, though, that the fantasy I'd drummed up in my mind vanished and mutated into a nightmare that I still struggle with to this very day – years after the fact.

Being in the military isn't easy, especially when you're a woman. It's quadruple hard as a Black woman. The staunch attitude toward African American women in the Navy not only is a disservice to the women who have to jump through hoops simply to be acknowledged but it perpetuated the stereotypes that we deal with on a daily basis.

As if our layers of melanin were a secret layer of armor, Black women are expected to endure, endure, and then endure some more. We have to work three times as hard simply to be acknowledged in comparison with our white counterparts. In addition to the unspoken requirement that we be work-horses until we nearly break our backs, we are expected to smile and be polite through it all.

Displaying any emotion other than blind happiness to be a part of the Navy isn't a privilege that Black female sailors get to have. For us, if you're not happy, you're instantly pegged the bitter Black woman. If you have the audacity to stand up for yourself, you're labeled angry and aggressive.

It's stressful enough to simply exist on a ship in the middle of the ocean when on deployment, being a part of the most marginalized sector in the fleet makes it that much worse. The pressure mounts quickly when you must suppress fundamental parts of what make you human to make it through each day. That's why, when I was invited out with some of the other sailors in my command for Cinco De Mayo, I hopped at the chance to get some air.

Normally I kept my work and personal life separate. Being a local of the area where we were stationed at the time, I was able to be in touch with my civilian friends, but I still enjoyed meeting and connecting with new people. Especially when they were supposed to be some of the best and brightest according to the Navy.

Like I've stated before, I've never felt naïve until I became a sailor. Civilians don't get to see behind the smoke and mirrors of what the service portrays itself to be and what it truly is. It isn't until you agree to enlist and are contractually bound that you see the true nature of the Navy: a beast that will chew you up and spit you out with no remorse if given the opportunity. For the monster that would change my life forever, he found his window that very night I agreed to go out with some of my sailor friends. He was supposedly one of those friends.

To this day, I can only recall fragments of the evening: lots of loud yet festive music, an abundance of drinks, and dancing. I was feeling the vibe of the night. As the night continued and the liquor began to settle in my system, I became more and more comfortable around my colleagues, until my stomach began tumbling uncontrollably, and all the drinks I'd knocked back became determined to rush back up my esophagus.

Head in the toilet vomiting and barely able to see, let alone walk, I was faded off my ass. Completely blacked out, I was incoherent and needed to literally be carried back to my friend's room and placed in bed. For that, I will forever be grateful for those who helped me with no ill will but, unfortunately, there was a person in our party with sinister intent.

Because I was sound asleep when I'd been placed in bed, the sailors who'd helped me to my room left the door unlocked just in case I needed assistance or got sick again later in the night. This was how my abuser was able to get access to me. Lurking in the shadows, the predator crept into my bedroom when the coast was clear.

Because I was so heavily intoxicated, I never felt him unbuckling my pants or even penetrating me; however, I'll never forget hearing his raspy, guttural groan echo in my ears and head. "Mya, I've been waiting so long for this."

I woke up with him casually lounging in bed beside me like we'd been doing that for years. He was comfortably lying on his back, shirtless, in a pair of basketball shorts. *What the hell*? was my first thought as I looked around the room trying to get understanding on what was going on. Looking over myself, my pants were up on my waist, but they were both unzipped and unbuttoned. And along with most of my memory, my panties were missing.

Head throbbing and still not quite sure of what happened, my gut told me that something wasn't adding up. "What happened? Where's everybody at?" I asked him, waking him up.

"I don't know," was his smug, casual response. "You want some water? You were pretty gone last night."

I DON'T KNOW! I screamed internally, immediately getting up and leaving the room. I was still slightly inebriated from the night before, but I was certain that I'd never invited that man into my bedroom. I'd never thought of him as more than a colleague or friend for him to have been so comfortable lying beside me.

It was clear he wasn't going to be helpful in filling in the gaps. So instead, I found the friend I was looking for that I remembered had helped me into bed and started asking him questions. "Why are my pants unzipped?" I started growing short of breath. "And where are my panties?"

His eyes bulged as he looked over me before sadness settled into his features when he pointed to a hole in my pants. "They're right there."

Unexplained holes in my pants, misplaced panties, skewed memories, and the randomness of waking up with a man I had no intimate attraction to, the world officially caved in around me. Something wasn't right. There were too many unanswered questions for everything to be okay.

Nerves shaken, mind still trying to retrieve and fill in the blank pieces of the prior evening, I followed every protocol the Navy had in place for sexual assault.

During boot camp and accession training we were instructed that if we were victims of assault ourselves to go to the hospital and choose between the option of making either a restricted or unrestricted report. With a restricted report, the victim is able to speak with and get treatment for their assault while remaining anonymous. If this were the route I'd chosen to take, things could stay confidential, and a full-blown investigation wouldn't be triggered.

Then there was the choice to file an unrestricted report. An unrestricted report would get both the military police and civilian law enforcement involved in the case. I felt it deep in my core that the military would take care of everything. After all, my abuser wasn't one of the best and brightest that the Navy so proudly boasted about.

A vaginal swab verified that my abuser's semen was found inside of me, proof of the sexual assault that I couldn't fully remember. I was infuriated! Sometimes that anger was pointed inwardly at myself for letting my guard down and getting so drunk that I couldn't protect myself and other times it was spewed at the lowlife who took advantage of me in such a vulnerable state. I wanted to hurt that man as much as he'd mentally and physically hurt me, but I maintained zero contact with him as instructed. I was determined to keep my composure to ensure I didn't hurt my chances at getting justice.

After it was confirmed that I was raped, I was given medication to thwart off any possible pregnancies, STDs, or STIs that might have resulted from the assault. I was also given the choice to stay or go. Either stay with the command and run the chance of seeing my abuser's face every day or be transferred elsewhere. I left without hesitation.

The Navy interviewed everyone who may have been involved with that night. If I remembered a person being anywhere around the party or my room that night, they were interviewed. It brought relief, thinking that they were taking my case seriously until everything came to an abrupt stop when the COVID-19 pandemic put a firm pause on the proceedings. My efforts to be patient and remain optimistic were tested and eventually ran out after the case was stretched out for almost two whole years.

Meanwhile my assailant was out and about, just living his life like it was golden. He didn't have to constantly remember what happened or make any changes to his day-to-day life – he was not impacted at all by what he'd done.

Two entire years after the assault, the Naval Criminal Investigative Service, or NCIS, finally got the trial underway. TWO YEARS. In an instant all the healing I'd done between the aftermath of the assault and the actual day the trial started was wiped away when I saw his face again. To say it was unnerving would be an understatement. Everything in me wanted to run, but I knew I couldn't. He'd already been free for two years after he'd attacked me and who's to stay there weren't more women he'd assaulted?

I refused to be part of the reason he got away with what he'd done.

During the trial I was able to watch his NCIS interview where he'd recounted his events of what happened. My eyes were closed the entire time as I listened to him tell the story like he was going over the details of a sports game instead of a sexual assault. Like he'd done nothing wrong.

He'd told the interviewer that he'd entered my room that night without permission and that my eyes were indeed closed. Where most decent people would take that as a sign to go away, my abuser plainly stated that he'd done otherwise. Instead of leaving the room and since I hadn't told him to go away, he didn't.

After noticing that neither of us had a negative response to him being in my room without permission, he admitted that he tapped my shoulder. When that did nothing, he took it upon himself to start having sex with me. Those were his exact words: "I started having sex with her."

Not only did the jury get to hear a confession come directly from my abuser's mouth but I had key, expert witnesses on my side. The nurse examiner confirmed that she did indeed find the accused's semen inside of me when I went to the hospital. There was an entire sleep expert that verified what common sense should tell any person: that many people have slept through sex – especially when intoxicated to the point of blacking out and that consent cannot be given when someone has been drinking to that extent.

Even all my friends that were out with the defendant and myself that night had taken time out of their own busy lives to testify on my behalf. They retold the story from their various points of view; all landing back at the same *he was acting shady the entire night* conclusion. Then, when it was my turn to take the stand, I upheld the oath to tell the truth. The whole truth and nothing but the truth is what came out of my mouth. I didn't remove parts of the story to make myself look better or withhold information out of fear.

My abuser, being the coward that he always has been, couldn't bear taking the stand to defend himself.

Instead, he allowed his attorney to speak for him and concoct some stupid defense: "What happened between these two was akin to two married people who got a little too drunk after a night of fun."

To say that my mind nearly exploded wouldn't accurately describe how I felt to hear that defense. We weren't like a married couple because we weren't a married couple. We weren't even a couple that was dating or even having those types of conversations.

Apparently, I was the only person in the entire room to consider those questions as the eight-person jury found him not guilty. He wasn't reprimanded in any way and was completely cleared of all charges. When I'd joined the Navy, I left behind everyone that I love and trusted that I knew without a doubt had my back because allegedly the Navy took care of their own. I found out firsthand that was a lie from the pits of hell.

In my case, they'd decided that even though I'd been good enough to sign my life over to them for the length of my contract, I wasn't worth protecting. To make matters worse, the only person that could have related to me on my jury was the one woman. A white woman who'd decided she couldn't relate to my experience as a sailor let alone be bothered to care about my well-being and safety.

Now, I'm counting down the days until my contract is up because once that day arrives, I will bid the Navy goodbye forever. There isn't enough money in the world to make me consider reenlisting. I'm no longer blind to the lies that they use to rope naïve civilians into lengthy contracts and dangerous situations.

I no longer participate in anything that is outside of what's required of me. I don't take on any extra responsibility at my command, and I definitely don't fraternize with anyone on my personal time. Whenever I am asked, the answer is a firm and resounding *NO*. Emotionally deplete and void of all trust in the military, I can't fathom putting in any extra to an organization that wouldn't even give me the bare minimum.

My advice for anyone in the Navy that goes through a situation like mine would be do not depend on the NCIS to handle your case. Transfer to a new command and file an unrestricted report. No matter how much you're encouraged to keep your case in-house or who could possibly face repercussions because of it. Get *every* law enforcement agency involved that you can. Local authorities can use not only semen samples but blood samples in court. The American justice system as a whole is fucked up, but by doing this you stand a far greater chance at actually getting results.

Always follow through with your case, no matter how long it drags out because you need justice for yourself and because speaking up could potentially save others from becoming victims in the future. Keep yourself safe because the Navy has no intention of doing so, especially if you're a Black woman. And if you weren't able to get justice the first time around, never, ever stop fighting for it. Your day of redemption will eventually come.

PART III

SEX, MARRIAGE, RELATIONSHIPS, AND BOAT BOOS

8

SEX

Sex on Deployment

Let's talk about sex because, let's face it, it's a part of human nature. Without sex, we as an entire civilization would no longer exist. So, as important as sex is (consensual sex of course) on land to everyday civilians, those yearnings don't just cease to exist once you're sworn in as a sailor. If anything, our instinctual, hormonal urges are heightened – severely.

Especially while on deployment.

If you partake in sex while on deployment, you should consider yourself one lucky S.O.B. However, by Navy law, you *are not* to have sex when you're stationed upon a ship and deployed. As we are all adults with certain needs, going out to sea can become extremely challenging in this area. After a few long months underway with no action, it's not even about the physical act of sex anymore – just human contact is enough.

Being on deployment will almost make you feel like a sex addict considering how much you will desire it.

You'll start craving hugs. Hugs that have stopped feeling so innocent. Regular old hugs will fly out the window and everything will feel more intense. Suddenly any contact from another person feels like those deep, sensual hugs you'd receive from your spouse or someone special. You'll find yourself *dreaming* about simply hugging them as you absorb their smell.

"Yo, how'd you get that big ass bruise on your forehead?" I asked one of my female shipmates as a group of us were hanging out in our berthing lounge.

"Y'all, I was having the *best* dream about my husband last night." She stated on this typical, boring deployment night. This was our thing to pass the time away: catch up on juicy gossip and anything related to sex was juicy gossip. "It started with his big, strong hands . . . I mean, they seemed *massive*. They were sliding down my waist, gripping me tight. Like I was a winning lottery ticket that he refused to let go of. It was a bit hard, but it turned me on even more as he drew me in closer. Then... we made eye contact," she detailed to me and two other shipmates as we leaned in with open ears. "He started doing *the lean* you know, so I started leaning in too. I closed my eyes...."

I was both hanging on to her every word and trying to stop myself from laughing at the faces and emotion she projected in her hands as she attempted to exude the same surge of energy that she'd felt during the heated wet dream and from the looks of it, it was working.

She continued to passionately describe the dream, and our eyes were big with interest. "Right when I'm about to taste those beautiful, delicious lips...bam! *Aaaaaaannnnnnkkkkk, Aaaaaaannnnnnkkkkk, Aaaaaaannnnnnkkkkk*!"

We all gasped and jumped at the sudden, loud wailing she demonstrated.

"Oh my goodness," I laughed, slapping my hand over my chest, trying to regain my breath.

Our other colleague chuckled as well. "What was the noise?"

The storyteller kissed her teeth and rolled her eyes. "That was my fucking alarm going off and that shit scared me so bad, I jumped up and hit my forehead on my rack light! That's why I have this stupid bruise," concluded my friend as she pointed to her head. "I was so mad, I just got up and went to take a shower and start another stupid day on this stupid boat."

I understand that there are civilian jobs that take spouses and lovers away from each other, too, and I am not demeaning that experience at all. All I'm saying is that at least you guys can keep it sexy with phone service – maybe a little naughty FaceTime and some phone sex here or there. Try getting freaky through your email and some spotty internet.

You will quickly realize how *not* sexy this endeavor is. Because honestly, the old colon and parenthesis duo that creates a winky face is not exactly a thing anymore in this day and age. Also, trying to get sexy on the community phone lines of your ship with a line of people behind you who are also waiting on their ten to fifteen-minute phone call is not exactly ideal either. But we sailors do what we have to do. Even if you have to ask your homie to airdrop you a few porn videos because you've been looking at the same porn for the past three months and it is just not working for you anymore.

However, not all sailors are married or in serious relationships. Some sailors join the Navy single and have yet to find that special someone. But according to the Navy's rules, regulations, and instructions, God forbid that deployed sailors meet, vibe, click, or are remotely attracted to each other while underway. Sailors hooking up, kissing, having sex, holding hands, or even just being a little too close to each other on board our warships is a huge no-no.

It does not matter that we are cooped up in metal floating tin cans for months, sometimes longer than expected with unscheduled extensions and have a hard time forgetting what human contact feels like. Sex on a warship is a no-go. Let me say it a little louder for those in that back. Under no circumstances, none whatsoever, are you allowed to have sex on warships.

Sex. On. Warships. Is. Prohibited. Forbidden. Banned. Unconstitutional. Unlawful. Unauthorized. Illegal. Sailors are not allowed to have sex on warships! Eh, but do you think these rules stop sailors from having sex on warships, though?

I have gone three months on a deployment without seeing a blade of grass but guess what I do see every day underway? The same damn people. Guess what I do every day underway? The same damn things. With terrible internet service, minimal access to outside line phone calls, absolutely no cellular service, and cancelled port visits, sailors start to get a little antsy. People start to need people and then mistakes are made.

When I say mistakes, I'm mainly talking about married sailors who just couldn't take it anymore. If two consenting adults get caught having sex underway, it's not uncommon for them to accept their punishments *happily* – especially single sailors who weren't spending their pay checks, now cut in half, anywhere else! It's sad but true. There are sailors who have broken their vows to their spouses on deployments simply because their appetite to have sex became too large to ignore anymore. Married sailors cheat, fall in love with other people, and make mistakes that they will regret forever; this is common.

With the litany of circumstances that come with being an American sailor, it is an unfortunate reality. As a person who takes marriage seriously and has witnessed an extremely high adultery rate within our organization, it truly baffles me that there are regulations with the *audacity* to state that even a vibrator is unauthorized on board a ship! I commend the married couples that have kept and keep their loyalty intact while deployed. It is truly a tough task for many.

Sea Story
By: Logistics Specialist Seaman Apprentice Ashley McClendon
Twenty-four years old. Haitian American. Cancer.

I met a guy while our ship was in port. He would see me at work or shortly after work and compliment me, you know, doing his little charm thing. To me he was fine as hell. We never actually had a conversation, just short, flirty encounters. Eventually, we started our deployment and maybe a week into deployment or so, I saw him! He stopped to talk to me and was raining compliments. At that time, it was obviously the beginning of deployment, so everyone is now recruiting for the *boat boo/bae*.

I would flirt back, although I had a gut feeling that told me he might not be good for me. I still played into the flirting though. We were deployed, okay? It's not that I was lonely yet, it was more like, I'm in the Navy and I don't hear compliments often. I can't go home, and I don't have a boyfriend so for me, bada-bing-bada-boom! That's how it happened.

We flirted for a while. And then when we finally hit our first port visit after sixty-plus days straight out to sea, got back underway, and were at about day seventy-something on deployment, I ran into him again. Wanting to see how he was doing, considering that we had been out to sea for a long time, we started talking and catching up.

"I don't know how you work down there in that hot ass space all day and still look this good every time I see you," he would say. Of course, he was saying the same things that were cute and charming; raining with compliments like he used to, making me blush. Outside of the compliments he was really a good conversationalist, too.

I was hot and ready, like a Little Caesar's pizza! So of course, we ended up talking about other things. I'm grown. I wanted to talk about sex. Like I've mentioned before, this was a fine man who knew how to use his words. One thing led to another, and we'd intentionally go to a secluded space from time to time. One day, we were having sex and the boat's security walked in on us. We were caught. I wasn't upset about getting caught. I was thinking more along the lines of *Right now? Really?*

When you've got sex on your mind, people can make some really dumb decisions, especially when you're around someone attractive. You want to be filled with love, you want to feel a touch and affection. It's a lot to ask of us to be out to sea for so many months while meeting so many people. We don't have boyfriends, girlfriends, or partners on the boat to just talk to. Phone calls and emails aren't enough sometimes. But yeah, we were put into security and had to make statements about what we were caught doing. We were put on restriction a few weeks later.

Although it wasn't the getting caught having sex part that made me feel bad, it was finding out the next day that the man was married with a child. I don't regret doing what I did as a grown, adult woman because whether I was in port or I wasn't, if we were still flirting and talking and having great conversation, it would have been the same situation. I do feel like it's my fault for not asking him if he was taken. That really mattered. But it had already happened, and I couldn't go back and cry about it.

I was crying because I've been in the Navy for damn near four years and I came in undesignated. I worked my ass off, worked hard, and then I lost it all because I had sex on a boat. That's what hurt me. And the Navy is like high school – everyone is talking about it, coming up to me, showing me fake love, asking me what happened, telling me it's okay – like I don't know that it's okay!

I didn't spiral into depression or anything, but I did have really depressing thoughts. The only thing that kept me going was the fact that I didn't want anyone to see me cry. I just kept asking myself: *Why am I crying about it? What the fuck am I feeling bad for?*

9

BOAT BOOS

Infidelity on Deployment/Having a "Boat Boo"

Usually at the beginning of a deployment, married and single sailors go on the hunt for the infamous "boat boo." I personally wouldn't consider single sailors who pursue other single sailors a part of the boat boo category because they are S-I-N-G-L-E. But the term is still commonly used for sailors that meet each other while underway and begin dating, flirting, hooking up, or whatever the case may be.

What is a boat boo, you ask? The term refers to a sailor who is currently seeing another sailor but is assumed to only be a thing underway. In other words, once our ship is back at home in port and the deployment has concluded, the romantic duo that emerged during deployment will be no more because our real lives will have commenced again. Married people go home to their spouses, engaged people move forward with their fiancées, and the boat boos that once were turn back into a strictly work-related relationship.

For sailors it's the equivalent to the civilian's side piece or work husband/wife. A boat boo is the person we connect with on a level that is close to what we miss at home while out to sea. Like any other case of infidelity, it might not make sense to some while others understand perfectly well. So why do people go on the hunt for a boat boo in the first place? There are several reasons:

1. After spending so much time around the same people for months on end, naturally, attraction and feelings may arise; that is, until we arrive back home and sailors have zoned back into reality, which could be that wife and three kids back at home.
2. When dealing with loneliness or the lack of human connection, some sailors search for or just happen to find someone they can talk to everyday and be themselves with.
3. Sometimes sailors intentionally search for a boat boo while underway as a form of entertainment, just to see if they've "still got it." Nothing more, nothing less.
4. Some sailors may not be enjoying their situations at home and view their deployment as a bit of a getaway and look forward to being free from their lives back at home for a few months.
5. Some sailors are just horny, unfaithful, selfish human beings.

An Opinion on Male-Female Relationships
Logistics Specialist Seaman Apprentice Roxsana Herrera
Nineteen years old. Latina American. Pisces

"I hate the amount of unfaithfulness there is with relationships in the Navy. That, and the disrespect that comes from a man to a woman or from rank to rank. I respect it. I just don't agree with it."

Boat Boo Proposals

One day, during my second deployment on the carrier, I was doing my regular tasks as a logistics specialist. After dropping off some receipts to another supply work center to complete my shift for the day, I was about to leave when a male's voice caught up to me.

"LS3, LS3!" I noticed it was the person that I left the receipts with. Once he caught up to me, and I noticed his rank of petty officer second class and I asked him if there was an issue with the receipts. After responding with a no, he inquired about my position in supply.

"So, you're TAD to the S-6 Repairable Asset Management (RAM) division on board, correct?" he asked.

"That's right," I confirmed.

He followed up with another question. "Where exactly is your work center at?"

"I'm on the way to my berthing now. I can show you if you'd like," I told him, and he took me up on my offer.

During our walk toward my work center, we discussed the deployment. He asked me questions like, "Is this your first deployment?" and "Would you prefer to be stationed on a destroyer or a carrier?"

"This is RAM," I told him after we arrived.

Once we arrived, I was prepared for us to part ways and graciously thanked him for the company. "I really enjoyed talking to you and—"

My words were cut short when he blurted out. "What are you doing later?" He interrupted.

"Probably just going to sleep. I had a long day," I clarified.

He paused briefly but continued with his interrogation. "I was just wondering if we could have some coffee later or have lunch together tomorrow?" he asked boldly.

Wait, he isn't asking me what I think he is, is he? I wondered silently. But there was no other explanation. Mouth dropping in surprise, I realized I was being asked out on a date, on a warship of all places. *I thought everyone knew I was in a relationship.*

It was never something that I hid, however it seemed this sailor missed the memo. I politely replied, "Oh, I see where this is going. I'm not single. I'm going to decline." Thinking that my reply would end the conversation, I gave him a moment to respond.

"That's good! Congratulations," he exclaimed, beaming with excitement. Where I thought my announcement would be the silver bullet to kill all further conversation, I continued to be surprised. "That's good. Very good . . . see, I'm married. Huh? See us two people, we both have a lot to lose..."

Creeped out by his shady proposition, I grew offended at his implication as soon as the words hit my ears. It was clear he had no real respect for the union that he had with his spouse; however, I wasn't going to violate my person the way he did. Rest assured guys I cursed him out and proudly exited that conversation with my morality intact.

He was really trying to make me his boat boo, I thought to myself, shaking my head. All I could do is laugh. I truly cannot make this stuff up.

INTERLUDE TWO: AN UNGRATEFUL, ENTITLED, MILLENNIAL SAILOR

It was during my second deployment, after I filled up my first journal, when I started asking myself, *Am I just another entitled millennial? Am I a brat? Should I be more grateful?*

Because the truth is: if it wasn't for the Navy, I would have really struggled to upgrade my life with no degree, special talent, trade skill, or job experience other than serving tables at restaurants. So, for me to remotely speak negatively about the organization that changed my life for the better really made me take a hard look in the mirror.

I came down with a cold while deployed on the carrier, far before the COVID-19 pandemic, and decided to drop in on medical for some cold medicine. Once I retrieved my medicine and was headed back to work, I stumbled upon a wall of pictures in medical's p-way that described the heroic actions of sailors dating all the way back to the late 1800s. The picture and description that stood out the most to me was of a white male sailor receiving a medal from Barack Obama. I stopped to read the description of Senior Chief Special Operations Combat Medic Byers. It read:

"Then-Chief Edward Byers was trained as a Special Operations Combat Medic at Fort Bragg, North Carolina before going through SEAL training in 2002. As part of a hostage rescue force in Afghanistan, he assaulted, tackled and fought the insurgents in hand-to-hand combat and then threw himself on the hostage to shield them from small arms fire. While shielding the hostage, Byers subdued others with his bare hands. The 36-year-old is still serving on active duty after 11 deployments. He is the most decorated living Navy SEAL."

Eleven deployments? Still active duty? Did I just read that right? Was all that I could think after reading that. I felt like a complete bag of ass, and I wanted to rip up *every page I* had written. I began to think of all the African American women and men who risked it all in the military for our freedom and equality, and to pave the way for ungrateful people like me so that we would have the right to peacefully stand in the middle of an American warship's passageway as I was doing. Yet, there I was, writing this book and showing my unappreciative Black ass.

Fortunately for me, I read many books while deployed and the very first book that I cracked open on this deployment took me right out of that mindset. It was *Bossed Up: A Grown Woman's Guide to Getting Your Sh*t Together* by Emilie Aries. I ran across some of the author's advice shortly after my moment of insecurity in the medical p-way and right on time. I've listed some quotes from her book that slapped the doubt right out of me and encouraged me to continue pushing forward with my opinions:

- "We've been told for far too long that 'work-life' balance, whatever the hell that is, is a challenge that women will face and women will have to deal with. But it's not on us alone to figure this out. In fact, it all depends on who we're negotiating that balance with. Who's on your team? Who's part of your support system? And more importantly, how does your employer feel about personal lives and families?
- **Yes Emilie, preach!**

- "Whether it's negotiating for the benefits you need from your employer or what you need from your partner to make it work, we have to be clear on our vision for the life we want for ourselves and have the audacity to be assertive in making it a reality. As the boss of your life, you get to negotiate those terms and conditions for yourself, with a community of courage that has your back."
- **Yes, ma'am, you are correct! I *do* have the audacity!**
- "Because, listen, it's never been more important for women to sit in the driver's seat of our lives. Watching your life unfold before you, happen to you, from the passenger-side window is no longer an option."
- **Nope!**
- "The way things have been done does not need to remain the way things are. But you gotta be willing to risk it, to put yourself out there, to be bold with your leadership, in order to push for progress. We can't be scared as we ascend in achieving our goals. We have to think about lifting as we climb: growing *our* power on behalf of those women and girls who come after us."
- **I felt like the epitome of this statement.**
- "You have to give yourself permission to dream big and articulate those dreams—not just when it comes to your career but in your personal life too."
- "You have to be willing to be patient in your pursuits and treat yourself with compassion, self-care, and resilience through the process of realistic, strategic goal setting."
- "Helplessness is not a good look. No, we're *grown* women, as Beyoncé says. And not only do we know what we want, but we can proceed with the calm confidence that we're gonna get it too."

Are you guys feeling as uplifted as I am? I *deserve* to complain! It's my mouth, my body, and my life! I wish someone would have written a book like this for me when I was considering enlisting. Hell, even after enlisting I would have loved to have something like this to read in A-school when I was terrified about what was to come next. So, I am going to continue saying whatever the fuck I feel like saying. Thank you, Emilie Aries.

Now, as I was saying . . .

PART IV

LADIES? OR FEMALE SAILORS? PICK ONE

As women who serve the country through military service, our challenges are our own – no matter the rank, rate, or title. The challenges we face on a constant basis while still maintaining or simply mustering up the strength to carry on should be applauded.

Without fail, we face our trials willingly, toughly, beautifully, and with sheer grace. Women, undoubtedly, are one of the best things to ever happen to the military. Yes, men, we know: you guys go through your own challenges as well. Understood. However, you are constantly patted on your back for simply existing or having a penis between your legs.

In some way, shape, or form, the idea that men are the superior sex rears its ugly, egotistical head on a daily basis. Not only is it displayed – it is perpetuated. But we're not going to focus on any of that. Right now, our focus is solely on the servicewomen of the Navy.

Are we ladies or are we simply female sailors?

It's ridiculous that this is a question that needs to be pondered, yet here we are. Granted, as a servicewoman you don't have the time to spend hours on hair and make-up, but why should a career in the military attempt to strip away every piece of a woman's femineity? There can be a balance.

We *are* the balance.

Both innately fierce and the embodiment of grace by birth, our natural dualities give any command we are a part of an automatic advantage. It's not something that should be taken for granted. So put some respect on our names.

10

EQUAL OPPORTUNITY

First and Foremost
Master at Arms Seaman Alexandria Smith
Twenty years old. Filipino American. Pisces.

"Even now, after so much has changed with gender identity and racism, there's *still* so much sexism within the workplace that doesn't get talked about. Especially when you're as young as I am; you get here and people undermine and disrespect you just because they know that they can get away with it because they are senior, and male, and white."

Equal Opportunity

Ladies, prepare to have your nerves amplified regarding our right to have equal opportunities in the military. And for women who are already serving, I'm sure you can relate. Women *deserve* to be considered and respected for everything that a man can be considered and respected for, not only within the workplace, but in life. Period.

Here's the issue: I do not appreciate the shade and obnoxious comments we deal with from our male counterparts because we want equal opportunity. I have seen, heard, and experienced men who will throw equal opportunity in our faces like it's a comical subject. Let's imagine that a male shipmate and I have been ordered to physically transport two boxes throughout our ship. One box is extremely heavy, and the other box is extremely light.

Unfortunately, I attempt to lift the heavy box and can't even make it budge. I decide to ask the sailor I am working with, who is much stronger than me, if he could grab the heavier box. "Nah bro you got it. Equal opportunity," is his response.

Yes, this is likely to happen to you, especially if you are a female with a low rank. It burns me up inside when I encounter situations such as these. It happens more often than one would imagine. It is a laughable matter to some men when we ask for help. Honestly, for the men who are guilty of this, what is it? Is it because you are still upset that women can serve in the military? Does it upset you that even though I can't lift a heavy box, I can still make rank as fast as – if not faster – than you?

Inherently Weaker
Gunners Mate Second Class Beverly Stroud
Twenty-five years old. White. Leo.

"If I complain about anything, I'm just being 'soft.' GM is a heavily male dominated rate and I have to work twice as hard to be taken seriously only to still not be taken seriously. I hear statements like, 'Choose your rate choose your fate,' and 'If you don't like it, maybe you should just get pregnant,' on a regular basis from the men I work with.

"Listen, I'm 115 pounds, I can't lift 100 pounds! Being considered weak or lazy simply because the men around me are better at physical labor than I am is something I will never get over. Just because I refuse to lift heavier things doesn't mean I am trying to get out of work; it means that I know my limits. I'm not going to throw my back out or pull a muscle just so I'll look good, or to be taken seriously. I hate the mentality and culture that assumes I am inherently weaker and anything that I do to admit that is considered laziness. If I admit any weakness, it is thrown in my face."

Advice to Salty Men
Navy Counselor (Career) First Class Elon McDuell-Briscoe
Thirty-six years old. African American. Taurus.

"It can no longer be a dick swinging contest and a good ole boys club when women are added to the equation. I'm the primary breadwinner in my household and I am so far from the typical stay-at-home mom mold! Think about it; most women run the household *and* the family. So that means that we are the most levelheaded because we must multitask so many things at once unlike our male counterparts!

"We are methodical, analytical, and even strategic in decision making.

"Instead of embracing, helping, supporting, and guiding us, they shun us. To this day, I get crazy looks because I have three children and chose to do this job for as long as I have, and I am successful in my own right. I can provide, take care of my family, take care of my household even when I am away for long periods of time, and be a major contributor to our mission and a boss all at the same damn time.

"Is it easy?

"No, of course not, because I am literally in a constant prioritization cycle of life all the time. So, stop trying to put the multi-faceted, powerful woman in a damn box because we will roll over that shit in a bulldozer and turn it into what we want to see in the world, in spite of what 'they' want or refuse to believe."

An Opinion on Equality
Aviation Structural Mechanic Safety Equipment Third Class Karissa McCorkmick
Twenty-seven years old. White. Scorpio.

"As far as sexism goes, I've seen that. I feel like females have to prove themselves in the military. We deal with the whole, 'Don't cry, it's a form of weakness.' If you do cry, a man's going to feel sympathy toward you and is more inclined to help a female before they help a male that's in tears. Women are just as powerful as men. I'm not saying we are as strong as men or as fast as men, but I am saying that we are equal to them and should be seen as such."

Menstruation Underway

Here's a sea story of mine. It was the third day of my second deployment, and I remember it like it was yesterday. My body was *so* tired. No, actually, I'd be willing to say that my body was exhausted. *I cannot wait until I have finally adjusted to these twelve-hour shifts*, I thought as I stepped out of the shower to finally hit my rack. I slept like baby for the next eight straight hours.

When my alarm went off at 0640 the next morning, I shut it off and rolled over to become aware of the insane amount of wetness between my legs. After reaching down in curiosity, I took a glance at my index and middle fingers now soaked with blood. It's one of the worst ways in the world to wake up out of your sleep.

No! No, no, no, no, I thought, mind scrambling to figure out how I'd clean myself up and avoid embarrassment simultaneously. I was not at all mentally prepared to receive my period. Due to my birth control, I hadn't had a period in months, so that meant I hadn't needed to even think about tampons, sanitary napkins, period panties, or anything else because I was enjoying the sheer luxury of cycle-less months.

Three days in a berthing full of women changed that, and fast.

My sheets! Oh my God these are the only sheets I brought! I cut on my rack light, eased my butt in the air, and peeked to ensure that the coast was clear. My heart was threatening to break my ribs it was pounding so hard. *Nothing. Thank God. Okay. I've gotta get out of here before I leak on my sheets.*

The entire berthing of women that worked the day shift was up, bustling around and getting ready to start their day. All I was wearing was a sports bra and a white pair of granny panties and I knew exactly what was to come as soon as I stood up. I peeked through my rack's curtains and took note that there were three women outside of my rack and that over on the nearest wall were my sweatpants and my hoodie, located at an arm's length away.

Wondering if I should just ask one of the three women moving around outside of my rack to pass me my pants, I decided it would be too awkward considering that I didn't know them and I kind of didn't want the extra attention as I climbed out of my rack. *I'll just wait. They should be done by seven. Please let them be done by seven.* I crossed my legs and just laid there.

Once it was finally quiet, I peeked out of my rack to see no one. *Game on.* After looking at my phone to notice that it was 0703 and I had twenty-two minutes until I needed to be at work, I grabbed my sweats off the wall, slowly and carefully slid them on while lying in my rack and hopped down. And that's when it happened. I felt the blood gushing out of me like a geyser and raced down my legs trying to stain as much of the sweatpants as possible.

Things going from bad to worse in a hurry, I scrambled to unlock my rack and grab a tampon. Praying, *God, please don't let me leak on the floor!* I put my legs together, grabbed my tampon, towels, and toiletry bag, and rushed up one ladder well to enter our female head.

After I entered the shower in the head, I stripped as fast as possible, stood under the water, relieved as I watched the blood rinse off me and be washed away down the drain. *I could really use a little more fucking privacy on this gaddamn boat!* I grumbled to myself knowing without a doubt that had I been home, this would have been a far less traumatic experience.

Once I was showered and dressed in the uniform of the day after a terrible rush, I entered my work center right on time, showcasing a fake smile to hide the fact that something close to traumatizing had just happened to me.

Go with the Flow
Aviation Maintenance Administrationman First Class Janelle Delgado.
Thirty-four years old. Trinidadian. Gemini.

"I hate that no matter what I am dealing with mentally and emotionally, I have to tough it out and deal with it internally because I will be the emotional female that can't handle her shit. I hate that I have to cry to myself when I am feeling down; I don't feel comfortable seeking help because it doesn't flow into the Navy mindset – which I know is unhealthy, but somehow is easier; to just say 'fuck it' and go with the flow until I don't care anymore. But these are also the reasons I remain because if I can simply influence one mindset to see that there is more to this shit than that mindset, I can influence another and the domino effect begins; and we make change."

11

HARASSMENT

Expect Harassment

Even though I do not wear clothing that is revealing to work or have sex with a bunch of men on board my ship, I absolutely cannot avoid harassment solely due to my sex. Even with the professional demeanor that I make sure I display, harassment is inevitable. I never understood why so many men in the Navy felt comfortable enough to address my looks and my figure.

Sometimes I felt as if I *had* to be walking around with a sign on my head that read: I HAVE A BIG ASS. COMMENT ON IT IF YOU LIKE! I couldn't see it myself, yet it had to be there because I heard those comments often. No matter how loose fitting my attire or how I carried myself, my ass got its fair share of daily attention.

It's uncomfortable and the fact that I'm simply expected to suck it up and keep it moving is ridiculous. That's life in the Navy, though. Either get used to it or walk around bitter and angry about it daily.

I know women who wear fake wedding bands to work on board their ships because they are less likely to get harassed by their male counterparts. Although, it still happens to married women on board as well, it's not as bad. Well, I'll take that back. The frequency that we, single and married women alike, are hit on at work is probably around the same; the major difference, though, is that it's a lot less overt with married women.

As a seaman at my first command, I encountered a male petty officer second class who would whisper. "Shake something," to me each and every time we passed each other in the p-way. Like I was a stripper strutting past simply for his arousal instead of treating me like an equal.

That wasn't the only clown that I had to deal with on a consistent basis. I also had a petty officer first class within my duty section who was in charge of making the watch bill for our entire duty section, and he would harass me as well. It was subtle at first; he would always schedule us together for the same watches. This way I was forced to spend hours alone with him. Not only was it a situation that was extremely creepy, but it could have gone too far at any moment.

I went out of my way to avoid talking to him about anything, knowing full well that if I did it would circle back to some uncomfortable question or inappropriate comment. But even with adding things to my workload that would keep me busy, he would still do his best to make eye contact with me just so he could lick his lips suggestively or give what he thought was a sexy week. Sometimes, if he was feeling especially bold, he'd do both.

Until one day, after his hundredth time of asking me if he could get to know me better, I told him that I was in a serious relationship, which was a bold face lie but I was completely fed up, and suddenly, we didn't stand watch together anymore. Had I known that was all I had to say to get rid of him, I would have done so a lot sooner, but I was grateful that he finally left me alone.

Trust me, I've had more experiences similar to these, but with these two were the worst.

When I was a seaman, I remember feeling so helpless and believing that no one would believe me over the word of these men who were higher ranking than me. I felt like reporting it would be pointless and constantly walking around with those sentiments in the back of my mind while enduring unfair treatment was torture. Those feelings constantly raised anxiety in me that I never anticipated when I joined the Navy. Why was it *so* hard for me to tell anyone what was going on? That was the big question. Or why couldn't I simply exhale the word, "Stop"?

It was probably because I would then be known as the sensitive, female snitch around the boat who couldn't take a "joke." Because, trust me, word would get around. Contrary to popular belief, men gossip and spread rumors further and faster than women any day of the week. They're simply a lot better at doing it quietly. If I had the nerve to stand up for myself, somehow that brave action would be flipped on its ear and my reputation would be the one to suffer. I'd be looked at as weak and it would be even harder to gain the respect of the men I worked with.

All that would be the consequences of speaking up for myself. Don't let me have the gumption to snap the fuck out, like I often wanted to, and that raggedy but often used label would be slapped on me. You know the label I mean. You guessed it: angry Black woman. As a seaman, utterly unaware of the level of sexual harassment in the Navy before I made the decision to enlist, I just ignored these incidents and acted as if they didn't make me feel uncomfortable. I'd rather do that than be the new female on board who reported everyone's *favorite* second class. It is harder than you think to simply say, "Hey, it makes me uncomfortable when you do that. Please stop."

A Warning
Logistics Specialist Seaman Katie Tillinghast
Twenty-one years old. White. Libra.

"I arrived at my first command and then we deployed ten days later. I only had ten days to adjust to the Navy lifestyle after arriving to the fleet and I went straight out into the ocean, not really knowing what I'm doing. I had to figure it out. My first deployment was wild. I was getting a lot of attention from men because of the physical assets that I have; you know, big tits, nice butt. All the personal training only added to my stacked physique, and it definitely got to my head a little.

"I was feeling myself because of all the new attention, not really understanding that it came from more of the culture of environment than a genuine place. Of course, as a civilian you still get attention if you're a pretty girl, but there are millions of other pretty girls out there. When you're on a warship, it is more intense because there's only a select few women. Especially when you have big titties and a big ass, straight up, you're going to get sexually harassed, even if you're not a flirtatious person. You don't even have to have big boobs and a big ass. Honestly at that point, just being female is enough."

Defense Mode = A Side Effect of Harassment

About three weeks after I checked into my second command, I was alone in my work center organizing some binders. At this point I was a new petty officer third class, and the new female at work. A male walked into my work center and asked if we had a pair of gloves available for him.

I began my search for some gloves for the young man and found them. As I handed them to him, he commented, "You look sleepy."

"You look sexy," is what my ears had heard him say, though – a by-product of men constantly making slick comments and advances.

I gave him the meanest glare that my facial muscles could form, flinging visual daggers at him nonstop. "I'm fucking reporting you, you piece of shit," I snarled.

Baffled, he replied, "LS3, I said you look *sleepy*! What the hell?" He grabbed the gloves, shook his head, and walked away.

As I stood there feeling like a complete bag of ass, I decided to give myself some compassion. Although I heard him wrong, I didn't blame myself for the assumption of what he said instead of asking him. At that point in my career, I was finally bold enough to defend myself at all times.

Unfortunately, the male that I verbally attacked never spoke another word to me again. I am probably known as the crazy new female now. But I can deal with that. What I can't deal with is being harassed.

12

GIRLY WOMEN

The Struggle Is Real for Girly Women

Being a feminine woman, often referred to as the girly type, genuinely sucks when you deploy. Personal maintenance truly becomes a thing of the past. You can say goodbye to the routine manicures and pedicures along with the relaxation that came along with each. While you're at it, go ahead and kiss the hair salon goodbye, too.

Oh yeah, and those quality beauty products at your convenience aren't a thing when you're on a ship, so that means no beauty supply either. Now, if you're truly brave at heart, you can definitely bring makeup and wear it if you like, but on a day-to-day basis during a deployment I personally don't apply makeup. I need the extra sleep! I refuse to be barefaced and tired looking.

And what if I run out of one of my daily products?

Mail is never guaranteed to arrive on time and the products that are provided in the ship store aren't exactly the best brands, so it's a huge NO for me. I only apply makeup in port and, depending on your rate, you may or may not even want to apply make up at all! Imagine being one of the sailors with a job that requires you to work outside in the heat or within a very hot work center, a job that makes you sweat all day because it keeps you running so much. Yeah, no. At that point, you're asking for acne.

By the way, when you've been deployed for several months, you'll start craving civilian clothes, too. I completely stopped using my internet time to scroll on Facebook and Instagram because it genuinely made me sad seeing my friends and family dressed up, looking cute, and living life, while I was stuck in my uniform.

It may seem shallow, but it honestly gets depressing! Meanwhile, I've worn the same coveralls for three days straight, the inside of my boots stink, and although I just cleaned under my fingernails yesterday, they are dirty again! It's even more depressing to have everyone else around you looking exactly like you. It minimizes subject content for conversation. I'm sure it sucks for more than just girly women in the service, though.

Listen, if you're the type of person who enjoys dressing up, trying new hairstyles, and making individual choices of personal grooming a top priority, a job in the Navy that requires you to deploy often may not be the job for you. I'm telling you, it gets so rough. You'll find yourself pulling out your phone to show your military friends pictures of yourself and saying things like, "This is what I really look like."

But some people like this lifestyle.

Waking up and knowing what you are going to wear because you are told what, when, and how to wear it, along with having written regulations of hairstyles to choose from actually makes the lives of many servicemembers much easier, which is okay, too. But ladies, check it out: we know that we can do this military thing. We can do literally anything we want when we put our minds to it! We've proven this fact time and time again. I just want you all to make the right decision for yourself when you consider joining the military. Because mental health matters, and these naval grooming and uniform standards mixed with the lack of individuality can seriously take a toll on your mental health. Or at least it has for mine. Make sure you are making the right decision for your happiness and sanity.

For the Female Sailors That Don't Believe in Being Ladies
Parachute Rigger Second Class Nyomi Ellis
Thirty-five years old. African American. Pisces.

"I hate some of the female leadership in the Navy because, although I'm going to do my job, I'm still going to look as pretty as I would like to look – within regulation, of course. I've always had problems with that in the Navy, especially when it comes to my hair and my nails. 'Why do you have to put on lashes?' or, 'Why do you have to look like that to come to work?' That doesn't affect anything. Just look at my record, I'm a good worker! Maybe it's the way I present myself that makes them think I'm too prideful. I've gotten a lot of backlash from female leadership because of my priorities to be girly. When I feel good, I do good work! I think that women in the Navy should have each other's back more."

Fingernail Regulations

Want to know what really grinds my gears – something that pisses me off deep down in my soul? The dumbass fingernail regulations! That's right, the regulation states: "Fingernails for women shall not exceed one-fourth inch measured from the fingertip and shall be kept clean. The tips of the nails may be round, almond/oval, or square in shape. Nail polish may be worn, but colors shall be conservative and inconspicuous. White, black, red, yellow, orange, green, purple, grey, glitter, striped or any sort of pattern/decorative nail polish is not authorized."

Yes, because white, black, red, yellow, orange, green, purple, grey, glitter, striped, or any sort of pattern/decorative nail polish on my nails is going to prevent me from doing my job, right? There's some mystery chemical within those colored polishes that severs the nerves in the fingers and renders them useless. Obnoxious.

I've been told that the regulations for fingernails were because it is believed that fancy nails will cause too much of a distraction from our uniforms. But does it really? As long as there's no glitter or lettering or something, I believe it's just a nail color. I can understand the instructions on length, but not the color.

Before I joined the Navy, while I was conducting my research on the fingernail regulations, I really thought it would be okay. No biggie, it's just a nail color. I should be able to deal with this, was my initial thinking. What I've come to realize now more than ever is how much I love getting my nails done and how different the experience is in the civilian world versus military regulation.

I love the way my freshly done nails look and enjoy the relaxing setting while they are getting done. When my nails are done to my liking, I smile a little on the inside throughout my day every time I look at my hands or when I receive a compliment about them.

I also hate being corrected because my nail color is out of regulation, which means I will have to go and have a color change or remove the coloring. I never expected the amount of anxiety that comes with trying to pick a nail color that is within regulation. While in the salon my thoughts are along the lines of: This one's too bright; this one is way too dark and ugly; nope, can't have purple.

What do they even mean by conservative? Should I just get brown? Then, I'm not even relaxed anymore. After that I'm usually sad because not only does the civilian girl next to me have the tone of purple that I wanted, but she also got the coffin shape which is my favorite shape!

Damn.

13

PARENTING

Parenting While Deployed

While on my second deployment, I really took note of the strength of parents in the military. Being a parent in general is a phenomenal blessing but being a parent while active is a completely different level. I worked beside a male third class and a female third class, both of them parents, and my heart went out to them both on a daily basis. The male's wife gave birth to their second child, a baby girl, while we were deployed.

I watched his child grow up right in front of our eyes. In the moments where I thought time was moving at a glacial pace, the growing child was proof otherwise. His daughter was getting bigger and stronger, smiling a lot more, and could lift her head up on her own. Every day his wife sent him pictures and videos of his baby girl, and every morning I saw him watch the new videos of her. He replayed those videos several times and would stare at his computer screen while they played. I'm sure he couldn't wait to hold his new baby – who looked exactly like him.

I'm not a parent, so I can't imagine the heartbreak of watching my own child grow up via a computer monitor or cell phone screen.

The mother I worked with had a son in grade school who was old enough to recognize his mother's absence. She watched her son grow up without her, too. She watched him develop new interests and knowledge about life that she was minimally an influence of. His new interests and his new knowledge were coming from his daily life and the people he interacted with on a daily basis, which was not his deployed mother. I can't imagine the toll it took on their mother-son relationships and the lasting emotional effects it could unintentionally have. I don't know how hard it must be to constantly have to reconnect with your own child when you arrive home.

In the past two years, this mother had deployed twice and wasn't able to experience *months* of her son's life. I think about the impact her absence has had on her son, especially on his birthday or during holidays because mommy is in the military. One day, she told me about the time that she surprised him at his school to have lunch with him and what stood out to her the most about this day was her son's excitement to tell his friends, "See, I told you guys that I have a mom!"

Hearing her repeat her son's statement tore me into pieces; I can't fathom how it didn't completely shatter her. Of course, he had a mother – he was a living a breathing person. Yet for her to be away so much that none of his friends had seen her with their own eyes was sad.

Serving the country as a parent requires a different level of strength. It requires a level of strength that has to be pulled from the deepest part of your soul in order to press on. For these parents, the feelings and emotions that come from the effort it takes to utilize their strength has to be suppressed on a daily basis simply *because* they are in the military or lower ranking, enlisted people who have to climb ladders to acquire a significant amount of respect. And you know what else probably sucks for these parents? Telling their kids and families the date that they've been given to return home, and then having it change two weeks prior because the deployment has been extended for an extra forty-five days.

Mission first, right?

Robotic Women
Logistics Specialist Third Class Laura Baxley
Twenty-eight years old. African American. Aries.

"The Navy expects us to be robots, especially women. They don't take into consideration that we're all people. Women are emotional. We go through all kinds of changes with our bodies throughout each month, and we're expected to show up to work like everything is cool. Our natural hormones and emotions are not taken into consideration in the Navy. When I found out I was four weeks pregnant, I was forced to go on my command's scheduled underway simply because there is an instruction that details that it is not prohibited because it's a short underway. I did not feel safe at all. You're just expected to show up and not say anything just because there's an instruction, which can be very vague by the way. No one's considering the fact that I am pregnant, I'm going through a lot of stuff that I'm not used to, I'm always fatigued, and being underway with a 0600 reveille and working hours wasn't exactly meshing with me. But they don't see it like that. They only see me as a sailor. What if it was your pregnant wife?"

Sea Story
By: Aviation Maintenance Administrationman First Class Janelle Delgado
Thirty-four years old. Trinidadian. Gemini.

During one of my deployments, there was an Aviation Maintenance Chief Petty Officer (AZC) who hated me. I did everything to not let her make my mind stray to the negative. *Fuck her*, I thought and kept on pushing forward. I got my enlisted surface warfare specialist pin and my enlisted intelligence warfare specialist pin that deployment but with much sacrifice. I spent mostly twenty out of every twenty-four-hour day working and staying awake to work on my qualifications because that AZC did not want me to finish my quals before her and refused to let me work on them during working hours.

One day, I received an email from my boo thang. I was so excited when I saw the name in my inbox. It felt like we hadn't spoken to each other in a lifetime. My heart fluttered to life trying to guess what he'd tell me about life back at home and I couldn't wait to spill all the happening with me while on deployment.

I'd drafted up a thousand possibilities of what he'd say but none of it was what I actually saw when I double clicked the message. The same excited heart that fluttered at seeing my lover's name transformed into disdain and disbelief. I wasn't being told how much I was missed or how my face couldn't wait to be seen again...oh no, no. Instead, my excitement was thwarted when I read the body of the email only to find out I was being dumped!

That's right, instead of the sweet nothings and letters of yearning that I'd stupidly assumed were in the email, I was being advised that things weren't working out and he needed space. SPACE. How much more space did he need? We were *thousands* of miles apart. My head started spinning so fast I thought it would detach itself from my neck. Here I was, doing all this bullshit for us and our future. Though *I* was the one dealing with all the foolishness, I was trying to ensure that *we* were set for life – a sentiment that I thought we both shared, but boy was I wrong! As I sat there pissed, I got the worst cramp I'd ever felt in my life!

As a woman who's had a menstrual cycle for years, I've had my fair share of cramps, but I'd never experienced such an excoriating pain before. It felt like I was being knifed in the gut. *Ouch*, I complained internally.

I tried to shake the sensation off, but when it was followed up with another, equally excoriating pain, it couldn't be ignored further.

To try and figure out what was going on, I hurried to the bathroom to investigate. When I pulled my pants and underwear down to discover that the cramps had been accompanied by a pool of blood that had now soiled my clothes. *What the hell*? I felt that I was bleeding *way* more than a normal period.

Well damn! When was my last period?

I couldn't remember.

I had been too busy running around doing shit like a mad woman that I didn't have the time to keep track of my cycle on a calendar! Crazy, huh? But in the Navy, there is always something to do which, afterward, leaves very little room for self-care.

I jumped in the shower to try and clean myself up. I initially planned on going back to work but as I was standing there in the shower, more blood kept coming out of me. This time in thick, dark red clots. My eyes almost popped out of my head when I saw this *thing* come out of me!

I was standing there in a daze . . . staring at this bloody, mass on the floor. I couldn't believe what I was seeing. I picked it up and immediately broke down in tears.

This was my baby that I was holding.

A baby that I didn't even know existed.

This was my baby that I killed by overexerting myself to gain what?

Just some quals?

A Deployed Mother's Mindset

One night on deployment, I was lying in my rack before taps reading a book and I overheard a conversation between two women who were standing outside of my rack. One of the women was a petty officer second class and the other a seaman. I assumed that the seaman was upset because the second class was asking her what was wrong. Crying, the seaman explained how she had recently checked in to this command on deployment; once she finished A-school, she was flown out to her new command, the ship that we were on.

She described that she was having a terrible time adjusting to the fleet so far and felt more than overwhelmed with the lifestyle of living on a warship mixed with leaving her son at home and being unable to contact him while on deployment.

The second class was sorry to hear about her terrible experience and presumed to comfort her. "I have a daughter myself. This is my second deployment and on my first one I wasn't a mother yet. I can't explain how it feels but somehow, I just try not to think about it, about my daughter. Don't get me wrong, sometimes I look at pictures of her but for the most part I just do not think about it, and it makes things easier."

The seaman responded, "I get that. Today while I was working, I thought back to a happier time and before I knew it, I was off work. It still sucks but at least in my head for a few moments today, I wasn't *here*."

Sea Story
By: Boatswain Mate Second Class Tushanna Brown
Thirty-four years old. African American. Gemini.

We had a hurricane one night before we left on our current deployment and the deck department was instructed to stay on board. We were only supposed to stay on board for one night. I was okay with that. I made plans for my daughter to stay with somebody for *one* night. By the end of that first night, we were told that plans had changed. Our leadership told us that we were staying on board for two nights instead.

I went to my chief and said, "Hey chief, I made plans to have my daughter stay with a friend for only *one* night. Would it be okay for me to leave the boat for a little while so I can move her somewhere where she can stay for another night?"

I was willing to drive through the *storm* to go and get my daughter.

"Well, where's your family care plan?" he asked.

"I'm sorry, does the family care plan cover storms or when she gets sick? A family care plan is for extended hours or for coming in early. I have that covered. You're stating that we have to stay on board for two nights instead of one. I can stay on board tonight; all I'm asking is, can I go move my daughter?"

He told me no. He said, "Fuck it, figure it out because I don't have to worry about these types of problems."

I told him, "Yes, chief, I know *you* don't have to worry about this because your wife is a civilian. I'm a single mom. Can I go move my daughter?"

"No," he stood firm. "It's something you're gonna have figure out on your own."

So, I went to the ship's bos'n, an officer, and asked him the same thing.

He said, "Well I'm just trying to figure out where your family care plan is? Is this a failed family care plan?" He asked.

I was trying my hardest to maintain my cool, but my patience was wearing thin. Through gritted teeth, I responded, "Sir, I wouldn't expect you to understand because you're not married, and you don't have any children."

All the curse words I could think of screamed in my head at once as watched him continue on, obviously unbothered by my needs. It was a lost cause, trying to grovel to a bunch of people who could care less. Fed up, I also told him not to worry about it and that I would figure it out. This was my child we were talking about, my own flesh and blood. Yet the Navy which publicly promotes family, unity, and pride, left me and mine hanging.

I took that knock on the chin the best I could, until I found out a few hours later that another sailor on board needed to take her sick cat to the fucking vet and guess what? They let her go! These people prioritized a fucking furball over my human child.

Here I am trying to get my *daughter* situated and all I'm hearing from this leadership is *where's your family care plan*? When they came around later asking me, "Hey BM2, did you figure it out?"

"Yes." I kept my answer short and to the point. "I sure did."

As a mother, I will always figure it out.

Single Mothers in the Military Are Aliens
Navy Counselor (Career) First Class Elon McDuell-Briscoe
Thirty-six years old. African American. Taurus.

"When you have men in leadership positions whose wives don't work and only take care of the kids and home, it is foreign to them to have a female sailor that is actively climbing the career ladder. There is limited understanding when encountering female sailors that are single moms and still desire to excel, which causes them to say the most ridiculous things like: your child(ren) didn't come in your sea bag, so you need to figure it out."

Why Do I Do This as a Mother?
Aviation Maintenance Administrationman First Class Janelle Delgado
Thirty-four years old. Trinidadian. Gemini.

"I picked orders back to sea duty and I have been away from my boys for two years now. With as many qualifications as I have now, I still ask myself daily, *why do I do this shit*? Why do I deal with motherfuckers talking to me crazy, like I'm not the same age as them?

"Officers constantly belittle me or chiefs ask me, 'When are you going to finally pass the E-7 exam?'

"Why do I deal with people automatically trying to get me spun up because I am the Black girl with the 'attitude?'

"And then I think about my boys at home, and I pray that one day they understand how close I am to retiring and why I am away from them so much. I do this to guarantee I can spend as much time with them as I want when I retire. I do this to make sure they are taken care of without struggling. I do this to give them everything they ask for.

"Of course, I think about the time lost and how I know I can't get that back, so I force myself to *not* think about it. Every time somebody tells me to smile, I want to say, 'Go fuck yourself.'

"Or when someone says that I have an attitude, I think: *You have no fucking idea*."

PART V

BUT WHAT CAN YOU DO ABOUT IT? NOTHING

While serving in the military, you will encounter situations, events, leadership, interactions, and sometimes cultures of working environments that you would have never expected. You'll wish that someone would have warned you! You'll wonder how it is possible that no one told you about certain things being a thing.

You won't understand how people within your organization accept the things that should not be acceptable. And after you've been confronted with surprise, frustration, sadness, or any of the emotion you feel from your experiences, you will then realize that there is simply nothing you can do about it.

Absolutely nothing.

You move forward by dealing with your circumstances and figure out exactly *how* to deal with them.

But here's what I *can* do, will do, and what I wish more people would have done for me: tell the truth about how things go down in the Navy.

I'm going to talk about it!

14

IT'S A NEW NAVY

Early in my career I overheard a senior chief petty officer give this advice to another junior sailor: "It isn't the Navy's job to adjust to you. It is your job to adjust to the Navy."

I think that's exactly the problem.

The Navy's Adjustments
Logistics Specialist Seaman Apprentice Ashley McLendon
Twenty-four years old. Haitian American. Cancer.

"When I joined, the Navy was on a roll of being more open to people, but it was still extremely traditional. Even with all the changes, I honestly do not see it being any better at this time. How can I say this . . . basically, the Navy is making so many changes so quickly that nobody has any time to adjust. They are making so many changes in the Navy that the Navy itself is failing to adjust to the Navy."

This Is Our Navy

One experience that I really enjoyed on a carrier versus destroyer was Sunday brunch! The culinary specialists (CSs) and food service attendants (FSAs) host a large brunch that consists of waffles with all the works and toppings: maple syrup, chocolate syrup, pineapples, strawberries, and nuts. There are always other choices, of course. I've seen baked and fried chicken, ribs, shrimp, spaghetti, grilled cheeses, grits, oatmeal, broccoli, corn-on-the-cobb, etc.

One morning as I was in line for one of the famous Sunday brunch waffles, I noticed a difference in the crew that was serving us. Our servers were members of the Junior Enlisted Association (JEA), Gay, Lesbian, and Supporting Sailors, (G.L.A.S.S.) and the Multi-Cultural Heritage Committee (MCHC). All the sailors who were serving waffles to the crew were young, vibrant, millennial sailors of all sexes, races, backgrounds, ethnicities, and sexualities. This made my heart smile to see my peers doing the damn thing!

They were making statements without even having to speak.

It hit me, right there that morning: this was *our* Navy. Ours. Us. Me. This is my Navy, and the Navy is as it should be. There is more work that needs to be done and more issues that need to be addressed within this organization that would benefit us and our beliefs more, but to look around a room full of millennials and generation Zers, E-1 through E-6 that morning, I realized that is not us that need to adjust to the Navy. It is the Navy that needs to adjust to *us.*

Without us, there is no Navy.

15

HURRY UP AND WAIT

"Hurry up and wait."

A phrase that, upon entrance to the Navy, you will get familiar with extremely fast. It refers to a sailor doing the absolute most to ensure they will either be on time, get off work at a certain time, or perform orders for higher ranking personnel in the allotted time *just* for that sailor to end up disappointed and forced to wait on who knows what without explanation, or just to get re-tasked.

When I was a seaman, the days that my time was wasted were the days that I hated the most. Busy work for adult sailors is infuriating! For example, being told to do a quick sweepers at 1630 after being done with the day's work for over an hour is common. Why? We don't know. We have to do exactly as we're told and there is nothing we can do about it.

That always sucked because even though I was a seaman, I was still a twenty-four-year-old woman with shit to do. Getting home after 1700 left me with less than five hours until 2200, my preferred bedtime, so that I could successfully wake up early enough to beat the morning traffic and make it back to the same bullshit work before seven o'clock every morning.

Also, before bed I need the time to wind down. This can be done in a variety of ways since I like to switch it up. Maybe I have homework that needs to be done for my online classes, fix myself something to eat, or even get a quick at-home work out in. Once that is done, I jump in the shower in effort to wash the entire day off me and relax my mind.

I also love to spend time with my significant other, call my mom, do laundry, and just live a decent life!

When you're done with work for over an hour, it's extremely frustrating when your LPO can clearly see that you are waiting around in hopes to go home and says, "Hey guys, let's do a quick sweepers around our spaces. Then I'll ask senior if he's ready to let us go for the day."

No! Tell the senior that your adult sailors have finished their work for the day! Tell him that you cut us loose for the day because you are sure that we have things to do! Why should we all suffer because our LPO is afraid of his higher-ranking boss? That extra hour that we were sitting around doing nothing would have really helped me out!

The sad thing is, we will probably deal with the same exact situation the next day and the next day after that, too.

Sweepers

I'm going to take this opportunity to talk to you guys about sweepers more in depth. Sweepers is a term that describes the crew cleaning around their command's spaces at certain times of the day. It is an all-hands evolution. Just know that if you enlist into the Navy, you will automatically acquire the alternate job title of ship's janitor. We do sweepers all the time and there is no way it can be avoided.

You will sweep and swab, it is inevitable.

Every day, several times a day. Especially while stationed on board a ship. Guess what you do when it rains? Yes, you sweep water off your ship. Get ready to sweep water for years in your career as a sailor on sea duty. It gets really old, really fast, and you begin to notice how it is usually an evolution that E-6 and below are conducting while being supervised by the higher ranks. It is not fun.

Be a L. E. A. D. E. R
Personnel Specialist Second Class Dominique Lucas
Twenty-four years old. African American. Gemini.

"I wish some first classes knew how to be a leader. I have met many who don't know how to take a stand for their sailors and always feel like they *need* the chief to make the decisions."

Politics
Logistics Specialist Third Class Laura Baxley
Twenty-eight years old. African American. Aries.

"Everything is so political. If I have an issue with something, I have to run the details all the way up my chain of command. Which is like running down a band of celebrities who sometimes feel like they are too important to be bothered or think that their time/problems trump yours simply because of rank.

"I feel like the Navy doesn't really want to help you with resolving your issues; they only pacify you with Band-Aid-over-bullet-hole solutions.

"Oh, you have an issue? Here's the instruction for that!

"Having problems? There's an instruction for that!

"They try to make everything so black and white and that's not how life is. We live in a world that dances in the gray area yet the Navy refuses to acknowledge that. They'd rather maintain the same old, antiquated guidelines and protocols that were laid down back in the 1700s at the

Navy's inception. It's 2021 for crying out loud. These instructions are old too! Some of this stuff doesn't even make sense anymore."

You're Just a Third Class, You Can Wait

One day during deployment, I locked my keys in my rack.

Fuck! My ID is in there! I thought to myself. *Oh well, I'll just get a master-at-arms to come and break the lock for me.* No biggie, right?

Wrong!

I found out from the male master-at-arms third class in security that a second class or above would have to escort me through the entire process. Of course, I asked him why and he explained that it was to ensure the lock being broken was mine.

Oh okay! That makes sense because a second class couldn't possibly be capable of trying to break into someone's rack – because rank is an immediate determination of a person's character.

Got it.

I politely walked back to my TAD office and shamelessly asked my TAD second class if he could escort me to security to handle my lock situation. There was no backing down here. My twenty-two-year-old second class told me, a twenty-six-year-old woman, about how busy his morning was and about how he had too much to do and had to help the chief at the moment. Not only that, but he'd help me soon as he got done because his work was oh so much more important.

There are probably still balls of wax in his ears from not being able to clean himself properly. This was practically a child, yet he was disregarding me, his elder, simply because of his title. It was a gut punch for sure and although I was frustrated, he was nice about it.

"Okay," I started calmly. My calm started to wain after fifteen minutes. Once an hour went by, I asked him *again.*

Again, he was *still* too busy to be bothered.

"Get in touch with LS2," he suggested, referring me specifically to who he thought could help. "And she's a female, ya know? So, it would probably be better if she went with you anyway, right?" he offered.

"Sure LS2," I replied with my eyes flipping towards the sky. I called the female LS2's office and she wasn't available either. As I hung up the phone, a female LS1 walked into my office. I was very happy to see her as she'd always been nice. "Hey LS1, are you super busy right now?" I approached.

She shrugged her slender shoulder. "What's up LS3?"

I explained the cliff notes version of my situation to her.

"Yeah, I can't go with you to your berthing right now. I've got some stuff in my hand for Chief that I need to do."

Argggggghhhhhh, I exploded internally but I kept my cool outwardly.

I didn't get upset and thanked her anyway. My next move was to call my actual boss, my LS2 in my squadron.

"Hey LS2, it's LS3 Pearson," I started before testing the water to see if he was busy. Come on, I grumbled inwardly, waiting for his response. I was relieved to know he wasn't busy and explained my situation.

"Yeah, I don't think I can go with you to your berthing LS3," he replied.

The initial rejection had me ready to lose my shit. *Stay calm*. "Yes, you can! Males are allowed in a female berthing on official business." I explained.

"Yeah, thing is though, I don't *want* to go in a female berthing," he made the distinction clear. "Why don't you call—"

At the absolute end of my rope, I cut him off. "I'll figure it out, thanks!" I interrupted and hung up. I exhaled hard, expelling a long puff of air from my cheeks. *Now I'm pissed!*

One thing about the Navy, the people are going to test your patience. Every process that we go through, even one as simple as having someone walk to my berthing with me, is an entire obstacle course. Smooth sailing is rarely ever a thing for enlisted sailors. There is a million-step process for everything. It's a real pain in the ass.

Three hours later, I still had no escort. There was nothing in my rack that was super important for me to get – it was the principle! I bet if there was something in my rack that the Navy needed or that even my chief needed, everyone would have been willing to help me. It would have taken no longer than ten minutes. But since there wasn't, fuck what you need petty officer third class.

You can wait.

Because the Enlisted Don't Have Lives Outside of the Navy. That's Absurd!
Airframer Third Class Sarah Adame
Thirty-one years old. White. Capricorn.

"My time in the Navy has been frustrating! It's hard to get anything done on your time. You have to be on the Navy's timeline for you, as a serial number and not as a person with needs, and feelings, and what not. I hate the lack of concern that Big Navy shows for the junior enlisted. It feels like, to get anything done, you have to have anchors, or butter bars, or something other than a chevron."

Duty Days

Duty days are something that no one tells you about *before* you sign that dotted line. A duty day is a day that you are on board your ship for twenty-four hours. At my first command on the destroyer, with a crew of a little less than 400 people, we were able to divide the crew into six duty sections.

Each section had duty once every week. If you had duty on a Friday this week, then next week it was on a Thursday, and the following week it was on Wednesday, and so on and so forth. Turnover time for swapping duty sections at my first command started at 0645. After your turnover and unless approved by your section leader, if you were in the new duty section, you were no longer allowed to leave your ship until the next day at 0645.

The only thing that sucked about the next day for the relieved duty section was that if it was a workday, you could *forget* about leaving until the *end* of the workday, unless you lucked out with a very lenient chain of command. As an undesignated seaman with my very strict chain of command, the chance of leaving was *highly* unlikely.

Each watch ranged between four and five hours and most watches were armed watches. Personnel wore bullet proof vests and carried pistols; sometimes they had an M9 rifle slung across their chests. Once watch commenced, we stood around, walked around, and patrolled until the watch was done...hours later.

In addition to working all day on your duty day, standing multiple five-hour watches through the night, we also have to wake up the next day to work a full shift before *finally* being allowed to go home. Seamen were averaging thirty-two and thirty-four hours on board my ship once a week. During the duty day, unless it was Sunday, the Navy's holiday routine-day, we also have to muster for duty section training on whatever the training was scheduled to be that week.

Sometimes it was a fire drill, flooding drill, or medical emergency drill, but most of the time after working hours we were doing training with our duty sections. Sailors *pray* that they don't get the 0200 to 0700 watch. If you're the unlucky one who gets assigned those hours, your ass is grass the next day. You'll be *begging* someone to allow you to take a nap!

I understand duty days, believe me, I do. That doesn't mean that they suck any less though. We *need* security on board our ships, even if we are our *own* security.

Why, might you ask?

Because civilian and Navy people are fucking crazy! No, seriously. As you've read throughout this book, being a part of the Navy is taxing mentally, physically, and emotionally. If you're not careful or grounded enough to realize that it's only a job, it can be completely overwhelming.

People will come on base and on ships shooting, committing suicide, driving crazy, and all kinds of stuff. I get it. It's just that I don't get paid enough for this. I need duty day pay! Give me my overtime if this is what I deal with for my measly little seaman check. It also sucks trying to be productive before, during, or after a duty day.

You prepare as much as possible before, you can't even leave during, and after you are exhausted. As draining as it is, you really must recover from a duty day but are rarely given the opportunity. It sucks.

You Need Us, So Treat Us Better
Airframer Third Class Sarah Adame
Thirty-one years old. White. Capricorn.

"In the grand scheme of things, it just makes me think: If they're bullshitting me about this and that, then the higher ups are just bullshitting everyone about *everything*, thinking we are not noticing. They think that we are all just blindly following them because we *need* this job, right? But the truth is, they need us more than we need them."

Structure
Retail Service Specialist First Class Kimberly Fleming
Thirty-three years old. West Indian. Capricorn

"When you look at the Naval structure, your petty officers, your chiefs, etc. — over time you learn that sometimes you don't have to respond to everything. It becomes a matter of: you're not going to win this battle because you are low on the totem pole. You're here to do your job. If your third class or your second class tells you to do something, if it's not hurting you, understand that this is something they've probably had to do too or that they were told to tell you to do. Just saying, 'Roger that PO3 or PO2,' would decrease a lot of stress."

16

JUST ANOTHER BODY

Bodies

It's so weird to me how we use the term *bodies* in the Navy. It's a common term, and I hear it every day. That is, generally, what sailors are referred to on a consistent basis. Whether it's a part of the whole mental mind game that the Navy plays, another way to strip sailors of their individuality, or a covert way for the system to let us know that we're looked at as nothing more than a couple cogs in a gigantic machine, it is unclear. But, in my opinion, referring to sailors as bodies while treating us like robotic vessels is insane.

Sometimes my first class would walk into our work center and tell my second class something along the lines of, "Hey, I need you to send me two bodies later to help with painting a space." *Bodies.*

It's extremely cringey isn't it?

What makes it worse, no matter how fucked up it sounds or how much I cringe when I hear someone being reduced to merely a body, is I've even caught myself using this term. I hate that shit and I try to push it out of my mind every time it slips out of my mouth. It is normalized in this culture of work. Everybody does it. Sailors refer to other sailors as bodies, which means that deep down, that's how they refer to themselves or how they are used to being referred to.

Then again though, maybe it is appropriate because that's ultimately how I feel every single day in the Navy. It's not like I'm in a situation that is beneficial for both me and my employer. They take far more than they give at any given moment. I'm unable to enjoy or highlight the features and traits that make me unique as an individual. I'm just another person in uniform. Another body.

When someone refers to you as a body, in that moment you're not a wife or husband, a daughter or son, a friend or foe, a female or male, or even a *person*. No, no. You are no longer any of those things that you worked so hard throughout your life to be. In that moment, you are reduced to essentially being nothing more than a living, breathing, space filler.

I do not know when, where, or why the mass use of the word "body" originated in the Navy, but we use it often. Too often.

Your Body Belongs to the Military

On one particular day I was informed that I had to receive a mandatory anthrax shot. Apparently, anthrax is a serious disease that can affect both animals and humans. It is caused by bacteria called Bacillus anthracis. People can get anthrax from contact with infected animals, wool, meat, or hides. I learned that information from the pamphlets the hospital corpsmen (HMs) were handing out while sailors stood in line waiting on their shot.

I stood in line for about fifteen minutes. When I finally reached the top, there was a table surrounded with HMs and filled with sterilized needles and bottles of the vaccine. I walked up and rolled my sleeve above my shoulder. The HM stuck me with a needle, pushed in the fluid, and I was done. "Good to go!" he said as I rolled my sleeve down. I went back to work.

I assumed we had to receive these shots because we had now entered the Middle Eastern seas during our deployment.

At this point in my life and career, I was a pescatarian. As such, that meant my diet no longer allowed me to eat land meat. I tried my very best to only drink alkaline water with a P.H. above 8.5 when I was in port. I moisturized my skin and hair with the best and most authentic natural products I could find. I exercised regularly. I had significantly cut back on eating junk food and desserts. I had developed a serious interest in gardening and having plants around me to create better oxygen in the air.

I didn't even utilize plastic as much as I used to! I owned several tote bags that I used to grocery shop with. I even had a tote bag that held bottles of wine. Dedication. I was taking several steps to not only help myself protect and take care of my body, but the environment, too! I made healthy choices and gave a shit about what I put in my body.

But I had been ordered to receive a shot without warning and with little education about what the concoction consisted of. It didn't matter if I agreed or disagreed with its components or was fearful of the side effects. I had to take it because otherwise I would have been punished under the Uniform Code of Military Justice (UCMJ) for refusing to. I hate that. I *could've* refused to take it, gone to court, gone to jail possibly, and messed up all the plans that I had made for after this deployment due to my beliefs. *Or* I could just take it and go about my day like a good little sailor. Things you don't think about when you sign on the dotted line.

Pearson's Journal

Urinalysis

Today I was informed that I am on the hit list for urinalysis. I've done it plenty of times before; but today was just odd. Maybe I was thinking too deeply into the situation, but I just really did not appreciate the urinalysis. I understand that we the people of the United States Navy are not allowed to do drugs same as most government jobs, but the way we conduct our urinalysis just makes me feel like such a criminal.

I walked into the office where the urinalysis was handled. I was told to remove any watches or rings that I was wearing and to roll up my sleeves. I presented the urinalysis coordinator with my ID, and he gave me a little plastic cup and a little plastic bottle. He asked me to inspect them and, after doing so, I accepted the cup and the bottle. A second-class female escorted me to our nearest head. On the way there, I had to hold the bottle up in the air and out to the side where my escort could see it at all times. Upon arrival to the head, I had to leave the door to my stall open while my escort stood in front of it, watched me remove the lids of my cup and bottle and then remove my coveralls. She watched me squat over the toilet while I pissed into the cup. Then I transferred the piss from the cup to the bottle. Threw the cup away and washed my hands. I kept the bottle of my piss out on the sink where my escort could see it at all times.

After I finished washing my hands, we were on our way back to the urinalysis office. Once again, holding my bottle up in the air and out to the side, but this time with my piss in it. It felt like I was passing by hundreds of people – all eyes on me. Why do I feel so ashamed right now? I don't even do drugs. My piss is clean. Why do I feel so embarrassed? I shouldn't feel this way. I felt humiliated. Everyone could see my bottle of piss. I'm a good sailor and I shouldn't feel like a criminal.

Souls
Airframer Third Class Sarah Adame
Thirty-one years old. White. Capricorn.

"I think about how they call us bodies all the time. I need bodies for this and bodies for that. Have you ever noticed that when you're on an airplane, they say souls? 'We have X number of souls on board.'

Souls.

Human beings.

People.

Thoughts.

Feelings.

Emotions.

SOULS.

"But the Navy – which uses us until we are broken or worse – just calls us bodies. We're unimportant to them. They promise us a steady paycheck and the bare fucking minimum of the things that we need to live anyway. But, when you try to get out they say, 'You need to go through a TAPS class so that you can learn how to live as a civilian – where you're not getting a guaranteed three square meals a day and you're not getting a steady paycheck. Are you sure you want to do that? Don't you want to stay here where we're going to give you all these things and then use you until you can't fucking stand up anymore? C'mon, just re-enlist. Four more years. Give us four more and we'll make sure you have a VA loan for your house that you're never going to fucking buy because we're going to keep moving you around every couple of years. Or the GI bill! You could give the GI bill to your kids if you give us six more. Six more years and then you can give the GI bill to your kids' . . . maybe."

17

MEDICAL

Sick Days

Here's the thing about sick days: they don't exist in the Navy.

Granted, you might get sick but you're never truly *off*, so we don't exactly have sick days in the Navy while on sea duty. Most times, no matter how bad you feel, you're supposed to tough it out. Always.

As a matter of fact, if at any time you feel like you want to call out, the process of doing so while make you rethink the entire thing. It's like being forced to jump through rings of fire with gasoline drawers on. We have to go through and deal with a lot to call in sick to work. If you wake up with a sudden stomach bug, vomiting, and shitting all over the place, you're *still* required to come in to work because you have to be accounted for.

You are not allowed to take time to heal yourself without first getting proper dismissal for the day. This requires that your medical team on board your ship (or any medical team on base) deem you sick enough to receive a Sick in Quarters (SIQ) chit for the day or for however long you need to recover.

Then you can go back home and officially be sick. There is no such thing as not coming into work.

Sailors need to pray and/or hope that they are lucky enough to have some cool and understanding leadership within their chains of command, otherwise your sick ass will be at work until someone tells you that you are *authorized* to be at home, sick.

Medical on Board a Warship

Receiving proper and compassionate care from the medical team on board our naval warships has often been quite challenging for many lower ranking enlisted sailors. Medical on-board warships is designed to look for the quickest route to stabilize sailors and/or bring them to a fit-for-duty status. Lower ranking sailors are vital. Therefore, it is hard for us because we're *needed*. Let's put it this way: unless you are knocking on the door of death, expect to be stuck on your warship with your medical needs.

On larger ships such as carriers, however, there are more options for medical attention. While I served on board a carrier, there were minor surgeries and X-rays performed, usually by officers. Again, whatever is necessary to stabilize sailors and make them fit for duty is the focus of medical care. If your condition absolutely cannot be handled by the medical team on board your ship or any ship within your strike group, *then* you will be flown off your ship to acquire more advanced medical attention.

I have seen deployed sailors with broken and fractured bones be put in quick-fix casts and be forced to stay on board the ship; anything to keep from having to send them off the ship while in the middle of the ocean. It's a bit different on land where these situations aren't such a burden on convenience. But once you're onboard the ship out to sea, it truly takes a person knocking at heaven's door before you can leave the ship.

Even sailors who have attempted to end their lives in one way or another remain onboard and are placed on suicide watch. There is a team assigned to ensure that no further harm comes to them. It can be intense.

Once on my carrier I saw a chief petty officer, a man who was missing an entire hand, on board during our deployment. His medical condition was something acquired long before the deployment and seemed to be under control, but I was absolutely baffled when I saw him regularly walking around.

The enlisted hospital corpsmen (HMs) have been trained for a few months within their A and C schools provided by the Navy after graduating boot camp and prior to entering the fleet. These are the caretakers of the sailors at their deployable commands. Typically, HMs have not gone to medical school or even a prestigious college. As a matter of fact, some have only had medical training through the provided Navy schools.

They are not doctors.

Good luck.

Sea Story
By: Skyla Pearson.
Twenty-seven years old. African American. Scorpio.

On my first deployment, as an undesignated seaman, I woke up in the middle of the night because of a sharp pain in my stomach. The pain would come and go but when it came, it was intense and kept me up all night. By morning, I barely made it to our 0700 muster because of the pain. "I need to go to sick call," I grimaced to my LPO.

I conducted, well more like pretended to conduct, our morning sweepers and waited until 0815 to go and wait in line outside of medical. On my destroyer that held fewer than four hundred sailors, we had an HM1 and two HM3s to cater to the entire crew.

Finally, after waiting a few minutes, I was inside of medical being seen by our HM1. "What's going on," the HM1 asked.

"I'm having sharp...like super sharp, pains in my stomach," I started describing my symptoms. "Sometimes when I try to take a deep breath, I get a strong urge to throw up, but it ends up only being dry heaving since nothing comes up."

She scribbled down information before continuing to probe. "What about your appetite?"

"It's gone."

"Alright, let's take your temperature." Doing as she suggested, she looked at the reading on the thermometer. "Well, no fever. Go ahead and de-blouse so that you can lie down," she ordered.

After removing the top half of my coveralls and lying on the table, she began to press on different areas of my stomach. "Does it hurt here? How about here? Here?"

My reply was a continuous yes.

Suddenly she stopped, looked at me with eyebrows raised in suspicion. "Look, if you're just trying to get out of work, you can stop pretending. I have other sailors with real issues that need to be seen."

The accusation that I was faking just because I didn't want to work took my already high temperature through the roof. I'm not a dirt bag by no sense of anyone's imagination so to insinuate that I could be that lazy to come up with a lie and go through all of this just to avoid work took me out.

I was livid!

"What are you talking about HM1? Why would I come in here to play? I've never even been seen by you before. I only come to medical for mandatory, routine shit."

She just stared at me with a blank, emotionless stare.

"HM1, I am not pretending! I am in pain!" I screeched.

She rolled her eyes and replied smugly, "It's probably just gas. Come back and see me later if it doesn't pass."

Probably just gas, her voice echoed in my head. Here I was, coming to this woman for medical help for real, actual pain that I felt but she had the audacity to turn her nose up at my discomfort, dismissing it as something trivial like gas. I sat there for a few seconds and watched her busy herself to ignore me.

That was her verdict, and she had no plans to change it.

I was shocked. I was in pain. I was infuriated.

I went straight to my rack! Yep, that lady had me fucked up if she thought I was working in the condition I was in. My stomach was hurting so bad that when the pain came, I'd have to stop what I was doing to let it pass. It felt like someone was taking my stomach and wringing it out like a wet towel.

Once my LPO caught wind of the fact that I had left medical and was not issued a sick-in-quarters chit, he continued to send my fellow female co-workers down to my berthing to tell me that I had to come back to work. I wouldn't move. I absolutely refused to do so. Since I was in indescribable pain and the only person taking that pain serious, I had to look out for my best interest.

I told them to tell him that if he wanted me back at work, he'd have the HMs help me, give me medicine, or just go ahead and give me my SIQ chit.

Honestly, what were they going to do? Write me up for not feeling well? Tell my senior chief to come and drag me out of my rack and work even though I told them I was in pain? Exactly. I'd make myself SIQ, damn it. Consequences be damned.

Eventually, the female of the HM3 duo showed up to my rack. She informed me that HM1 believed I had gas built up and since it wouldn't pass, the gas bubbles that were stuck were causing the pain in my stomach. "Just lie on your back, bring your knees up to your chest, and rock yourself back and forth. This should help the gas pass. Here are some laxatives and here is your SIQ chit," the HM3 explained, mapping out my treatment plan.

I really wanted my mother more than I ever had before in my life. I felt so unsafe, uncared for, and scared. But all I could do was hope for the best.

Medical Does not Rush for the Enlisted Often
Aviation Maintenance Administrationman First Class Janelle Delgado
Thirty-four years old. Trinidadian. Gemini

"Shortly after having my miscarriage in the shower while on deployment, I got dressed and was escorted to medical. I had the sweetest HM but even he couldn't erase what I had just seen. The only thing he did was give me pain medicine, a few other drugs to knock me out, and a SIQ chit for the week. I laid in my rack that entire week crying and sleeping and crying and sleeping over and over again until they finally flew me off of the ship almost two weeks later. Then my command had the nerve to advise that I needed to go to base medical ASAP to make sure it was all out.

"Well, where was the rush when I was bleeding in my rack for two weeks?"

PART VI

YES, YOU CAN BE BLACK. BUT YOUR HAIR CAN'T!

Yeah, I said it. And I'll add more to it before I take it back.

You'd think since hair is a natural part of the human anatomy, that it wouldn't be such a big deal. I mean, it is hair after all. It grows, gets cut, and grows back again. Seems simple enough right?

Well of course nothing can be that simple when it comes to the Navy.

The hair police are alive and well in the military and, apparently, look for every opportunity to regulate hairstyles. For those with silky straight hair, it's not that big of a deal because all they have do is pull their hair back and keep moving. But of course, the ordinance wasn't crafted for those with the silky straight hair.

If your hair is naturally kinky, coiled, frizzy, easily intertwined, thick, or thin, you will have a difficult time abiding by the naval regulations for hair. Sometimes it's not even the regulations that are the difficulty; it's the people who enforce them because, depending on the day, someone's perception can determine if you're out of regulation. That being said, my natural hair journey happened *because* of the Navy.

This is the case for a lot of African American sailors. We're forced to go natural because we don't have access to our typical hair care products, but those same forces attempt to limit the way we express ourselves through our strands. For me, returning to my natural roots was monumental.

So much so that I felt the need to dedicate an entire chapter to it.

18

OUR HAIR

First and Foremost
Aviation Ordnanceman Airman Danielle Lowe
Twenty years old. African American. Libra.

"First of all, I don't give a fuck what anybody says, race plays a big role in the military! I'm a female, but because I'm Black, a Black female, and that plays a big difference in it. When it comes to progressing, the Navy has this thing where you have to take away so much of yourself so that it can make 'this' and 'that' out of you. The Navy is not supposed to be taking everything out of my personal beliefs and how I naturally am to transform me into some kind of robot. I'm going to do my job, but I'm going to keep me in it while I do it."

The Most! Okay? The Most!
Logistics Specialist Third Class Laura Baxley
Twenty-eight years old. African American. Aries.

"Black women really have to do the most to fit their hair into regulation just to come to work and deal with someone still having something to say about it. This is a subject that I feel is never going to be right for us."

A Letter to the Ignorant

Dear ignorant (I said ignorant, not all) white people in the Navy,

Let's just first address the really big elephant in the room. All sailors are NOT created equal. We with melanin are aware of the fact that *you're* aware of our hair that's worlds different from yours. It bends and twists, scales towards the heavens and can even be ironed silky straight at any given moment. It amazes you. We get it.

What we're also aware of are the regulations regarding the grooming standards and instructions associated with how we are to wear our hair while we are members of this organization.

We have a few questions for you: Are *you* truly aware of the fact that our hair is different? Are *you* aware of these instructions, regulations, and grooming standards before you attempt to correct and/or criticize our hair? Are you sure? Can you stop sending and asking other white people to correct issues they know nothing about? I'm sorry but a white person CAN NOT tell me what to do with my hair. If you have the audacity to assume without education or even have the correct assumption that our hair is out of regulation, why are you so afraid to correct it yourself? Also, can you please find the time to educate yourselves on *how* and *why* our hair naturally grows and looks the way that it does before you presume to correct or criticize it?

By the way, did you know that there is nothing wrong with nor is it against regulation to wear different wigs, extensions, and weaves that may also include different hair color and texture, every day, or every other day if we choose? Have you taken into consideration that perming and straightening our hair is not natural and we have the right to choose if we would prefer that method or the other? I just need to know.

One more thing; this goes out to the indelicate, undiplomatic, melanated leadership and members of the Navy as well. How about a little more support and less criticism? Stop doing your own people wrong while these white women walk around with whatever hairstyle they feel like throwing together today. Don't let that shit slide either.

What's Going on with Your Hair?
Personnel Specialist Second Class Dominique Lucas
Twenty-four years old. African American. Gemini.

"As a Black woman, some things that I feel other ethnicities do not have a hard time dealing with while in the Navy are the hair regulations. I am natural and I wear my natural hair to work in natural hairstyles. With that, I'm always having to deal with the constant question: What's going on with your hair? Even when I get braids, I hear, 'this bun is too big.' It gets so bad that even if I just freshly twist my afro with moisturizer and take it out, I will still get that same question: What's going on with your hair?"

Different Textures = Different Results
Logistics Specialist Second Class Briana Williams
Twenty-four years old. Panamanian American. Leo.

"I'm expected to look a certain way or what they deem is professional and well put together. However, what is not taken into consideration is the fact that everyone's hair does not react the same way."

It may be a shocker to some but just like no person has the same dental profile, DNA, and fingerprints – no two people have the same hair profile.

Especially when it comes to Black hair. We have different textures, porosities, thickness, etc. There is no one-product-cure-all for African American hair. Our hair is just as multifaceted as we are.

Learn to deal with it.

It's Twisted
Logistics Specialist Third Class Laura Baxley
Twenty-eight years old. African American. Aries.

"Having to try and figure out how to keep my hair in regulations and be able to wear my hair how I want to wear it while being natural is stressful. I feel like even if I do wear a really nice hairstyle like a twist out, people are still going to look at it as unprofessional and I think it is so fucked up that it's up to their interpretation."

19

MY RELAXED, CIVILIAN HAIR

Before I joined the Navy, my hair was relaxed. My mother started perming my hair when I was in third grade, and we never looked back. I couldn't even imagine myself without a perm after receiving my first one. I loved it! I was just happy to ditch that dreadful hot comb! Every six weeks, it was on. My mom would relax my new growth like clockwork. Growing up, my mom *always* did my hair – whatever I needed. A perm, braids, cornrows, pig tails, flat iron, curl set, you name it, mama did it. As the oldest of two with a younger brother, I never saw a reason to learn how to do my hair or anyone else's hair for that matter. I did have Barbie dolls' hair to do, but even the Black Barbies back then had relaxed hair. So, to me, this *had* to be the way to go. Even when I moved away from home at twenty, no matter where I went, I always found a salon with a woman I trusted to perm my hair just the way I liked it! Eventually I started rocking sew-ins with some leave out that I could blend into my extensions. I was also a huge fan of the clip-on, long-ass ponytails that I could wear with a little swoop-di-swoop of my hair in the front. You couldn't tell me *anything*.

When I joined the Navy at the age of twenty-three, I even made it through boot camp with no problems. Since it was only a nine-week adventure for me, the fresh perm I had gotten prior to shipping out lasted better than I expected. By the end of boot camp, things began to get a bit rough, but it was nothing that a little edge control couldn't handle. I slid through boot camp with zero hair issues.

Undesignation + My Hair Texture = Hot Mess

After I arrived and settled in at my first command in Norfolk, Virginia, found a hair salon, and accepted my role as an undesignated seaman, I realized some things rather quickly:

- Wearing a bun every day was breaking the hell out of my kitchen and something had to give.
- After I took my bun out every night, my hair was dented and flimsy, so in order for me to go out and look remotely cute, I would have to flat iron my hair or rock my tired-ass, clip-on ponytails that still required a little flat ironing of my new growth so it could blend. I was flat ironing my relaxed hair at least three to five times a week.
- Every single time I got a fresh perm, the undesignated lifestyle had me sweating it out within the next two to three weeks!

Having a perm with my new position in the Navy was starting to become extremely unhealthy and damaging for my hair – not to mention expensive and hard to manage. *Something* had to give. With much research, observation of the Black women around me, and consideration, I decided that getting a wig would be the way to go. This decision didn't bother me. I was not familiar with wearing wigs, but I was exceptionally ready to become familiar with anything that would make the day-to-day maintenance of my hair an easier and healthier task!

Ponytail and Bun Damage
Logistics Specialist Third Class Laura Baxley
Twenty-eight years old. African American. Aries.

"And even when I tried to conform to standards by wearing a ponytail – which is more like a puff for me – it would break my hair. I was wearing that *every* day. It's damaging."

Logistics Specialist Second Class Briana Williams
Twenty-four years old. Panamanian American. Leo.

"I know people who have gotten out of the Navy because of the regulations dictating how we are to wear our hair. I would prefer *not* to damage my hair as we are constantly forced to put our hair in ponytails."

Manhattan Beauty on East Little Creek

I'll never forget Manhattan Beauty on East Little Creek in Norfolk, Virginia. It is literally the best hair and beauty store on the East Coast hands down, and better yet it is Black-owned and affordable! It was wigs *galore* in that place and they were on sale 100 percent of the time! *And* active-duty military members received a 10 percent military discount on top of whatever sales they had going on! I know it sounds like I'm advertising for them, but I'm not. Manhattan Beauty did not pay for their inclusion in this book. I'm just stating the facts. That store will forever have a special place in my heart.

So, four to five wigs later, it was definitely a thing. I felt like I had solved all of my hair problems. I even had a specific work wig that stayed in its 24/7 bun. I usually just popped it right on in the morning and popped it right back off at night after my day was done. I had fallen in love with wigs and the many varieties and style options. But by the time I had undergone a few short under ways with my command and experienced living on board as an undesignated seaman 24/7, I was not at all interested in popping my now very itchy wig on and off all day and night. Between watches, random drills, and evolutions that vitally required my presence, I was *beyond* over having to remember to pop on my wig. I honestly just started to show up in my raggedy, quickly thrown together, wig braids/cornrows. If I was going to be underway for more than two weeks, I decided to have my hair braided straight to the back. I felt helpless. I settled into the mindset of, *well I don't have anyone to impress so, fuck it.* But slowly and surely, this way of thinking started to take a toll on my self-esteem and my feeling of freedom.

Deployment with Relaxed Hair

It was my first deployment that gave me the worst hair issues. Fortunately for me, by the time the deployment started, I had made friends who would braid my hair – even my mentor, an information systems technician petty officer (IT1) at the time braided my hair on a regular basis. I actually used to love our pep talks when she would braid my hair, and rocking my cornrows underway was definitely the best thing for me as an undesignated seaman on a destroyer. All of the sweating and vigorous participation in drills, exercises, and evolutions made it hard to upkeep a cute "in regs" hairstyle – especially when you *live* in a hard hat.

After several weeks of rocking the same old, tired cornrows, I started to become jealous of the Black women with rates who did not stand watches underway. For example, I was jealous of the women in admin and supply. Every evening after I was relieved from my first watch of the day and finally made it to my berthing, there would be Black women of these certain rates in the berthing lounge and/or head listening to music, watching movies, and doing their *natural* hair, making the entire berthing smell *amazing* with their hair products – meanwhile, my stinky ass was more concerned about making sure I ate something filling, showered, and received a decent amount of sleep before my next watch. I could not afford the time to do hair! It bothered me so much.

After about three months into the deployment, I had so much new growth that trying to wear a decent bun was damn near impossible! And frankly, I was sick of looking at cornrows or braids. "Well, why didn't you bring a relaxer with you and either do it yourself or have someone perm your hair for you," you ask? Well, didn't I mention that unless you were my mama or a professional I had grown to trust, you weren't touching my hair with a perm? Oh, and I'm pretty sure I mentioned that I never really learned or had a reason to learn how to do my own hair. I was a little embarrassed and shy about the fact that I did not know how to do my hair when every woman around me was so knowledgeable about theirs. *That's* why. Do not judge me.

My goal was to wear braids the *entire* deployment – unless we hit a port visit and I had a few wigs packed away for that occasion, of course. But every Black, female, junior sailor I knew on my first deployment was natural. Witnessing them strand twist, flat twist, and braid their hair at night and then walk around the next day with perfect puffs and fros with beautifully, manipulated curls was beginning to become heart wrenching. Even the women who wore their twists for a couple of days before they took them out had me in complete envy because I knew that there was no way I could possibly manipulate my hair to do that and *stay*, not with damn near an inch of new growth and relaxed ends.

"Fuck it."

Oh yes, I was determined to stand up to my hair and feel good about it for once on that deployment.

But in return to my rebellion, I created the worst hair day of my life.

The Worst Hair Day of My Life While Deployed

One evening before holiday routine in the Middle Eastern seas, I stayed up a little bit later after my first watch. I had the brilliant idea that I would do Bantu knots. In my head, I calculated that this style would allow me to twist and roll sections of my hair into little balls so tight, it would twist all the way to my scalp and manipulate my new growth *and* relaxed ends. Brilliant! I, too, would have a nice holiday routine, damn it! I, too, would look kind of decent for once on this deployment.

Eager to boost my own morale, I did it.

For about an hour and a half, I was posted up with the other females in the head doing *my* hair and jamming to *my* music. One of my good friends, Personnel Specialist Third Class (PS3) Lucas, was in there at the time herself. She was twisting her hair per usual. To me, she seemed surprised that I was doing my hair because when I started she gave me a weird look and when I finished, I noticed her staring at my beautifully twisted Bantu knots.

Yep, get a load of me girls. Tomorrow is my day! You will see a new seaman walking around! Deck seaman can be cute, too, damn it, I thought to myself as I proudly strutted out of the head and to my rack to carefully wrap up my Bantu knots before napping until my next watch.

I rocked a baseball cap to my next watch, which was a night watch, and no one noticed my hair. It was a good thing, too, because hidden underneath the cap were my Bantu knots; a style that is considered out of regulations. By morning, after watch and before reveille, I skipped breakfast and ran straight to my berthing so that I could undo my Bantu knots.

Full of excitement, I started to unravel them. Because of the versatility of African American hair, I knew that having the Bantu knots served as two styles in one. While I'd worn the knots under the hat, unravelling them was supposed to reveal a gorgeous, well- defined set of curls. I couldn't wait to see how it would look.

One by one, they came down and by the fifth or sixth one, something just wasn't adding up. The new growth looked nice and curly, but when it came to those relaxed ends, it was struggle bus central. The relaxed ends were straggly and limp, leaving it to appear as though someone had held my head down, ruffled my hair, and gave me a noogie. Frustration swelled within me, and I wanted to cry!

Since Bantu knots were unauthorized, I had no choice but to finish taking them down.

Once they were down, and I looked like a ratchet version of Medusa herself, I was in a panic to figure out how in the hell I could recover my hair before the entire command woke up to witness this disaster. I tried everything I knew, which wasn't much. I put a head band on and attempted to wear some sort of a puff/fro thing, but nope. It looked like shit to me.

I tried to slick it back into a bun. *Hell* no! My hair was so coily, curly, intertwined, and confused. Without a handy spray bottle and a jar of holding gel, a bun didn't stand a chance. My hair was such a thick and tangled mess that rivaled anything I'd ever had to deal with before. I was clueless.

Running out of time, I was stuck and had to try *something*. So reluctantly, I slicked it back the best I could into the head band and went with the puff thing, with even that being a struggle. At least, it was holiday routine, and I could try my best to fix it before my next watch. Insecure about the state of my hair, I felt hideous. I mean, I literally *hid* in my rack for about three hours waiting for the chaos of women who had just awakened and were starting their days to calm down to avoid being seen in that state.

After it was quiet and low-key empty around our berthing, I called everywhere to find my mentor and friends who usually braid my hair, but they were either on watch or MIA. Feeling extremely hungry – considering that it was around lunch time – I couldn't hide any longer. So, I decided to attempt to fix it myself once again.

I hopped in the shower, washed my hair, and after my shower I began to aggressively apply moisturizer and brush my hair into a bun when PS3 Lucas walked into the head.

"What happened to the Bantu knots?"

I gave her a very mean glare. "Bitch, they were a *mess*! Terrible idea! They did not look anything like what I thought. I had to wash them out," I responded. The inspiration that led me to test out the hairstyle was so cute but when it was placed on my head, not so much.

"I could have told you that was going to happen," she snickered, shaking her head.

I immediately stopped what I was doing and turned toward her. "*What?* Well, why didn't you stop me?" I exclaimed.

She shrugged. "You looked like you were happy and in your zone, so I didn't want to kill your vibe. I will tell you this though, you're *never* going to be able to do a style like that unless you go ahead and cut that perm out of your head."

I was baffled! Cut my perm off? I couldn't imagine! I was planning to get a fresh one as soon as we returned home. "Look, I can't do that! I don't know the first thing about taking care of natural hair."

She shrugged, "Well you're going to either have to learn or keep perming your hair because whatever you've got going on there, ain't it. You need to figure it out. And I can help you Pearson. *We* can help you. Just do it," she suggested as she left.

Cut my perm off? Isn't that called a big chop? I don't think I have the balls. Like, I don't want to go through that ugly stage that everyone talks about. But I can't deal with this shit either... I don't know, maybe... I thought to myself as I continued to wrestle with my hair. Finally, after getting my hair under some sort of control so that I could stop hiding and eat, I called my mentor.

Later that day, she was able to braid my hair. I never attempted a hairstyle outside of my lane again on that deployment.

20

MAMA, CUT IT OFF!

After I made it through my first deployment, my new growth had grown to a little over two inches. I was still rocking my wigs and battling with the decision to cut my hair; and although I couldn't seem to decide out loud, I still conducted lots of research on Google and YouTube, soaking up information about how to take care of natural hair just *in case* I decided to go ahead and cut off my relaxed ends and ditch the perms. I learned everything I could about natural hair as I waited to take post-deployment leave.

When I finally took leave, I was headed straight home to the Sip! Whatever I was going to do to my hair – perm or chop – it was going to involve my favorite girl: my mama. I think I already knew that I was going to cut my hair, but I was probably just in denial that I did not want a perm anymore. I wore one of my favorite wigs home for the long-awaited reunion with my family.

The moment I told my mom that I wanted her to cut off my relaxed ends, she was in complete shock.

"What? Why?" she asked.

"Mama, I just think it's time. I want to make this change." After telling her about all of the natural Black women I had met in Virginia and everything that I went through with my own hair on deployment, she was assured that I had given it enough thought.

The next day, we took down my cornrows, and washed and conditioned my hair. The moment had arrived. My mom asked me for the last time, right before the first snip, "Are you sure you want to do this?"

Boldly, I replied, "Mama, cut it off." I watched the hair fall. I felt *relieved*. I kept trying to cop a feel, but my mom kept popping my hand. Nerve wrecking as it was, I couldn't help but feel warm inside from the nostalgia of having my mom help me with my hair. There I was, at the age of twenty-four, and my mom would *still* pop me. But from what I could feel, it felt so short! I was nervous and excited at the same time!

I'm going natural! Oh my God, oh my God!

When she was finally done and told me to look at it, I took off to the bathroom. When I saw myself, a wide smile stretched across my face. The woman looking back at me was so *beautiful.* The woman looking back at me was ME. Only now, I was reborn.

Staying in Regulation as a Natural Was Easy. Until It Wasn't.

After my leave and much more research, I started getting pretty damn good at twist outs! My puff was just growing and growing. I even found the products that worked for me and my hair texture. Although I had to stay up a little late some nights to twist and moisturize my hair, going natural was the best decision I could have ever made. For me, being natural made it much easier to maintain my hair and keep it within these naval hair regulations, until it didn't.

One night, when the destroyer was in the yards after our deployment and well after my natural hair journey began, I had fallen asleep before I could moisturize, twist, and wrap my hair. I woke up the next morning before work thinking, *Fuck*!

At this point in my journey, my hair measured out to around five to six inches without shrinkage, but with shrinkage I could definitely manipulate my fro into one to two inches. The actual instruction for hair bulk states that hair bulk (minus a bun) as measured from the scalp will not exceed two inches.

Since my night hadn't gone as planned, on this morning I had no choice but to spray some leave in conditioner, pat down my fro, and go with it. It was my duty day, I had to be at work early and did not have the time to wrestle it into a bun/puff. This was the first time I had ever worn my actual fro to work and although I was a bit shy, I received several compliments upon my arrival to my ship.

In the yards, there was a barge messenger of the watch whose duty was to keep an eye on who was coming in and out of our barge, answer and communicate through the duty radio as needed, and maintain cleanliness of the barge entrance. I was scheduled to stand this watch this day. My job was to literally stand at a podium, unarmed for five hours.

As my afro and I were on watch minding our natural business, the command master chief, a white, middle-aged male walked by. He stopped and briefly stared at my hair.

"Pearson, did you cut your hair?" he asked.

"Yes, Master Chief, I did." I answered with a smile.

"It looks very nice! *However*, I can't help but notice that it looks a bit bulkier than two inches. Am I correct?" he asked with a raised brow.

Confused as hell, I head jerked back. I just knew it was a haircut and that I didn't know the exact dimension of the look. I answered, "I'm pretty sure my hair is in regs, Master Chief." With a bit of a tsk, he replied, "Yeah, I don't think so shipmate. I need you to find a relief and correct that." He walked off.

Within the next ten minutes I found a relief, went to my berthing, and started the attempt to manipulate my "bulk."

"What are you doing off of watch?" someone asked. I looked over and it was my good friend PS3 Lucas who fortunately was in the same duty section as me. I told her what happened.

"He tried me like that before, too, girl and I corrected his ass. Let me go and grab my ruler out of my rack." she stated as she stormed off. I laughed, "You have a ruler in your rack?"

"Girl, yes! These white folk will try the fuck out of you with they aggravating ass. You have to be ready to educate them at all times," she said.

When PS3 came back with her ruler, we both patted my fro until it measured all around to two inches. Yes, my hair was actually *measured* in real life. Honestly, when she initially measured it, it was at two inches and one quarter. This really upset me. Seriously, was there anything else better master chief could have been worrying about besides criticizing my hair? I guess a fourth of an inch was going to prevent me from doing my job and standing a proper watch. I wholeheartedly believed he only stopped because my hair was different.

It was in a new style, and it was noticeable. Why couldn't the compliment on my haircut have been enough? I truly believe that what he wanted was for me to put my shit back in a bun so that he could prove whatever point it was that he wanted to prove or to have a power trip. Who knows! But was that really necessary?

Eventually, I was back on watch, standing at my podium with PS3 Lucas standing right beside me, ruler in hand, ready to bat for her friend. "You don't have somewhere to be?" I asked her.

"Yep! Right here with you waiting for Master Chief to walk by," she affirmed. And that's exactly where she stayed until she saw him off in the distance. "Excuse me, Master Chief? Would you mind if we had a word?"

With energy, he replied, "Sure PS3!" and cruised right over.

"Master Chief, I took the liberty of measuring her hair bulk and it is *exactly* two inches in bulk. I have a ruler right here if you would like to check." Lucas held out the ruler for him. Our master chief looked at the ruler, at me, and then back to Lucas. "No that's okay PS3. I trust you." he alleged stiffly. "Thank you for helping out your shipmate."

With complete sarcasm and a smile, PS3 Lucas replied, "*Anytime* Master Chief."

As Master Chief walked off, PS3 stood there until he was out of sight. She looked at me, gave me a wink, and continued about her day. I cannot describe to you guys how powerful I felt in that moment.

Two-Inch Bulk Is Bullshit
Personnel Specialist Second Class Dominique Lucas
Twenty-four years old. African American. Gemini.

"I wish the regulation that basically states that your afro can't be more than two inches would change. It might as well say, 'Hey, if you're going to wear your natural hair, and it's growing, you need to wear a wig or something.' Two inches is bullshit."

Stay in Your Lane Black, Female Sailors; Whatever That Is
Navy Counselor (Career) First Class Elon McDuell-Briscoe
Thirty-six years old. African American. Taurus.

"They try to stifle the tenacity and passion that we possess because they feel like we should stay in our place and fall in line with the status quo."

Address the Grey Areas!
Logistics Specialist Second Class Briana Williams
Twenty-four years old. Panamanian American. Leo.

"Okay, our hair is appealing. That doesn't mean that it's faddish. I want the Navy to address the grey area; but what is the grey area? A grey area for me is the volume of my hair. Although it has been addressed as hair bulk in our regulations, what happens when my hair naturally exceeds the required bulk due to the humidity outside on that given day? Now I have to somehow try and bring my fro all the way back into a bun. I'm damned if I do and I'm damned if I don't."

Sea Story
By: Logistics Specialist Second Class Briana Williams
Twenty-four years old. Panamanian American. Leo.

On my deployment, I was hanging out with a few new African American female friends of mine and I had just taken my twists out. I had cornrows in the front. My twists were becoming a little aged and I tried to add a little pizazz to them. Once I took them out, I felt like someone was going to say something eventually, but this was me trotting in that grey area. Although I was aware of my grey area, I was still triggered when someone called me out on it.

So, I was laughing with my friends, and a senior chief walked by. He looked and continued on his way, without saying anything. Soon after, he came back, wanting to know who was in charge. Then, he proceeded to reprimand that person instead of me and passive-aggressively gave *me* a printed instruction with a boldly underlined portion about cornrows. I would have appreciated the senior chief saying something directly to me or openly reprimanding me instead of doing it with no words, almost as if I didn't deserve the respect as a person, African American, or woman.

All he had to say was, *Hey, I believe your hair is out of regulations. Here's the reason why, A, B, and C. I'd rather you set a better example because of your rank or whatever the case may be.*

The printed instruction said that my braids had to be cornrowed from the front of my head to the nape of my neck and had to have rubber bands of the same color as my hair at the ends. But who's *really* wearing straight back cornrows these days? And to be honest, even if it was braided all the way back, it still would have gone past my collar.

So, I proceeded to pull my hair back into a ponytail right there in front of my friends and in that moment, I felt stripped. It had me upset for a little bit but then I realized that, when we signed that contract, we became slaves to the game. So, I just had to learn how to play it better. I'm still going to teeter in that grey area. I'll just be *well* aware of my audience.

PART VII

COMMIT SUICIDE OR GET WITH THE PROGRAM

Before entering this chapter, I would like to offer an official trigger warning. I apologize to those people who may be specifically touched by this portion of the book. This title and subject are in no way comedic nor are they intended to produce shock and awe.

I named this chapter with the intent to draw the attention that the subject matter deserves. Though it is taboo and rarely ever talked about, suicide in the military is a rising issue that is tearing families apart. Despite the programs, training, and support provided for service members, there are still sailors out there who need help before it gets to a deadly point.

One suicide is too much.

In this chapter, you are presented with opinions, stories, and events that pertain to military members who have either considered, attempted, witnessed, or successfully committed suicide. If you yourself or someone you know is having suicidal thoughts, please reach out for help, even though it might feel like there is no help available.

You are not alone. Your life is valuable. You matter...

If you or anyone you know is struggling with thoughts of suicide, the National Suicide Hotline is always an option: 1-800-273-8255. You can also visit their website at https://suicidepreventionlifeline.org.

Mission First
Gunners Mate Second Class Beverly Stroud
Twenty-five years old. White. Leo.

“The job and the mission always come before the sailor; no matter what they tell you. They will always put the mission before you. And when I say ‘they’ I’m talking about the higher ups or anyone that has anything to gain by the mission getting done. Nothing about a Sailor’s mental well-being is taken seriously until something serious happens.”

21

THE DAY SUICIDE MADE SENSE TO ME

By the time I made it to the middle of my first deployment, being undesignated started to really take a toll on my mental health, and the more I stood watch, the more it hurt. I began to truly believe that people in the Navy were extremely senseless. I did not understand how sailors cared so much about the Navy, its operations, or its equipment.

Don't you guys realize how much the Navy does not care about you? I thought to myself every day.

Being deployed on that destroyer in the Middle East is what hurt me the most. It was the ten to twelve hours of watch I stood outside in the heat that ranged from 115–130°F every day while profusely sweating and standing in one spot, unable to escape the sun. My sleep and shower times were continuously interrupted, and all of that occurred in days that *still* included working hours outside in the sun or within the bos'n locker that felt like a sauna. We were undermanned, so to get a relief from watch to go to the head was an *enormous* and inconvenient task.

After the seventh cancelled port visit, I stopped counting. We hadn't seen land in months, and the continuous cancellation of our replenishment and supply (RAS) due to our multiple movements for our everchanging mission – which meant we were running low on food, snacks, and beverages, and were not receiving care packages – was not helping the stress either.

One day I worked my ass off all day in the Middle Eastern heat. Hungry, I went inside the ship for lunch and our culinary specialists were serving us sandwich meat, tomatoes, and pickles as our entrée. We didn't even have bread, only tortillas and a few other items like apples, oranges, and a salad bar. My pride was hurt.

To think about how I *volunteered* for this. Nobody made me join the service. I volunteered to join the military. I decided to serve my country. A noble decision, right? But this was what the "World's Greatest Navy" had prepared for its hardest working sailors to eat.

This was what I had to eat before my next six-hour watch. After I looked at the food on the line, I laughed. I decided to eat a few granola bars that I had stashed away in my rack and went to lie down for about thirty minutes before reporting to watch.

As my watch began, I stared at nothing but water, thinking. I was about to spend the next six hours staring at the ocean, just thinking. That's a lot of time to stand and think. Day in and day out with the sun beating on you during the day, turning your thoughts into a blurry haze and a quietness at night that made your thoughts haunt you. It's kind of like being in some sort of adult time out.

After a few hours, once my hunger started to kick in again, my wheels started turning. A long list of questions popped into my head, coming up with questions and creating scenarios before I could process it all. It was so much.

Does big Navy even care about our morale at all?

Why can't we hit a port visit? Just one port, even for just one day.

The mission always matters more. Just the mission. We're just bodies. We are all just bodies being put to use. I'm just another body to the Navy.

There's a number on my forehead and it's been there since the day I signed the dotted line. Recruit number 0080225643.

Damn. This ocean is big.

So fucking big . . .

I wonder how far down it really goes.

I wonder what the bottom looks like and what kind of creatures are there; creatures that are probably undiscovered.

These waves are getting crazy today.

There's no way I could stay afloat in these waves long enough for someone to save me if I fell overboard.

These waves would swallow me.

I miss my family.

If I ran to my mama, crying about this Navy shit, and telling her everything that it's doing to me, I bet she'd offer to cook me something nice for dinner. I would love that.

It would probably feel like all my troubles were gone.

I can't wait to hug you again, mama.

Wow these waves are really getting crazy!

If I jumped, no one would notice for twenty minutes. Guaranteed.

All this would end.

Everyone would wonder why I did it.

Would these watches even change? Would anything about my death change the Navy? Hell no!

But if I jumped, I'd be telling the Navy, 'Fuck your contract!'

Fuck this deployment!

It was in that moment, that very moment, that for the first time in my life, I understood why people commit suicide. I understood why *sailors* commit suicide. I did not want to kill myself. I recognized that I was having suicidal thoughts and brought myself out of that mindset. I forced myself to think about my family, about how my mom, dad, and little brother would feel if I committed suicide. They would be devastated.

Eventually, I started talking to and joking around with my shipmates who were also on watch in different areas of the ship but were connected to the same line as my headset that I had to wear while standing watch. I felt less alone once I did these things. But . . . I finally understood.

Instead of the Ocean
Personnel Specialist Second Class Dominique Lucas
Twenty-four years old. African American. Gemini.

"After being a deck seaman and transitioning into my rate of personnel specialist, I was the new seaman in the admin office. I always felt like I was being picked on because I was new to a job that I knew nothing about. I didn't get the opportunity to train for my rate in school like most PSs that come into the Navy as PSs. I was trying to study for an E-4 exam in this rate that I knew nothing about, I didn't make rank on the exam either, and I was also trying to study for my Enlisted Surface Warfare pin while on deployment.

"I was depressed, to say the least. I would go outside every night and contemplate my life. I felt like everyone was against me. I felt overwhelmed. I really wanted someone to be there for me but the one person I looked to for comfort during this time didn't really care. I always felt shut down. I didn't want to talk to anyone else about how I was feeling.

"To be honest, the only thing that kept me from doing it were the stars at night. I went outside so much that I would start having conversations with the stars because sometimes that is all you can see at night outside in the middle of the sea. I would give it all to the stars instead of the ocean."

All It Takes Is One Person
Aviation Maintenance Administrationman First Class Janelle Delgado
Thirty-four years old. Trinidadian. Gemini.

"When I transferred to my second command, I was challenged with more things than I could even fathom possible. I went through my divorce and a trying child custody battle. While thinking I could lose my kid at any moment, I thought the people around me would be there to help me through the worst time of my life. I was wrong. My new command gave me a P-eval, the worst evaluation a sailor can receive due to their "poor" performance so to speak, and told me I had too much going on and transferred me.

"I was losing my mind and losing my son. I got to the lowest point in my life because I had no one to turn to. Even my mother believed I was doing the wrong thing for divorcing my cheating husband simply because we are Catholic. I couldn't even turn to her.

"I tried to end my life because at the time I thought I had no other choice. I was, however, lucky enough to have a friend stop by on her way home because she hadn't heard from me in a while. She kicked my door in because she knew I was home. She found me passed out on the floor. She dragged me to the bathroom, stuck her hand down my throat, and spent the entire night by my side because she knew what I was going through.

"Since that day I try to stay as positive as possible, and I try to be that person for other people who just need one person to care. Just. One."

You May or May not Lose It a Little Bit While Deployed. At Least Once.

One morning, I woke up to a female screaming in our berthing. I checked my phone, and it was 0640. *Okay well I was about to get up in ten minutes anyway,* I thought. As I lay there and listened, this woman began screaming.

"Ahhhhhhhh! Fuck the Navy! Fuck this command! I am done! I'm done!" She screamed at the top of her voice. Frustration overflowing, she started throwing things, too. "Fuck this! Don't touch me! I gotta get out of here! I gotta figure out how to get out of here! Ahhhhhhhhh!"

I smiled at the woman's display of liberation. This was the best alarm clock I'd had the whole deployment. Someone was doing and saying *everything* that I wish I could daily.

You go girl, I thought as I heard her throw around more things.

I had to know who this woman was, so I hopped out of my rack, slid on my slippers, and peeked around the corner to see that it was *my* friend! I had only made two friends so far at this new command and she was one of them.

Oh my God! Oh shit, oh shit! I said to myself as I ran back to my rack, grabbed my hoodie and sweats, and ran out into our berthing lounge where she was located. There were three other women attempting to calm her down, but she wouldn't let any of them touch her.

For some reason I just stood there and watched. Knowing that there was nothing I could do or say that would make her feel any better, I just stood there. Completely frozen.

It was like I was in a trance because I felt like I was looking right at what the Navy was doing to me, except it was coming out through someone else. I was on her side. I completely agreed with her actions. I was jealous. I wished I was brave enough to express myself in this way, but all I ever did was break down and cry in the shower. Within the next few minutes, there were six masters-at-arms in our berthing prepared to break up the fight that someone reported. We let them know that there was no fight and that everything was fine. After assessing the situation, my friend was escorted to medical. I proceeded to get dressed to start my day.

I went back to berthing within the next hour to see if my friend was back. She was standing by her rack, folding some clothes.

"Are you going somewhere?" I asked.

"Nah. I'm SIQ for the day." She replied. Shaking my head while we stared at each other briefly, we understood what the other was thinking. I approached my friend and wrapped my arms around her. She hugged me back.

"I love you," I told her. "I love you, too," she whispered.

22

ANTWONE FISHER

I just watched the movie *Antwone Fisher*.

First off, don't judge me. I already know that I'm late. But late as I am, I can truly say that it was a beautiful movie. For those of you who may not know or never heard of the movie before, it is about a Black, male sailor in the U.S. Navy and the struggles that he goes through trying to navigate and adjust to life on his ship.

We *need* leadership like Lieutenant Commander Davenport in the Navy. Portrayed by the legendary Denzel Washington, Davenport truly cared about this particular sailor and was so admirable. That's the type of leadership that will make us reenlist. That type of leadership is what would make the Navy a greater Navy. Without a doubt, the military is an ideal option for people with similar circumstances as Antwone Fisher – homeless or struggling in life.

If I did not join the Navy, I would have had a hard time figuring out what to do with my life. The Navy and all its flaws mixed with all its resources really shaped me into the woman I am today. It cultured me, disciplined me, paid me, and challenged me. I only wish there were more leaders like Lieutenant Commander Davenport – *many* more.

I have come across only a handful of LCDR Davenports during my career in the fleet, just a handful who *really* gave a shit about me.

The Difference a Caring Leader Makes
Boatswain Mate Second Class Tushanna Brown
Thirty-four years old. African American. Gemini.

"I was hell on wheels as an E1 to an E3. After boot camp, I became angry. It was hard to accept being told what to do, how to do it, and when. It was hard to cope with being yelled at and unable to do anything about it. And when I checked into my first command, I was still angry.

"I was hell, and I didn't work well with others. Being rated as a BM has nothing on an individual basis – everything is teamwork. You work together for the bigger and better picture. I didn't understand any of that.

"There was this one BM2 back then, Caucasian guy, that I would give hell everyday just because he told me to do something. And you know what? I never got written up. Back then, your leadership pulled you to the side and figured out what was wrong first. Next, they would address the problem. They would figure out what was wrong with you mentally and if it was something they could help with.

"Then, they'd have to address your military bearing. If you had something going on, they taught you to open your mouth and say something and to at least see if someone could help you. I didn't do that. I was just pissed the fuck off.

"Extra military instruction (EMI) was something that only a chief or above could assign to you. 'Okay! You don't want to work with others? Then we will give you *one* person to work with.'

"I'll never forget it, my Master Chief Skeet. He would put his little glasses right at the end of his nose, pop his feet up, and read his book while I'm needle gunning the same exact area for two hours a day after work for EMI.

"But he invested time in me. He didn't give up. He didn't pawn me off on somebody else. He didn't delegate it down. He invested time in me and that is why I served for so long. I had leaders coming up in the ranks who invested time in me. They planted a seed in me that allowed me to grow into this tree when I couldn't see past the anger that I had for whatever reason as a junior sailor.

"Leaders now are different. They'll pawn 'it' off on someone else real fucking quick, and then the person that they pawn it off to won't even have an idea of what's going on. No one invests time into the people that they expect to take over after they're gone. It's 'Oh, I'll just get so and so to do it,' or 'Well, I'm just not going to say anything because I don't want to deal with how long that would take.'"

Are We Really Aware? Do We Really Care?

One evening after work on my second deployment, I was talking to two good friends of mine in our berthing lounge. One was a third class and the other a seaman. We were discussing the suicide rate in the Navy. During our conversation, the third class felt comfortable enough to share.

"I went to medical and told them that I was thinking about killing myself during this deployment."

Shocked, I asked her what happened after she told medical. She said that medical immediately referred her to the ship's psychologist, a white, male lieutenant. She told the psychologist about her feelings and her urge to take her own life. The LT asked her why and what made her feel that way before informing her that he would be emailing her a personalized schedule for counseling and sent her on her way with well wishes.

"It's been two weeks and I haven't received an email." she finished.

"Did he ask you to follow up?" I inquired.

"No. He just told me that he'd email me."

I know what you're thinking. *Why didn't she just go back and ask him about that schedule he was supposed to send? He's a lieutenant. He's probably super busy with other clients.*

Well guys, it is *already* hard enough to build up the courage and strength to seek help and admit to someone that you want to kill yourself. The least a person in that state of mind can hope for is that someone will actually give a shit and attempt to help. Reaching out again about your own urge to commit suicide? Come on. Some would just rather do it. It beats the embarrassment and shame.

On that note, we discussed the three sailors who committed suicide in 2019, in the *same* week, and were stationed on the *same* ship. We all agreed that the interviews on the news that were conducted shortly after those tragedies were bullshit!

"I have a male friend, who was once a fire controlman second class in the Navy, who posted about that news report and it low key went military viral." I stated.

The seaman perked up with interest asking, "What did the post say?"

Eventually, we discovered that she, stationed all the way in California, had caught wind of the post my friend wrote on his Facebook page while he was in Virginia and had reposted it herself, long before she and I knew each other. She also mentioned that she agreed with the post so much, she texted a screenshot of it to a few of her contacts shortly after reposting it.

I was so proud of the awareness that my friend was able to spread! His post read:

"They're talking about the Suicide rate in the Navy which was 67 people in 2018 on Wavy News. 3 sailors took their lives yesterday on the George W. Bush alone. And this dumbass news report decides to interview a Master

Chief and a Full Bird Chaplain. If you want to know why sailors are killing themselves, ask the ranks that are more prevalent to kill themselves E5-E1.

"Interview a Seaman that is cranking and smells of food and takes out trash 5 times a day, interview the E4 that just messed up on the 1MC and is frustrated because 'leadership' is screaming at them and they have another armed 5 hour watch later in the day, ask the E5 Work center Supervisor that just went through a divorce and had to get the force revision done by Friday and they have a dog and a child at home but they can't get off work until 6 p.m. after getting to work at 6 a.m. Don't interview a freaking Master Chief or Captain in the Navy. They don't know our struggles and they never will, they just say 'It would behoove you to work better because you get paid to be in the great Navy.' Get the fuck out of here."

His post received 1,800 shares and 326 comments, mostly from people currently serving in the military or veterans.

By the way, prior to that post, my friend had never received more than twenty shares.

Sad.

23

SOMEONE HELP

Pearson's Journal

The Realization That Something Is Wrong. Mentally Wrong.

This second deployment is really getting to me. I've been crying a lot in the shower lately. My shower time is actually the only time that I truly have a moment to myself throughout each day. I've cried in the shower for three straight nights. Just crying, sad, lonely, missing my home and family, and getting even more sick of this Navy shit!

I do not feel free. I do not feel like I have any control over my life or even my physical being. I feel like a caged animal. I belong to the United States Navy. At least in prison, your spouse can come to visit you from time to time. I've missed every holiday and even my birthday with my loved ones this year dealing with the Navy and all this moving around.

It hurts. It really fucking hurts. This deployment is affecting me. There are so many people I don't know, and I just want to lay in my bed and have a glass of wine while I try and pick a movie to watch tonight – but all I have to look forward to is attempting to focus on reading my book, trying to discretely utilize my vibrator in my rack tonight, and maybe scrolling through some pictures of my loved ones after I get my rocks off.

Earlier today I missed a step while I was coming down a ladder well. I rolled my ankle but caught myself. Although it hurt, after catching my balance I thought, You stupid fucking ankle! Why can't you just break?

Fuck!

This isn't like me. I love my body. I love my features. But this second deployment is really getting to me. Breaking my ankle doesn't sound so bad if it came with the option of getting sent home. I think I need to talk to somebody.

Seeking Help

I set an appointment but had to wait more than a week. On the day of my appointment, I arrived at medical ten minutes early and knocked on the door. No one answered but, fortunately, about thirty seconds after my knocking, a male lieutenant opened the door because he was on his way out.

Surprised by my presence he spoke. "Do you have an appointment?"

I smiled, "Actually I do sir – with the psychologist." The LT informed me that the ship's psychologist was absent due to an emergency. He explained that he had to be flown off the ship.

"Do you want to talk to HM2?" the LT asked.

Taken back, I asked, "Will the psychologist be back anytime soon?"

The LT replied, "He left because of an *emergency*. I don't know when he will be back." He walked off and left me standing there.

I'm not going to lie; I became very angry. I went to smoke a cigarette.

Damn man! I wish someone would have warned me about my appointment being cancelled. I mean, I get that he had an emergency, but this is what happens when you have one psychologist and a boat with 5,000 people! Who do I even talk to now? Should I email the Deployed Resiliency Counselor? Nah, not her. She's just a counselor. I want to see a specialist. Maybe I should write something to the captain about this and put it in his suggestion box – tell him how after I was told the psychologist wasn't on board, I wasn't even helped! That fucking lieutenant though, didn't even ask if I was okay! No real attempt to see if I needed anything. You know what? That's definitely not okay! I was there to see the psychologist. My appointment mattered. I deserve not only some decent help, but some accommodations as well, I thought.

I put out my cigarette and walked my right back to medical. I was on a mission, damn it. I arrived to discover a new sign on the door that read:

Medical is open today for ***EMERGENCIES*** *and* ***APPOINTMENTS ONLY****! For other assistance, please knock on the aft, starboard door.*

Thank you,

Medical

Okay... So, I went and knocked on the suggested door. I heard music playing and people laughing on the other side. I didn't get upset. Instead, I assumed that they didn't hear me, and I knocked louder.

An HMSN answered, "Hey what's up?"

I explained my situation. "Yeah, HM2 said since the psychologist had to leave, he'll start taking care of his appointments at 1400."

I looked at my phone to discover the time of 0940. "Okay, well from 1400 until what time, because I'll be at work during that time." I asked.

He shrugged, "I don't know. He just told me 1400." We stared at each other for a second.

"Okay," I replied.

"Okay!" He said as he shut the door. Once again, I was left there to just figure it out. What if I were suicidal today?

Receiving Help

I finally got my appointment with the carrier's psychologist! Eager to receive some help and hear what a professional had to say about what I was going through, I arrived ten minutes early – just as I had done for my first appointment. He finally came to the waiting area of medical to pick me up and escort me to his office. He greeted me with a handshake, and we were on our way. After shutting the door, he invited me to sit down with him. We broke the ice when he asked me about my day at work. I expressed to him that it had actually been a pretty smooth day.

After a little banter, he asked the big question, "What brings you here today?"

I told him I've been thinking about the answer to that question for weeks now, "but my answer is: I am here because I am not okay."

I told him about my anxiety, depression, and panic attacks in the shower. I gave him the details of my misery in this organization known as the Navy. I even became very emotional while explaining to him what I was going through. I made it clear to him that I was not suicidal, just miserable.

The psychologist took notes and asked, "What would it take to make you feel better?"

I sat straight up in my chair, looked at him in the eyes, and said, "Getting out of the Navy. I want to get out and I am sure."

He suggested I try some coping mechanisms such as meditating or reading. I informed him that I did both and that I had already read four books this deployment – not to mention, I meditated several times a day, every day.

"I know that the best thing for me at this point in my life would be to separate from this organization," I finished.

He asked me about what my plans would be if I were to leave the Navy. I told him. He also asked me if I was interested in counseling or medication. I said sure to counseling and no to medication.

"Well, I believe that changing the way you think would help you out a lot and would probably make your situation a lot better. Instead of being so focused on getting *out* of the Navy, shift your focus to *staying in* the Navy. Maybe focus on pushing through. If you push through the rest of your contract, you are likely to have a better outcome because you can say you did it! You can say you toughed it out and made it through," he finished with a smile.

"Sir, sometimes the toughest thing you can do is leave." I noted.

His facial expression dropped. "Well, if you're just going to throw cheesy quotes at me then I don't know how I can help you," he stated defensively.

Shocked and emotional, I replied, "Sir, what do you mean? I'm serious! I really feel that way. This entire situation for me is tough, sitting here admitting that I'm struggling mentally," I sat up in my chair, voice quivering but I was still determined to get it out. "I feel brave for setting this appointment!"

The psychologist gave me a blank stare for a second. He seemed to kind of snap out of it and set his clipboard down on the desk beside him. He made eye contact with me and said, "Well here's a suggestion for you that I believe could help. I think you should take some time and do some research. Try looking up slavery and concentration camps. I want you to compare and contrast the slaves that killed themselves with the slaves didn't. Place your focus on the slaves and members of concentration camps that did not commit suicide. Find out what it was that they did in order to push through and make it through *that* rough time."

I know guys. I know. I can go ahead and answer your question. Yes. Yes, he did.

The audacity of this man. I am not, nor could I if I wanted to, make this shit up.

Crabs in a Bucket
Airframer Third Class Tyler Vickers
Twenty-five years old. African American. Aries.

"You come here and it's like a crab-in-a-bucket mentality. Everyone is trying to make it to the top and no one gives a fuck about who's at the bottom. Even in the real-world mental health is non-existent in the African American community. It's a legit thing that if you're Caucasian or Asian or some other race and you go to medical, most likely they're going to take you seriously.

"I have not seen yet or heard of any African American since I've been in the Navy at whatever command I'm at, have their case taken seriously. I've never heard of that. I've seen other races go in to medical and leave the Navy within the same deployment type shit. Like what do we have to do? Do we have to almost kill ourselves?

"Do we have to legitimately slice our arm in front of them? Do we have to be suicidal to get some decent fucking help? It just doesn't make sense to me. Why don't we have experts? And why is there only one phycologist on a fucking aircraft carrier with 5,000 people losing their fucking minds? It baffles me."

Justice for Malpractice

So, I bet you guys are wondering, "Well, are you going to tell us what the fuck you did about that ignorant psychologist? There's no way you just left it at that!"

I'll tell you what I did.

I conducted his suggested research, typed up some bullshit, and emailed it to him with a request for a follow up just to see what he would say. To my surprise, he responded accepting the request, so I went to the follow up. I just needed to see if this asshole would *really* try and school me on the mentality of a slave who did not commit suicide and made it through their tough times. He did.

I left that last session with him baffled. I reported him to a *Black* representative of the carrier's Command Management Equal Opportunity (CMEO) group, which is designed by the Navy to issue policies and standards. They aid in the prevention of harassment and unlawful discrimination throughout the Navy, including sexual orientation as a basis for unlawful discrimination and gender identity as a form of sex discrimination, and process complaints of harassment based on race, color, religion, sex, gender identity, national origin, and sexual orientation.

And the wonderful representative that I made my formal complaint with was more than helpful and supportive. When a sailor submits a formal complaint through the CMEO, the command's captain is notified, an investigator is randomly selected for the case, and an investigation of the alleged incidents in the formal complaint commence. These investigations can usually take anywhere from two weeks to three months.

About three days after I submitted my formal complaint, I was notified by a chief at my squadron, my squadron's CMEO representative, that I had an appointment in medical. I figured that this was the work of the captain who had obviously read my complaints about the trash ass mental health help on board his ship in the statement I submitted in my formal complaint and immediately found me the assistance and help that I was looking for.

Wrong.

I arrived at my medical appointment ten minutes early to discover that I was meeting a Hispanic, female commander who just so happened to be the head of the entire medical department on board. So, the ship's psychologist worked for her. This woman was the person who was chosen as the investigator of my case. This was the woman I sat down to do my interview with.

The interview went well.

She asked the necessary questions and took on all of the documents that I insisted she review, including my emails exchange with the ship's psychologist and an angry letter of recommendation that I drafted up after the incident detailing my frustration with the Navy, my frustrations with the carrier's medical resources, and my desire to separate from the Navy due to pretty much the fact that I felt as if I was going bat shit crazy. The accused, of course, was notified of the investigation, interviewed, and allowed to make a statement regarding the accusations.

About two weeks after my interview with the female commander in charge of the medical department on board the carrier, I received word from a chief at my squadron, my squadron's CMEO representative, that my case results were in. I immediately went to review the results with him. The statement submitted by the commander that investigated my case read:

(I have substituted the ship's psychologist's name with "LT Ignorant Ass" and substituted official dates with the word "confidential.")

Subj: RACIAL HARRASSMENT COMPLAINT

Ref: (a) JAGMAN Chapter II PART E

(b) OPNAVIST 5354.1G

Encl: (1) Appointing Order

(2) Summary of Interview with LS3 Pearson, USN

(3) Voluntary Statement by LT Ignorant Ass, USN

1. Pursuant to reference (a) and as directed by enclosure (1), I conducted an investigation into the circumstances surrounding claim of racial and religious harassment made by LS3 Pearson against LT Ignorant Ass

2. I personally interviewed LS3 Pearson and LT Ignorant Ass separately and reviewed LT Ignorant Ass's statement. I reviewed emails and medical notes for the clinical encounters between LT Ignorant Ass and LS3 Pearson. LS3 Pearson also provided to me copies of her research, emails, and a statement she wrote expressing her desire to separate from the Navy.

3. Based on the evidence collected, I find that the complaint is not substantiated.

1. LS3 Pearson completed the assignment and emailed the research to LT Ignorant Ass on (confidential date) with a request for a follow up appointment to discuss

2. LS3 Pearson has repeatedly expressed feeling unhappy, anxious, and dissatisfied with the Navy. She expressed a desire to separate.

Opinions

1. The claim of harassment as defined in reference (b), is not substantiated. There is no evidence that LT Ignorant Ass specifically chose the topic of slavery for LS3 Pearson to research, there is only evidence of suggesting figures in history.

2. The Claim of religious/spiritual harassment is not substantiated. There is no evidence of discussions of religious spiritual nature between LS3 and LT.

3. The claim of malpractice is not substantiated. LT Ignorant Ass functioned within his scope of practice and licensing as a psychologist and engaged LS3 Pearson in behavioral health therapies/strategies that are in accordance with accepted standard of care.

Recommendations

1. The patient's concerns regarding her care were addressed through the medical patient satisfaction process. I recommend no further action in this case.

Oh yes, *unsubstantiated*! My case was the classic he-said-she-said. Join us next week for another episode of *Enlisted versus the Commissioned* where we will watch more evidence of how the enlisted could never win against the almighty commissioned.

Help Us!
Airframer Third Class Tyler Vickers
Twenty-five years old. African American. Aries.

"One day, our psychologist had to fly off our carrier and go to the small boy in our strike group because a sailor over there died. We were out of a psychologist, and we had someone in our berthing that was on suicide watch. What the fuck do we do then? Like, help us! We are going through some shit that most people have never even heard of!"

Jokes About Suicide

While deployed on board a ship, you're more than likely going to stumble upon some very unusual conversations every once in a while. I'm pretty sure in my three short years I've passed by hundreds of sailors discussing their desire to jump overboard. Hell, I've conversed with sailors myself that have said this directly to my face. Jokingly, of course – like that makes it any better. But what I want you guys to grasp from this passage is the knowledge of the insane sense of humor that sailors develop.

We literally laugh about our comments that pertain to jumping overboard. For example, when there are rumors in the air about the possibility of an extension during a deployment, it is not uncommon to hear a sailor say, "Yo, if we get extended, I'm jumping overboard."

"On everything, if they extend us, I'm going for a swim bro."

And most of the time, the sailor is joking – until they're not joking. This is a normal thing. It doesn't faze you. Maybe at first, when you're new in the fleet it may catch you off guard, but after realizing that these are just things that we sailors joke about, you'll keep walking. Why? Because you assume that they are probably just joking.

Reconnecting with Society

Speaking of a sailor's extremely fucked up sense of humor, it's this culture of environment we live in along with being *stuck* in a that environment for months that makes coming home an awkward experience for some. Reconnecting with your civilian family and friends can be very weird at first. You're so used to being in such a harsh environment that requires you to mask your feelings so much, recovering the person your civilian loved ones know and are used to can take time, you know, if that person can be recovered at all, depending on what it is you've been through mentally.

Being on a deployment changes people. It changes you. I don't care who you are. When you step on board that ship to leave for your deployment, six to eleven months later when you return, something about you will be different. I just hope that the odds are in your favor.

Sea Story
By: Retail Service Specialist First Class Kimberly Fleming
Thirty-three years old. West Indian. Capricorn.

Growing up in the Navy, I've seen how people are unable to figure out how to speak to junior sailors or deal with those 'problem' sailors. I always try to understand them or at least identify what it would take to get them to succeed and be a part of the team. I see the mental frustration behind people not listening or people not understanding.

People from the outside that are looking in, see the military and think that they have an idea of what it looks like, but they don't know the truth behind it. The little things that aren't so clean, the rework, the unnecessary work, and how the lack of communication plays a mental toll on sailors. People on the outside do not see how we are expected and sometimes forced to perform day in and day out as if we are robots.

They don't hear how our higher-ranking leaders use the phrase, 'well you're in the military' as a way to justify that 'you're going to go days without eating' or 'there will be days where you don't sleep,' like this is a thing or that it's functional. It's not right, not if you want 100 percent of your sailors.

Look at the situation we're in now, on deployment – we understand that we're in the military. Duh, we can see it. But think about it: barely any internet, no phones, and there's not that much going on around here for people to mentally decompress or find a balance. Well, how can you find balance if you don't have anything? I've lost many sailors through suicide, sailors that just lost it.

My sea story is about my junior sailor. I think about him all the time. Some people may think that it's not healthy, but I keep him to the forefront of my head, and he is why I treat my sailors the way I do – because not everybody can take this pressure. If you're working stateside, most people don't think that we're dealing with anything out here, but we are. And what is a big deal to you may not be a big deal to me, but a big deal is a big deal. There's no reason to one-up me with, 'Oh, that's what you're going through?'

'Well, I went through this, this, and this.' Maybe you handled that differently because of your upbringing. All mentalities and mental issues are important.

My junior sailor and I were stationed in Australia, and we were leaving. Wherever we were at, we didn't have a SOFA[1] guidance with that country, which meant that we couldn't fly. My junior sailor was TAD (temporary assigned duty) to me during this time. Every day, he'd ask me, 'Hey how are you doing RS1?' Until, one day after I had sent him back to his division, because his TAD was over, he walked past me with a very blank look on his face and he didn't speak to me.

He worked within the air department of our ship, and they work directly with our aircraft on board. The way the air department's leaders speak to their junior sailors, I get it. It's because of their dangerous work environment. They're harsh in that department. They yell and scream all day. They have little compassion to give. They work with jets all day, launching and catching real battle jets with real ammunition. So, the way they communicate to each other is a little different. My junior sailor had this weird look about him this day, and I didn't even say anything. I just kept walking forward to get to the hanger bay and help set up for a hanger bay sell. Where we were sitting, you could see the hanger bay doors, it was clear out there. Right outside of the door was a trash barge at the bottom where sailors would throw their trash out. While we were sitting there, an unexpected object whizzed down past us followed by a loud BAM!

"MAN OVERBOARD," we heard immediately afterward.

Everyone, even people who were out on liberty, ran over to the sound. He had jumped off the flight deck. And when you looked over, you could just see his twisted, lifeless body. Gone.

After learning more about him, we found out that his dad had passed away and his chain of command told him that he couldn't fly home to his dad's funeral because we were using SOFA guidance. And that completely broke him. He lost it.

Watching the surveillance footage is equally devastating. He could be seen walking backward, towards the camera. Before he made his final decision, he can be seen looking over the side, contemplating the distance of the fall. Then, he took off into a full sprint, fast as he could, and jumped.

I wondered, what was his thought process in that moment? Would it have helped if I stopped and talked to him like I usually did? Maybe I could tell from his tone that he wasn't doing too good that day.

His chain of command could have told him, 'Look, where we're at, we can't fly right now. But once the opportunity becomes available, we'll make sure that you're the first person out of here.'

Not being afraid to explain the why because everything is not a secret mission. That's the bottom line. People forget about the mental. That's what I've taken from that moment. Every day I take that with me when I deal with my sailors – when I talk to them. I have no problem explaining, I'll tell you why we're doing that. I'll tell you that 'No, it doesn't make sense to me either,' and we'll make a joke about it.

Because I know that it's probably hard and frustrating, but I want you to know that I'm just as irritated as you are and we're going to laugh about it, because it doesn't change the fact that we still have to do it. And look, I'm going to do it with you. And we're going to get through it and then when we're in port, alive, we're going to talk more shit about it. Because I believe in the mental."

Life Happens
Navy Counselor (Career) First Class Elon McDuell-Briscoe
Thirty-six years old. African American. Taurus.

"I don't like that higher ranking individuals forget that life happens and lack empathy for anyone else. We lose parents, siblings, babies; we begin and end marriages, and the expectation is for you to be a robot with no emotion is unacceptable. We're not robots. We are very human and should be allowed to have human reactions. A lot of times, those same higher-ranking individuals have experienced hurt at some point in their career and sadly their leadership chose not to care enough about them and their situation. So now the cycle of 'oh well, suck it up!' is established and fueled unconsciously instead of recognizing the harm it causes and breaking the cycle."

PART VIII

I'M JUST VENTING

vent[1]
/vent/

verb
gerund or present participle: venting

1. give free expression to (a strong emotion)

24

LET'S KEEP IT 100

First Class Petty Officers

I am really amused when a petty officer first class complains about anything Navy related. I understand that we are all entitled to our feelings and opinions but look, you've had at least one to three opportunities to make a plan and exit the Navy, and yet you continue to sign on the dotted line. It's like, nah petty officer . . .*hooyah Navy*.

When the Navy says jump, you better be the first one trying to jump out of the ceiling. And don't you even think about asking why! Just jump, dance, smile, and do. In my opinion, a petty officer first class needs to be the happiest motherfucker in the Navy. I should immediately be able to assume that you love it here.

Clown.

The Navy Comes First

One day I asked myself if I had time to take a shit. No seriously, this happened. I was at work during my second deployment, ripping and running, grabbing parts, and doing as I was instructed to do. I stopped by the head in the mist of my chaos to take a piss. As I sat on the toilet, I felt the sudden urge to take a shit. *No, no, no. I don't have time to sit here right now! I can hold it.* I thought to myself, trying to squeeze my cheeks together and seal my butthole shut.

I was really concerned about some high priority parts that needed to be picked up within a certain timeframe and the long distance I had to travel to pick them up. I caught myself. I was putting the Navy first – before myself and my body's personal needs. Now, I can understand attempting to "hold it" if we were in the midst of a war and a part was needed to win a battle against some terrorist, sure. But it was just another regular smegular day in the Navy.

As I took the time to sit and relieve myself, I began to wonder how often I mindlessly put the Navy before myself and my personal needs. Do I do this when I'm hungry? Do I do this when I'm sleepy? How many other people do that daily and how many times a day do they do it? What was it about the Navy that had driven me to this way of thinking?

Freedom
Gunners Mate Second Class Beverly Stroud
Twenty-five years old. White. Leo.

"All your choices are monitored, vetted, and screened – you're not completely free, and definitely not in a way that you want to be."

I Can't Relate

One night I engaged in an awesome conversation with two women in my berthing – a third class and the other a second class. We were discussing our mutual opinion on the South being the best area in the states to purchase real estate considering that we had all lived on the East and West Coast as well.

"I plan to move back to the South after I have finished my contract." I stated.

The third class replied by telling me that her husband was getting out soon, but she was planning to stay in and do the full twenty years.

Baffled, I asked the second class about her plans in the Navy. She replied, "I don't know. I mean, I *just* reenlisted for another five years. So, after my shore duty I'll be at *nine* years." She was emphasizing that she may as well ride it out until the end.

"Well guys I'm about to shower. I'll see you in the morning," I concluded with a smile and politely exited the conversation.

Wondering how in the hell they planned to purchase a forever home with all the movement the Navy will instruct them to conduct, I had nothing further that I wanted to discuss. My mother always told me that if I did not have anything nice to say, I probably shouldn't say anything at all. I did not know their personal situations, so I wasn't eligible to judge them and their decisions to continue their careers in the Navy.

What I do know is this: I don't see fit to continue mine and if you do, we can't relate. I don't care. I don't care.

Getting out of the Navy Is a Terrible Idea!

GRABS MICROPHONE

Excuse me military members, and Navy sailors for sure. After expressing that you do not want to reenlist, how many of you have experienced a superior of yours attempting to convince you that it would be a terrible idea? Show of hands please. Wow! Yes, that's exactly what I thought – all of us. I *hate* those super Joe Navy sailors who love to tell you that there's nothing else out there, describing how hard it can be in the civilian world. How nothing is guaranteed. The audacity of them to sit there and disagree with you about your life and your life decisions, right?

To those who try to convince us junior sailors not to leave the military, here's what I would like to say to you: first of all, I understand that you love your job. You support the Navy's mission! You love all of the benefits that you accumulate while supporting the Navy's mission. I understand that this career offers you a guaranteed paycheck. I understand that once you get out, getting back in is tough. Cool. I get it and I'm not knocking you for that. I just want you to consider this: people who make up today's military are about 1 percent of America's population. So, can you just, I don't know, maybe, shut the fuck up?

DROPS MIC

The Lifers
Personnel Specialist Second Class Dominique Lucas
Twenty-four years old. African American. Gemini.

"I hate when 'lifers' do not understand when you voice your desire to get out, which is usually the exact moment where they stop helping you. If I am a good sailor and I work hard, why not help me prepare for my post-Navy life?!"

A Love-Hate Relationship
Logistics Specialist Seaman Apprentice Ashley McLendon
Twenty-four years old. Haitian American. Cancer.

"So, I love the Navy. But I hate the Navy! I feel like it's that abusive relationship that you can't get out of. Every day I think about how much more money I could be making in the civilian world and how much more peaceful it could be to work in someone's office or library.

"Then I think, but what can the civilian world do for me?

"The Navy gives me good health care and dental. I get money to go and live somewhere. I get a regular paycheck even when I get in trouble. So, if I got kicked out today, where would I go? Because now, everything that I think about is Navy-established. You ain't going nowhere."

"Put Some Respect on My Rank!" Said No Seaman Ever.

I don't know why I've acquired so many qualifications. I think it's because, as an undesignated seaman, they are all I have. I don't have a job. I don't have rank. But I do have qualifications. I just can't stop getting them. I'm demanding my respect with these qualifications. You will respect me. You have no choice because I'm qualified. You can't tell me shit about shit because I probably already know it. I'm probably more qualified than your first class.

Your divisional officer just came to me for some training. You *need* me. This ship needs me. The Navy needs me. I am valuable. I am an asset. I drive this ship better than anyone else on it! The captain trusts me. And I'm only a seaman – an undesignated one at that. And as only a seaman, my qualifications are as follows:

Mess Deck Attendant
Scullery Operator
Line Handler
Deck Line Handler
Winch Watcher
Basic Communications
Craftsman
Maintenance Person
Repair Parts/Supply Petty Officer
Basic Damage Control
Advanced Damage Control
Basic First Aid

Basic Firefighting
Basic Chemical, Biological, and Radiological
Team Leader
Fire Watch Stander
Log Keeper
Basic Console Operator
Internal Communications Operator
External Communications Operator
Bridge Telephone Talker
Bridge/Combat Phone Talker
Lookout
Helmsman
Aft Steering Helmsman
Lee Helm
Master Helmsman
Color and Light Detail
Messenger of the Watch
Petty Officer of the Watch
Officer of the Deck In-Port
Reaction Force Member
Sentry
M16 (Series) Service Rifle Operator
M9 Service Pistol Operator
Enlisted Surface Warfare Specialist

I have also completed eighteen college credits while utilizing my tuition assistance through the Navy and received three early promote (EP) evaluations in a row! My performance as a master helmsman during our six-month ballistic missile defense deployment earned me the Navy and Marine Corp Achievement Medal that was presented to me prior to my detachment from the destroyer and transfer to my new command, the squadron.

Think twice before you come for this undesignated seaman.

But You Need to Respect Us Though
Aviation Ordnanceman Airman Danielle Lowe
Twenty years old. African American. Libra.

"You've got eighteen to twenty-year-olds launching million-dollar aircraft. I feel like I should be thought of at a higher standard because of this fact. But we do the grunt work. To my knowledge, we are the hardest working, the most underappreciated, and the least respected."

Kids in the Military

My heart goes out to these kids who join the military, specifically the eighteen to twenty-year-olds. They are babies with young, vulnerable, and easily impacted minds. I joined the Navy at the tender age of twenty-three. I am currently writing this as a twenty-six-year-old woman. I am grown and I still struggle in this organization. I feel for the kids who join and allow this organization to be their first job, never truly getting a full experience of freedom in the civilian world.

Eighteen and signing their lives away. Nineteen, signing some of their rights away. Twenty, growing and maturing in this intense culture of work, some knowing nothing else as a lifestyle in their young years as adults. God bless these kids.

And to the Recruiters: Stop It!

Stop sending recruiters to high schools to pressure teenagers into joining the military. Stop it! These kids hear the words *money* and *you'll be able to get out of your hometown* and are promised this by the most amazing sea stories in the world narrated by the *world's greatest sailors* who are just trying to make their quotas and couldn't care less about these kids' lives or wellbeing! It was extremely shitty of my recruiters to sell me the dream of undesignation without properly educating me. It was cruel.

They told me I would be able to join undesignated and shadow all of the jobs I wanted while I traveled with the Navy! It was also shitty that I could not find much information on the internet about the job title of "undesignated." My life was hell while I was undesignated! I was lied to! Hundreds to thousands of other sailors feel just as played as me. And I was twenty-two when it happened to me so I can only *imagine* the dreams that are being sold to these high schoolers! Stop sending recruiters to high schools!

And high schools, please stop letting them in!

Sorry to yell but I really needed this to be heard.

These are people's lives. Teenagers are not complete adults. They are real people who will eventually grow up into older adults with bitterness in their hearts and minds. Stop it. The military is a serious commitment and most of these kids have never even held down a job before.

How old is eighteen really? Why is it that an eighteen-year-old can sign an enlistment contract for four or more years, yet they cannot legally drink, rent a car from most places, or purchase tobacco in some places? You can put your life on the line for the military, but don't you dare try to buy your own vodka. That makes no sense and comes across as extremely predatory. They can be exposed to extremely dangerous circumstances and environments? What kind of shit is this?

It is sick!

No Regrets
Logistics Specialist Seaman Apprentice Roxsana Herrera
Nineteen years old. Hispanic/Latina American. Pisces.

"I joined the military because when I was a high school senior, I learned that by joining, I could grant my parents their American citizenship. I absolutely do not regret joining the military for my parents. Even if the military is super harsh on me and I felt like I hated it, I don't regret it. I knew the sacrifice that I would have to make, and I still keep that same purpose with me. No matter what I have to go through, I know that I did this for my people. I know that the happiest day of my life will be seeing that envelope arrive in the mailbox. Because of the look on their faces, I know it's all going to be worth it when they know that they are finally citizens of the country that they love so much."

Generation Z

There are kids joining the military now who were born in the year 2000! Let that sink in for a moment please. Kids that were born in the year 2000 were born into a world full of thriving and evolving technology. Technology in the early 2000s was delivering the early stages of the iPhone, iPod, camera phones, Blu-ray discs, internet speeds that were on the rise, Amazon Kindle, YouTube, Twitter, and even Facebook itself!

This is what these children were born with. This is what normal looks like for them. That being said, Navy, how in the hell do you plan to keep this new generation of sailors? Don't worry, I'll wait. Because the system that you're using today isn't going to work...at all.

These kids are not going to go months on months without phone service and internet, and then reenlist to do it all over again! These kids live their whole lives on the internet and do not know what a life without it is. Shit, I was born in 1993 myself and this crap is rough!

The Navy should rethink and rearrange this deployment on a boat thing. Somehow, someway, you guys better get with the times because these are the types of people you will be dealing with. It is your job, Navy, to adjust to them – with them. If not, good luck in about ten years when you're wondering, *why is our military so small*?

Mindfulness
Airframer Third Class Tyler Vickers
Twenty-five years old. African American. Aries.

"I'm just starting to see and realize things more clearly. While in the Navy, being this aware isn't good. It causes you to not take anything seriously at all – knowing that all of this shit is not real or that it's all like a show for the world. Yeah, I think the Navy is trying hard to force it and keep old traditions alive. Anything forced is not good. They're trying to force old habits on the new generation and it's just not really a good idea."

Adaptation
Navy Counselor (Career) First Class Elon McDuell-Briscoe
Thirty-six years old. African American. Taurus.

"When I was coming into the Navy, we were still using dial-up internet and technology was nowhere similar to what it is today. I've watched it go from a Motorola pouch that had a phone in it and the World Wide Web featuring AOL to now – a vast wealth of communication capability and information at the press of a button!

"It is absolutely necessary to acknowledge today's innovative minds because this generation is finding better, faster, and more efficient ways to execute the mission, which revolutionizes us as a military organization."

Access Denied

I'm about to lose my mind! I'm on this deployment attempting to use the internet and just trying to do some general research. It's holiday routine, and the office is slow. I just wanted to use the damn internet. All I was curious about today was some of the world's greatest, best-selling authors but I can't pull anything up on this God-forsaken internet.

Network Access Message: Access Denied

Once, just once, on this deployment, I wanted to dive into some research and can't. Why? Well, because in the middle of the ocean, internet connection ain't the best. The nearest towers are hundreds of thousands of miles away, and the Navy is too cheap to get service that isn't spotty at best.

This really sucks.

Not to mention, we are only allowed to pull up authorized websites like Facebook, Instagram, Amazon, Navy Federal, and select government sites. I simply cannot *just* do research. I can't even begin to describe to you this level of frustration I have while being on this damn boat. Having to ask my mom to email me research on certain things because I can't do it myself is beyond irritating. This is the type of minuscule pet peeves that you deal with for months. This is the stuff that you don't think about until it's gone. These are pleasures and luxuries that sailors appreciate so much more after a deployment. These are the little things that will drive you bat shit crazy while on a deployment.

For me to do extensive research on whatever I feel like researching, I have to make note of it so that I can remember to look it up whenever the Navy decides to allow my ship to pull in for a port visit. I also have to hope and pray that the Navy decides to pull us into a port that is included in my international phone plan. Duqm, Oman, surely isn't covered by AT&T and we *surely* pulled in there once already on this deployment.

I utilized my phone after not being able to for damn near three months. The Wi-Fi there was surely shitty and forced me to use my own data. *Whew, okay*, I thought to myself in that moment, temporarily being satisfied to just be able to use my own phone again. After being in Oman for four days, experiencing terrible phone service the entire time, and then receiving my next phone bill that was $512.00, those feeling changed!

I just absolutely cannot deal.

Food on Board

The food here in the Navy is trash! Okay, maybe that was a bit harsh, so let me try that again. The food here in the Navy is not the best in the world, let's just put it that way.

First, I pay way too much money for the food in port that I barely eat. That's right, the daily not-so-great cuisine comes out of my paycheck. The Navy takes a little over three hundred dollars out of my measly seaman check every month to pay for my food consumption while on board. I can totally understand this expense underway when the food that is prepared on board is damn near the only food I have to eat, but when my ship is in its home port, do you think I eat on board? *Barely*.

On my duty days, when I have to stay on board overnight, I bring leftovers from home, order a pizza and have it delivered to my pier, or ask one of my friends to drop some food off for me. On a regular workday, I take my little lunch break elsewhere unless I am in a rush and need a quick bite – *then* I will eat on board. If not, you'll probably find me in my rack taking a nap for lunch.

I would prefer to have the option of paying for my meal *by* the meal. If I ate the food, I would be happy to pay for it, but I don't even have the choice! That three hundred is coming out of my paycheck whether I eat on board or not. No one wants to eat the shit we are served 90 percent of the time. It's barely real food.

It is extremely processed. Extremely bland. You can ask the junior sailors who have yet to acquire a place out in town and still live on board. Yes, they eat on board from time to time, but they also prefer to go out and eat too. Sheesh.

And I won't even blame the cooking on the culinary specialists because they can only make do with what they had. Of course, we have those CSs who cannot cook and should not have the rate of CS, but for those who can cook there's a limit to their creativity. Like any other rate, they, too, have policies, rules, and regulations that generalizes our food so that it is fit for consumption by all. I just want the world to know that the food here in the Navy is ~~trash~~ not the best in the world.

A Sailor's Relationship with Food
Gunners Mate Second Class Beverly Stroud
Twenty-five years old. White. Leo.

"A lot of people gain weight in the Navy, especially on deployments. I remember that, during my deployment, I would miss out on so much sleep, I was living off of candy or granola bar for breakfast, a whole container of coffee, and more candy. Deployment creates this weird relationship with food because once you're off of deployment you just want to eat anything you want because you are finally free to eat anything you want and not just what is available to you on a ship – and you definitely don't want to work or work out. You want to do nothing. And those three hundred dollars that is taken out of my check every month just for me to eat crunchy rice and soggy waffles three months into a deployment makes me really bitter."

Fed like Animals

Again guys, I don't think you hear me. But that's okay because, as always, I can elaborate.

The food while out to sea is one of the *few* perks of a sailor's day, something we look forward to. Food that is prepared and served to sailors on board a warship has the potential to either boost or lower a crew's morale. Sadly, most times the chow is a *huge* disappointment. We mentioned those soggy waffles earlier, right? Well, I've also had the pleasure of wringing out the occasional deployment omelet in my day, too. I know what you're thinking: *But how is that even possible?* And believe me, that is a great question.

Imagine you work on a farm with thousands of other farm hands. You live on this farm, and you perform manual labor for the farm's owners for twelve to twenty hours a day. Three times a day, the farm's indoor workers provide you with a square meal. This morning you had an avocado that was 85 percent browned, two hard boiled eggs, and a piece of ham that damn near resembled the consistency of a gummy worm. The eggs were the most decent of them all.

You didn't finish the ham because its texture really grossed you out so, you grabbed a cup of joe from the coffee stand on the farm and hoped that it would tie you over until lunch.

When lunch came around, you were excited to see that the indoor workers prepared corndogs, chicken breasts, and slices of pizza! And because of your close friends, who is one of the indoor workers, you were able to weasel one of everything onto your tray. The corn dog's breaded layer was burned and blackened all over, but you did your best to eat it by ripping off most of the burned areas.

To your surprise, the corndog was still very cold in the center. Once you moved on to the pizza, you were sad to discover that it was burned as well – to a crisp at that. It had the audacity to even break in half like a thick saltine cracker. The chicken, being the best option on your tray, had no seasoning at all. No salt, no pepper, hell...no paprika. It was just a plain, old, boiled breast. Blah. Nonetheless, you ripped it up and dipped it in ketchup anyway, finishing your lunch with a glass of the farm's weird tasting water and continuing with your work schedule.

Eventually, you hear the alarm notifying you that it is time for dinner. As you go to wash your hands you think, *I am starving! I really hope there is something good to eat for chow.* With optimism, you reach the chow line and stand behind the numerous farm hands that are ahead of you.

After patiently waiting for thirty-two minutes, you finally reach the top. You scan the dinner options and choose salmon, white rice, a vegetable medley, and a slice of cheesecake for your tray. Once you get to your seating area and dig in, you find that your salmon is raw in the very center. You're not a fan of raw fish so you move on to your rice and vegetable medley.

Since your rice was sticky and most of it crunchy, you end up slicing your serving of rice with your fork into bite sized pieces. Once one of the undercooked pieces of rice painfully becomes lodged between two of your teeth and causes your gum to bleed, you finally give up on the rice and the vegetable medley that tasted as if it were poured right out of a can and on to your tray. Even a dash of salt and pepper couldn't save your medley.

With your last shot at sustenance being your cheesecake, which was obviously store-bought, you dig in. Fortunately, the cheesecake was outstanding, and you are happy to end your day with at least one item that was easy to eat.

For the rest of the week, you encountered other entrees such as extremely dry, flavorless chicken wings, pita bread that housed spots of mold, overcooked corned beef, and an egg bake with surprise eggshells inside.

If you haven't gotten it by now guys, the ship is the farm but, unfortunately, the sailors are the animals.

Thick Thighs Save Lives

The physical fitness standards for women in the Navy are beyond absurd and, in my opinion, Europeanized. At no point does it take into consideration that the build of an African American woman is different. We carry much more weight in our hips, thighs, breasts, and ass than women from other cultures. We're naturally more toned, curvy, and muscular. But is that taken into consideration? Of course not. Here are a few random examples of the female height and weight standards in the Navy:

Height (inches) / Maximum Allowable Weight

'51 / 102

'53 / 110

'55 / 118

‘60 / 141
‘63 / 152
‘68 / 170
‘70 / 177
‘73 / 189

Now for me, my height checks in at 63 inches. I currently weight a little more than 170 pounds. I am not overweight, I am in great shape, and I wear a size small in shirts and a large size in pants. I am very active, and I maintain a healthy gym participation. But according to these standards, I need to lose weight because I am way too short to be packing so much weight. Well, my thick thighs, curvy hips, and slim waist would like to argue with that.

Europeanized Weight Standards
Logistics Specialist Third Class Laura Baxley
Twenty-eight years old. African American. Aries.

"There's a perception that, to be within standards, you have to be a certain size and hit certain scores for your physical readiness. That has been my biggest struggle since joining. My weight goes up and down. I've always been over my max weight for the standards. I've never been under because I have a bigger butt and hips and I carry weight there. Even after bootcamp when I was in the best shape of my life, I was still ten pounds over my max. The standards are definitely Europeanized and outdated to say the least."

Pearson's Journal

Petty Officer of the Watch

Three hours into my watch as the petty officer of the watch (POOW) and my back is already starting to hurt! I've got two more hours left of this watch, too, to make matters worse. This bulletproof vest is making my back sweat and I feel so gross. I know for a fact the person that had this vest on during the watch prior to mine was musty because this vest stinks!

Oh well. At least it's just POOW. I could have been roving – then I would have had to carry the M9 pistol on my hip and the M4 rifle across my chest on top of this vest. That stuff gets extremely heavy and uncomfortable after three to four hours. I need to stop complaining. But to be honest, the rover just told me that this watch is his only one for the day.

After this 1200-1700 POOW watch that I'm currently standing I have colors at 1748 because Seaman Timmy forgot his whites at home and another POOW from 0200-0700 in the morning!

Fuck! I think I could've dealt with the one rover versus my two watches and colors. My back is already starting to hurt.

Running Late

Being late for work when you're in the military hits differently. I don't care, I don't care. First, attempting to drive on any base during the morning rush while running behind is a different level of anxiety and road rage that I wouldn't wish on anyone! Second, when you're late to work in the military and you finally show up, it feels like you've been labeled *Dirt Bag of the Day*.

It's like your chief and LPO print out that label and tape it to your forehead to wear for the day. And okay, if you're always running late or show up late a few times a week, that's definitely shitty no matter what job you have. But in the military, try showing up late for work once because you simply didn't hear your alarm or were just having an off morning and you're a dirt bag. Period. Try crossing that quarterdeck late without being judged or feeling judged. It won't happen. It's like we're supposed to be robots! Like people in the military just cannot have an off morning! Gee, I am so sorry that I missed sweepers this morning. Whatever will the Navy do?

Care Packages

When deployed, you have three favorite days. First is the day you arrive back at home, of course. Second are the days that you hit a port visit, and third are the days when you receive mail! Mail days are like Christmas.

No matter how long it takes your mail to arrive, it is always a great day when it does. My mom had informed me of a package that she had shipped, and it took more than a month to reach me. My chip bags were all busted open and those that remained closed were all smashed. I had chocolate bars that were melted and hygiene products that were banged up.

Do you think I gave a damn? Do you think my stuff still got eaten and utilized? Hell no, I didn't care and hell yes it did! I'm sure I can speak for any deployed sailor waiting on mail.

But you know what sucks? When it is mail day and everyone around you receives mail, except you. You try and act like you are unbothered but really, you are. You want mail. You want new snacks. You're sick of the ship's food.

You want new soaps and new perfumes. You want the dumb stuff that your mom sends you that you've never used or eaten in your life, but you appreciate it because it's the thought that counts and somehow you end up using/eating it and liking it anyway! But you didn't get any mail, it will probably be another month before you do receive any. It's heartbreaking, but you take yourself to chow, just like every other day, and pretend to be okay.

Listen, if you're reading this book, and you know someone in the military who is currently deployed or about to deploy, *please* send them a care package because they are lonely and could use something to show that someone out there truly cares about their well-being. Not everyone will admit this because some people allow their pride to consume them, but are packages really are needed.

Send a box of popcorn, soap, hand sanitizer, a few candy bars, tampons and pads, perfume, lotion, and shampoo. Send them *something*. Go to the dollar store and pick up a few things for them. Send them one thing from a dollar store every two weeks if you can. I guarantee they will appreciate it. I promise that *we* appreciate it. This job is a tough job. Send someone you know a care package. Please.

Beer Day!

During my second deployment, we executed a beer day on board. Per instruction, when a ship underway has completed forty-five consecutive days out to sea without any port visits, that command is authorized a beer day! Each sailor on board, depending on their age and guidelines of whatever country that ship is in, can have two whole beers!

Now, this is what pissed me off: the day prior to our beer day, my division and I received countless briefs on how to act during a beer day, how we are not to consume more than two beers, the type of attire to wear during the beer day, the fact that we absolutely should not get beer just to give away or sell to friends, blah, blah, blah! Just give me my two fucking beers that I've been waiting forty-five days for and shut up! Geez!

Regular-Smegular Enlisted Folk

Most civilians love their military members. They treat us like kings and queens. Seriously! If you're in the military and haven't yet, go walk around the nearest downtown area or strip in your city and watch people stare at you, greet you, smile at you, salute you, and thank you for your service. I've gone into restaurants and gas stations before in uniform and I've had random civilians pay for my things, especially in those small towns who don't see military members often.

I remember the first time I came home to Mississippi after being away for a while, my mother wanted me to go with her to Walmart and, of course, with her being the proud Navy mom she is, she wanted me to wear my uniform. I did. Walking around the Walmart in my small hometown with my uniform on was like being a celebrity. We could barely shop because of the amount of people coming up to me, talking to me, and taking a picture with me – especially children. It was and always is a complete honor to receive such gratitude from civilians.

But in turn, to not receive that gratitude or to be treated like shit – like a regular-smegular person while actually at work on board my ship or within my squadron is so frustrating sometimes! Why can't we enlisted folk love and appreciate ourselves the way that civilians love and appreciate us? Why don't we treat each other as respectfully as we treat officers? Why don't we greet each other with the same hesitance as we would an officer? I get it. We aren't necessarily your average war heroes. Most of us, in the area and environments that I've worked in, barely know how to use the guns we carry and have definitely never had to use them before. Most of us are doing regular-smegular work – painting, serving food, paperwork, cleaning, or just being a security guard all day.

What is the point of us regular enlisted treating other regular enlisted like kings and queens, right? That's what we do for the officers. Our job is to simply do our job, under their instruction, and go home, right? It's hard to see how great you and your sacrifices are when the people around you, the people you work for, and the organization you work for have paved a path for you that is built to make you feel like a regular-smegular motherfucker. And when everyone around you feels like they are just regular-smegular, they treat their peers the same way. Ask a master chief what the difference between him and a lieutenant is. Ask him why. And ask him if he believes that master chiefs should or should not receive the same treatment as an officer in the Navy. I just want to see how this goes.

Starbucks for You but not for All

Yes, it is true, Starbucks is offered to sailors on board carriers. So yes, if you are deployed on a small boy like a destroyer for example, you do not have this luxury, it is not fair, and it is unreasonable. When I shipped out for six months on my first deployment on the destroyer, at any point in that deployment I would have fainted in happiness over the offering of a nice hot cup of Starbucks coffee.

The luxury of having that flavorful coffee could have boosted my morale on several occasions. But that was not an option of us – more than 300 – serving on board that ship during that deployment. I didn't know that it was an option at all for deployed sailors in the Navy until a little more two years later when I deployed upon my first carrier and stumbled on the coffee shop that was serving a menu listing of Starbucks coffee with numerous flavors out of Starbucks cups! Although I faithfully purchased a nice cup of SB joe during my deployment with the carrier, I always kept my anger and pity for the other sailors in our strike group who were serving upon their small boys who weren't afforded such a luxury at the forefront of my mind.

We Need More, More, and More! And no, We Are not Asking for Too Much!

If I am required to stay out to sea for three to nine months at a time, continuously extended, given curfews in port, forced to migrate in a group, restricted on where I can and cannot go in port, and live on board a ship that runs out of supplies every so often during these periods of time, here are a few of the things I'm going to require in order to consider ever reenlisting again:

1. We need an enlisted lounge on board with charging stations for our devices – and I'm not talking about the small, poorly furnished twenty-something-year-old lounges we already have within some of our berthings either. I mean a specific space loaded with couches, recliners, several big screens, Xboxes/PlayStations set up with a snack area.
2. In the snack area we need a bakery section that has cookies, pastries, cakes, and pies for our delight. I wouldn't even mind if they were on sale.

3. We also need several vending machines strictly for healthy snacks, a sandwich bar, soda machines, snack machines, and a minibar. Yes, I said it! A minibar! See, the problem with America's military is the closed mindedness. You can create rules and regulations for these luxuries to minimize risks of course, like certain hours, drink limits, age limits, or whatever would make the instruction feel better.
4. We need a mini spa, too, because I need a facial while out to sea. Being exposed to all this dirt, grime, sea salt, fumes, oil, etc., is terrible on my skin. I need a manicure and pedicure while out to sea every once in a while. I need to be able to get my hair done – like, *done*, done and no, not a bullshit trim. I need a protein treatment with my trim.
5. We also need a masseuse. Since I have to sleep in a metal rectangle fitted with a mattress that is smaller than a twin-sized mattress, hard as a rock, and overused by multiple people, go to work, work, and stand watch for more than twelve hours, go to sleep, and wake up to do it all again, I'm going to need the option to schedule myself a massage! The masseuse could even work in medical. Having us out to sea for half to almost whole years of our lives is strenuous, stressful, and hard enough on its own. We are away from life as we know it, our families, and our services – phone service to be exact. And what's crazy to me is this passage is going to be looked at as if I'm asking for too much when really, I'm not! The sacrifices I endure voluntarily to serve and protect my country deserve this treatment while out to sea. Yes, it does. I deserve luxury treatment, especially when off duty – no matter my rate and rank in the military.
6. Oh, and by the way, we don't want to be the ones providing these services for ourselves onboard either. Bring our beloved civilians in the picture. Contract civilians for these jobs. If you can bring them on board for the ride to grant us services such as counseling, fitness training, and printer troubleshooting *and* give them better treatment than your own enlisted members, you can hire them to treat, cater, and serve us at a higher standard as well.

7. We need more pay phones to make outside line phone calls on board.
8. We need every single head on every single ship in the Navy to be remodeled.
9. We need male, female, and unisex gyms on board our ships.
10. We need to do away with the restricted internet access. The restrictions dictating which websites we can visit are extremely irritating and demeaning. Only sites that are inappropriate should be blocked. People have bills to pay on websites that may be unheard of. We do have lives that do require internet use. We are adults. Do not restrict our internet freedom while underway.
11. Seamen need to make more money! THE LOWER THE RANK, THE HARDER THE WORK! Guaranteed. The lower the rank, the higher the danger exposure. Let's not ignore the fact that we waste money on things in the military that are way less understandable than the ones mentioned above. I need a better quality of life while out to sea. Period. It's ridiculous. And it didn't take me twenty years of service to realize it either. It's inhumane. Am I a slave or am I a sailor?

Look in the Mirror, Sailors!

Honestly, all generations and especially the new generation of the Navy has to take a hard look in the mirror. Why don't we have these luxuries out to sea that I speak of? Why do we have these relentless boundaries and regulations when at home or a foreign port? Why is the treatment of enlisted personnel so belittling? Why this? Why that? Why, why, why? The answer to most of those questions is because we are spoiled rotten, ungrateful, and disrespectful people.

Yep.

And the military is scared to relax most of its standards due to our entitled attitudes. They are scared that we simply will not be operational with added luxury. Have you guys ever heard of the saying, "Give them an inch and they will take a mile?" Yeah, that's us taking the extra mile. Here's an example: Remember my rant about the beer day we had on my second deployment after being out to sea for forty-five consecutive days? Here's what I didn't mention: there were some sailors on board that day who were acting like complete asses with their two beers. They were literally just showing out and acting belligerent like they had never consumed alcohol once in their lives or like they'd had zero home training.

You're probably thinking, *Well, this is what happens when you give sailors only two damn beers every forty-five days.* Sure, that may be the case for some. But for others it was the classic, I-know-three-people-who-don't-drink-so-I-asked-them-ahead-of-time-to-give-me-their-beer type of thing that was going down that had people on board drunk!

Some people just don't know how to act! They have no respect. None. We are proudly selfish and entitled. If we had some respect for simple shit like the instructions to ONLY CONSUME TWO BEERS, we'd probably have better treatment. And to be even more honest, most of us – I said most, not all – who join the military these days are not the most patriotic.

Let's keep it all the way real. We're in it for the B-E-N-E-F-I-T-S! Oh yeah. Join the military to pay for your college. Join the military and get insurance and health care provided by the government. Join the military and get guaranteed pay even when the government shuts down or the world suddenly closes due to a virus.

Well, yippie-kye-yay, sign me up! With that being said, who actually wants to die for this? Right? We're here to collect our checks and benefits and go the hell to the house every day.

Is it really our fault, though? What can you expect from an organization that broadcasts its benefits, uses them as recruiting tools, and continues to remind us of what we would lose if we left? I'll tell you: you can expect to be given those benefits, for sure, but also expect to be worked until you either break a bone or lose your shit.

Expect to sign that dotted line and enter a world unlike any other with rules, regulations, restrictions, and punishments that no one ever told you about. Expect to be used more than a bicycle in New York City!

Expect to go through hell, hot water, around the world in thirty days, and ungodly amounts of paperwork just to exercise the use of most of your benefits. Know that when you get stationed on a boat that's about to go out to sea, you might as well forget about returning home at the estimated date. Just wave goodbye to your loved ones and expect nothing else after that. Expect to hate this shit most of the time. Expect to consider, reconsider, and then consider again, the option you have to either get the hell out or reenlist.

And speaking of the large number of benefits and efforts offered to the young, potential service women and men by recruiters, there's this new way of recruiting that the Navy is now trying in the form of online/digital recruiting. They utilize video games and the internet to reach out to potential bait, I mean, sailors. How cute.

Anything to push more people in because of their expectation that people will get out. "Let's just trick 'em and talk 'em into it! We have contracts that are damn near impossible to get out of, that way although they might leave eventually, we can still use them for every and anything we may need as much as we need to while we have them!" says Big Navy.

Why in the world would we want to risk our lives for an organization that treats us as such? We don't! At this point, it's a never-ending cycle of *treat us better and we would act better* versus *act better, and we would treat you guys better*!

Now, how in the hell do we fix this?

Coming to a Realization
Logistics Specialist Third Class Laura Baxley
Twenty-eight years old. African American. Aries.

"What I've realized is all of the things that I like about the Navy isn't the Navy itself, it's extra shit. It's not 'I love being in the Navy because it's a great organization!' No, it's, 'I love being in the Navy because of the health care.' It shouldn't be like that. I should thoroughly love what I do for the country. If it wasn't for some of these benefits I probably wouldn't want to be in the Navy."

PART IX

THANK YOU, NAVY!

Although I may naturally have negative opinions toward the Navy, I would be biased if I did not acknowledge the magnificent services, expediencies, and benefits offered to me because I joined. The Navy changed my life for the better. This organization has been a significant contribution to my growth as an African American woman and the growth of several others in a way that we could never repay.

We can only thank the United States Navy.

25

WHAT A BEAUTIFUL DECISION

Damn it feels good to have guaranteed pay twice a month! And on top of that, the Navy is the only reason I would have moved to Norfolk, Virginia. I don't care what anyone says, I love that place and I really enjoyed Virginia. I mean c'mon – beaches on beaches within a few minutes of a drive.

I loved my little apartment that was close to nautical scenery and beautiful murals in the cities of Norfolk and Virginia Beach. Richmond, Virginia made me fall more and more in love with being a Black woman with its many Black-owned businesses, Black entrepreneurs, and artists. Thanks to the Navy, this little, country Black girl from Mississippi was sent to the East Coast!

I took myself to New York, a place that has forever inspired my views on fashion and expression, and to Washington, DC, where I had some of the best strip club experiences ever and said *hello* to The National Museum of African American History and Culture. What a life-changing experience visiting that museum was. I was introduced to Baltimore, Maryland. The cultural experience there was outstanding as well. That state produces the best crab cakes in America, hands down!

As aggravating as it is, joining the Navy introduced me to so many things that I had been missing out on culturally. I don't know where I would be today if I did not join.

Big Girl Moves, Big Girl Purchases

I bought myself a car!

All on my own, I made a big girl investment with *no* cosigner. I can freely afford this investment, too, as in I can pay my car note on time, sometimes early, put money in my savings, and go out with my friends if I want.

Three years ago, I did not have a credit history and I was still driving my 2002 Nissan Altima that did not have working heat or air conditioning. That car did not have door handles on the outside either. Although that car was my baby, I still had no idea how, when, or where I would be able to upgrade my car. But here I am with a new Nissan Maxima and a great credit score because I made the decision to join the Navy.

Health Care and Dental

I make a dental, doctor, eye, or really any kind of appointment I want and it's free. Okay, not free. I pay for my insurance monthly but it's so cheap that I never miss it or notice it taken out of my paycheck. I remember when I was a civilian, after I was too old to be covered under my parents' insurance, going to a doctor of any kind became very rare for me because it was too expensive.

Now I make appointments just because. I own six pairs of glasses, including a prescription pair of shades. I schedule myself STD exams once every three months, too. Why? Because I can! Why not? Any time I consider getting out of the Navy I wonder, *What the hell am I going to do for insurance?*

Completely Taken Care Of
Parachute Rigger Second Class Nyomi Ellis
Thirty-five years old. African American. Pisces.

"If it wasn't for the Navy, I probably wouldn't have had kids. I had a lot of reproductive issues and infertility problems. I had to have several surgeries and the Navy took care of it all. I appreciate the Navy for that. I have friends back home that are still trying to save up for the same surgeries with insurance. But as for me, the Navy referred me to a doctor out in town and took care of me."

Who's in the Most Pain?
Boatswain Mate Second Class Tushanna Brown
Thirty-four years old. African American. Gemini.

"When I was coming up, there were things that my family endured with medical and dental. My mom would ask us, 'Who's in the most pain?' and that'd be the one going to the dentist. I don't have to worry about that with my daughter. I can take her to the ER whenever she needs to go. I don't have to worry about not having insurance like my parents did."

Broke Dreams

I treated my family to vacation because I could afford it! I saved up for it and spoiled the shit out of them! My mom, my dad, and my brother all came up to Virginia for the Fourth of July. That year it was on a Thursday, so if you didn't have duty, you were off from Thursday through Sunday. In the Navy, we call that having a 96.

Guess who got lucky and had the entire 96 off?

That's right, me!

My mom, dad, and brother arrived in Norfolk on that Thursday evening to start the mini-vacation that my mom had obsessed over making a reality for six months, which was the last time I'd seen my family in person. Excitement was written all over their faces upon their arrival. I was anxious and ecstatic, too. It felt like we hadn't seen each other in years.

We were all ecstatic about our reunion! Being with my family felt like we were right at home. I immediately took them to see the fireworks in downtown Norfolk on their first night, and we took many wonderful pictures.

After the show, we walked around downtown for a little while. Since my family and I are some small-town country folk from Mississippi, the big cities were a rare visit for us during my childhood, so I really enjoyed watching my family people watch and absorb the hustle and the bustle of downtown Norfolk on a holiday night.

The rest of their three-and-a-half-day vacation included me taking them to Captain George's Seafood restaurant, one of the biggest seafood buffets on the East Coast, taking them to the Naval Exchange because the one in Norfolk is like a mall and my mother just *had* to go, taking them on a three-hour tour on The Spirit of Norfolk mini cruise boat that sailed them around the outskirts of Norfolk and Virginia Beach, treating my mother to a mani-pedi day, introducing my dad and brother to various styles of sushi, and even taking them all to Virginia Beach. That weekend was amazing for not only my family but for me, too.

"Look at where the Navy brought me, mom and dad! Isn't it cool here?"

"Beautiful right?"

"Big and busy, huh?"

"Let me show you guys the base!"

"Do you guys like all these big ships?"

"Can you see all of the ammo they hold?"

"Look, look! There's my ship right there!"

"Big, I know."

I gave my family a wonderful experience and I paid for it all. All they needed was the gas to get there and the gas to get home. I have a *career* now, and a *nice* car now. My family stayed in my apartment that I pay for. I'm doing big things! This is a version of my life that I was able to show my family and let them experience as well. These are moments I dreamt about when I was broke.

For the Family

One day I walked in on a senior chief mentoring some junior sailors. This senior chief was a logistics specialist, an LSCS. When I walked in, he asked me, "Hey LS3, you were undesignated right?"

I responded, "Yes Senior, I was."

He inquired, "How bad was it?"

I chuckled, "Terrible, Senior."

He turned back to the sailors that he was mentoring. "See what I mean," he continued, "You get no sleep, and sometimes when you try and sleep, or eat, or shower, it gets interrupted because of flight quarters. You have to man the boat deck. That life is terrible. When I made LS, I said nothing could ever hurt me because now I can shine."

He described his journey into the LS rate, discussing how he made every rank his first time up because he was dedicated and studied hard for his exams. He eventually ended up on the topic of how great the Navy is. Usually, I'd tune out anyone who believes the Navy is the best job in the world, but this day I was interested in what he had to say. It sparked my interest because I was really baffled that he was undesignated for more than twelve years and his situation was extremely similar to mine. He described his life in the civilian world prior to joining.

As an Asian American with a language barrier, it was tough for him to find steady work and move up in the chain in a work force.

"The last company I worked for," he explained, "I worked there for five years. I worked *hard*. I worked for ten dollars an hour for forty or more hours a week. It was past time for my raise and every time I asked about it, I would just get the run around with no good explanations because it wasn't my work ethic! It was hard to support a family of five and pay bills with that pay and those hours."

He then started his description of life after joining the Navy, saying that the Navy paid for his speech courses, provided him and his family with health care benefits, and all he had to do was perform well, study, and make rank to make more money, which is what he did. He loved it! This is where he belonged. No longer did he struggle to improve his lifestyle in the civilian world despite his amazing work ethic. In the Navy, it was inevitable. Hard work paid off.

I understood his opinion, and I did not disagree with it. Thinking about most working-class families, the circumstances are difficult at times. The fact of the matter is that in the Navy, if you perform well, follow orders, study, and rank up, life gets easier for you. No matter what rank you are, your family always has guaranteed benefits, even if you are underway or pass away.

You do not have to worry about being able to provide for your family. It is a guarantee in the military. Shit, it's a gig! I respect the parents and the people who do this specifically for their families.

A Proud Family = Instant Motivation
Parachute Rigger Second Class Nyomi Ellis
Thirty-five years old. African American. Pisces.

"The main thing that makes me excited about being in the Navy is my family. They are so proud of me. Being from Africa, a third world country, that is the main thing that makes me proud – my family. Because of them, I'm able to deal with everything I have to deal with in the Navy. They keep my motivation high."

The Navy Has My Back

It'd been an easy day because it was Sunday, holiday routine, and I only had one watch. I was sure I only had one watch because the first class who wrote our watch bill had a crush on me and was being 'nice' to get my attention, but he could keep dreaming because I was not interested. With that being said, I was having a smooth duty day up until I received an unexpected phone call from my mom with sudden news.

My mother explained that for the past few days she had been monitoring my dad's big toe on his left foot because he had stepped on a nail at work, but it didn't seem to be healing properly. He finally went to the doctor to have it looked at. By that evening, which was when I received the call from my mom, my dad had been admitted into the hospital because his toe was infected almost to the point of gangrene and that he needed an emergency amputation the following morning at 0800. She then told me that his doctor suggested that the immediate family should be there because with his level of diabetes mixed with an amputation, things could go left fast.

I was in complete shock. It was Sunday! How the hell was I supposed to get a flight for the next day, that late? Also, the money! This was going to hurt my credit card something serious. Although I was in a panic and stressed, I followed the Navy's emergency protocol. I had the hospital send a Red Cross alert to my command after my dad was admitted. I then quickly explained my situation to my section leader and command duty officer (CDO) who were more than willing to help me and cover my watch that I had later.

They assisted me in ordering my plane ticket through the Navy and Red Cross; all expenses were temporarily paid for by the Navy. I applied for fourteen days of leave, two whole weeks, taken on a whim and my CDO approved it on the spot. I was on the next thing smoking to Mississippi! I arrived at 0600. My dad's surgery was a success, and he was expected to make a full recovery! Did you know that even though I needed to take this amount of leave, unplanned, the Navy still paid me on the first and the fifteenth while on leave?

I was okay guys.

I needed to be somewhere, and the Navy got me there.

The Navy had my back.

Deployment Perks

Oddly, I look forward to deploying. It is during deployment that I get into great shape. Seriously, with the slow internet, if any, and the inability to use my cell phone, I have nothing better to do than either work out or do other beneficial activities. Even if a person does not work out, I guarantee they will be stair stepping the hell out of some ladder wells several times a day.

Your body is in so much motion for so much of your day that you really cannot help but drop a few pounds. And if you're actually trying then trust me, on deployment, it will happen. Personally, I make it happen so that when I come home, I can feel amazing about myself in my civilian clothes and live my best, healthy, and fit life. Deployment has its perks. Not many, but it has some.

Travel
Airframer Third Class Tyler Vickers
Twenty-five years old. African American. Aries.

"What I love about being in the Navy is having the opportunity to travel to the countries I've traveled to. The fact that I lived in Japan for three years..."

Rare Sightings

I'm not even going to front like I haven't seen some cool shit in the Navy. On my very first deployment we ported in Duqm, Oman. Now, there isn't much in good ole Duqm but at least I can brag about setting foot there and interacting with the Omani people, who are extremely pleasant. I tried shawarma and hummus, both for the first time, in Oman.

These dishes originate in the Middle East, and I've had the pleasure of trying them authentically. We also ported in Egypt on my first deployment. Yes, I said *Egypt.* You're probably thinking the same thing that I was thinking when we got there.

Now this is the type of shit I joined the Navy for! I remember what the sea looked like in this area.

It was like a blanket of velvet, flawlessly floating below our ship. I toured Cairo, and I saw the Sphinx of Giza! I laid hands on a pyramid that was so tall, it was uncomfortable for my neck when I looked up at it. It was mesmerizing. It was mind blowing to think about the man-made history behind it and the fact that it was still standing. I rode a camel in Egypt, you guys. I still can't believe it myself, but it happened.

Our last port visit was in Rota, Spain. I fell in love with that culture! It is so bright, beautiful, and lively. I only wish I would have had more time to explore Spain but from what I was able to tour, the culture was captivating, the food was mouthwatering, the people were welcoming and friendly, the women were beautiful, and the beach was perfect! I can't *even* with that place – just wonderful.

Can we all just take a moment to talk about and appreciate the sky when out to sea? I have been blessed to see some of the most breathtaking scenery at sea. The most beautiful sunset I've seen was in the middle of the Atlantic Ocean. It seemed like the sun didn't even want to go down because it recognized how beautiful it was in that moment. It lasted for what seemed like forever and I watched the entire, stunning thing.

The stars out to sea – there's nothing like a starry night underway. Miles . . . there are stars for miles, as far as the eye can see there are stars. I am certain that I have spotted the Big Dipper on more than one occasion.

There are jelly fish that light up the sea at night. The luminescence of these jelly fish is a rarity for some, but I've had the pleasure of witnessing it more than once in the Middle Eastern seas. It is absolutely breathtaking. You'll think you're dreaming. A picture couldn't possibly do this site any justice. You'd just have to sail the seas to see it yourself.

Blood, Sweat, and Tears
Personnel Specialist Second Class Dominique Lucas
Twenty-four years old. African American. Gemini.

"On my first deployment we went through Morocco and Spain. Morocco was on one side of the ship and Spain was on the other. That was the most beautiful moment. My friends and I stood out on the flight deck and just admired it . . . This was the motherland! We couldn't believe it! This was the first country we had seen. It was a beautiful experience. It's the traveling that we might pay for in blood, sweat, and tears; but we do travel. It's worth it. I've been to Africa three times."

The Open Sea
Aviation Structural Mechanic Safety Equipment Third Class Karissa McCormick
Twenty-seven years old. White. Scorpio.

"Deployment sucks, don't get me wrong, but you'll never get a sunrise or a sunset like you get on a deployment and out in the open sea anywhere else though."

Sea Story
By: Gunners Mate Second Class Beverly Stroud
Twenty-five years old. White. Leo.

We were underway. I was on the bridge while on lookout duty. It was around 0500. I was excited because I was about to be relieved and I was about to be relieved by Pearson, my best friend. We would always talk for a while after she relieved me. I was drinking shitty coffee out of my sparkly Beauty and the Beast mug, watching the sunrise over Africa, and all I could think was, *the mountains are purple*. That's when it hit me. I had this sense of, I'm right where I'm supposed to be right now. I'm with the right people. Yes, my life is shitty right now, I get no sleep, I work all the time, but it's for me and it's what I do. This is a choice I made for myself. It was a moment like that, that made me believe joining the Navy was the right choice.

Sea Story
By: Aviation Structural Mechanic Safety Equipment Third Class Karissa McCormick
Twenty-seven years old. White. Scorpio.

The first time I ever got to be on a naval carrier, my senior chief took me up to the flight deck and let me stand there. He grabbed me and said, "You're going to love this, just wait."

I got to watch a tanker take off. A tanker is an F18 with four drop tanks and an ARS pod. I've never in my life felt prouder than in that moment. It was really weird because people always told me, "You're going to get tired of the flight deck. You're going to get really tired of seeing this happen – seeing jets and helos recover."

I was just standing up there looking at this, and I started shaking and doing a little dance because I was so happy. "You good?" My senior chief asked me.

"You don't understand how breathtaking it is to know that this is something I get to do for a living," I responded.

I loved being on the flight deck during flight ops at nighttime when all you see are stars or the sunset or the sunrise. It was something that not a lot of people in life get to say they did. It was the first step for me to say I love the Navy. I loved watching that. I felt like I was fighting for something when I was up there. That moment made me proud to be an American and to be in the Navy.

That's my greatest Sea Story.

The Choice Is Yours

Each deployment I've been on has changed me. When I calculated the time that I had spent out to sea before I hit my three-year mark in the Navy, it placed me at a few months beyond a year! I had been out to sea for more than a year in less than three years! My first deployment was strenuous and rough on me as an undesignated seaman. I *hated* the Navy for what it put me through on that deployment. I realized that a career in the Navy was not for me, which is okay.

My first deployment inspired my desire to be an entrepreneur. I did a vast amount of research while underway on how to start a business, acquire LLCs, and more, and when we made it home and my feet hit the ground, I took off running! I took college courses, worked a second job, and modeled on the side while still working from 0700 until anywhere from 1630 to 1730 five days a week with my 24-hour duty day once a week in the Navy.

All of this hustle helped me pick up extra cash that I could use to invest in the businesses I was starting for myself. I learned so much about myself during that first deployment and I discovered my high and intense resilience level. All these discoveries contributed to my grind outside of the Navy and have continued to benefit me to this day.

My second deployment wasn't as physically demanding as the first. By then, I had picked up the rate and rank of logistics specialist, petty officer third class. It was, however, mentally challenging. When I heard that I was about to deploy again, I started dreading it immediately. For me, it was like I was going back to jail. Mentally, I was struggling to even get out of my rack most days on that deployment. I was miserable and depressed, but I knew that I had to find a way to make it through.

I discovered a love for meditation on deployment. Learning how to become centered became a valuable tool that I still use to this day. I became more mindful and very aware of my mentality. This for me was the most beautiful discovery of my lifetime. I drowned myself in books.

Knowledge is power and my self-education plus meditation was tremendously helpful in my life inside and outside of the Navy. I truly believe that becoming more mindful led to the making of this book, which has aligned me with the growth that I needed and one of my purposes in life!

It's all about how you use the deployment, how you *use* and not just spend your time, that is going to be important. You can come out of it better or you can come out of it worse. The choice is yours.

It's one of the few choices that not even the Navy can take from you.

Why Be Bothered When You Can Be Unbothered?
Retail Service Specialist First Class Kimberly Fleming
Thirty-three years old. West Indian. Capricorn.

"I think in this moment, I just realized how much I've changed in the Navy. If you had asked me what I love about the Navy four years ago, I would have told you I hate everything about it. But now, the Navy doesn't bother me. The Navy only starts bothering you when you start taking things and making them personal. When you see something that's not going to change and you still let it bother you, it's like, why? It's not going to change. You either conform to it or you do your part to make it work for you. There's no need to be frustrated."

Nothing But Respect

On one particular day when I was relaxing in my berthing lounge a Black, female first class – a woman that I am very fond of – approached me with news.

"Guess what," she stated with a smile.

"What?" I asked excitedly, picking up on her infectious smile and contagious energy.

"I made board!" she replied in a squeal.

My heart and my mouth dropped at the same time in a good way! I was thrilled for her! *Thrilled!* It was the first time that I had witnessed a first class's immediate reaction after receiving the news that they made board for chief petty officer.

I was so happy for her that I felt like I had made the damn board. Now look at me, always talking crap about these higher ranks. But it's different when it's someone you know personally. It hits differently when you witness the struggle and sacrifice of someone until they make it.

It hits differently when it's a Black woman.

She made it.

She achieved her dream.

She achieved her goal.

She made board, and I had nothing but respect to give.

The Storm
Gunner's Mate Second Class Beverly Stroud
Twenty-five years old. White. Leo.

"I'm happy I joined the Navy, but I don't thank the Navy. Anything good that has happened to me, I've done. The Navy didn't give me any of this, and I think that's where people fuck up. People start to think that they need to stay in because they don't know where they would be or what they would do without the Navy. Yeah, I got my car, I've pushed through, I'm going to college, and I have all the funds, but the Navy only opened doors for me. I'm still the one that walked through and started making decisions. You don't thank the storm for you weathering through it. You value it."

26

GRATITUDE

"Before joining, I was really stuck on the idea of not wanting to do the same routine every day. Here, every day it's something new. I love how spontaneous each day can be. Good or bad."

–LSSN Roxsana Herrera

"I love the relationships that you build here. I've never been one to get close to people in my past life, but in this life, my Navy life, I've made so many friends that I could not see my life without."

–MASN Alexandria Smith

"First of all, all of the people you meet – and I know that everyone says that but it's really true! That is one of the most important things being in the military. You guys are all here going through the same thing. The people that you meet are so important. I've met lifelong friends here."

–LSSN Katie Tillinghast

"I'm twenty-seven years old and a third class in the Navy. Low on the totem pole, yes, but I know I'm going to make my way up to the top. I'm not worried about ever changing my opinion of loving the Navy. I have nothing but respect for the people that are willing to raise their hand and serve this country. I love America so, hell yeah, guns and shit!"

–AME3 Karissa McCormick

"I love that I am financially stable for the first time in my life. I love most of the people that I've met and the friends that I've made along the way. I met my husband in the Navy, so I love the Navy for that."

–AM3 Sarah Adame

"I love the people. The people that I never would have met if I didn't join. It's the bonds that you create with these people that are suffering alongside you that will last a lifetime."

–GM2 Beverly Stroud

"It's the relationships and friendships that I have created. I have more friends in the Navy than I do back home. These people will be family forever. We are here for each other. All we have are each other. Those bonds are forever and to me, there is nothing like the bonds that you create while you're stationed on your first ship."

–PS2 Dominique Lucas

"I love that we can all share a memory at the same time. Like right now, it's five thousand of us on this ship and we are all experiencing the same life moments at the same time even though we might all see it differently. You become bound by helping one another through life experiences like heartbreak, losing loved ones, having children, getting married, getting divorced, personal growth, and different milestones in life. It's the unpredictable and life changing stuff that binds you all forever. I love that part."

–NC1 Elon McDuell-Briscoe

"I personally love being able to be there for sailors that don't recognize they actually need someone to be there for them. I am a mother so I suppose it's only natural that I look at my sailors as my babies and, in the end, if I can be the one person that leaves them with something good to remember or a goal they never considered possible, I have done my job. I love motivating people, that's just me."

–AZ1 Janelle Delgado

"I feel like being in the Navy and meeting new people is it! I don't really have too many sea stories, but I've got mother figures, brothers, and sisters. Not many of them either. I could probably count them all on one hand, but through the struggle and through the pain, they are always there.

"Yeah, you've got people back home that you're close to, but here it's a different feeling. If I dropped today and I lost everything, I know that the people I've met in the Navy are who I would call on. Because of that, I'm going to keep doing this shit, twenty years without a doubt. At the end of the day, this is all I know. I may wake up every day and complain, gripe, and moan but this is what I want to do."

–CS1 Skyler Gregory

NOTES

23. Someone Help

1. Status of Forces Agreements (SOFAs), generally establish the framework under which U.S. military personnel operate in a foreign country

ABOUT THE PUBLISHER

TACTICAL 16

Tactical 16 Publishing is an unconventional publisher that understands the therapeutic value inherent in writing. We help veterans, first responders, and their families and friends to tell their stories using their words.

We are on a mission to capture the history of America's heroes: stories about sacrifices during chaos, humor amid tragedy, and victories learned from experiences not readily recreated—*real stories from real people.*

Tactical16 has published books in leadership, business, fiction, and children's genres. We produce all types of works, from self-help to memoirs that preserve unique stories not yet told.

You don't have to be a polished author to join our ranks. If you can write with passion and be unapologetic, we want to talk. Go to Tactical16.com to contact us and to learn more.

CPSIA information can be obtained
at www.ICGtesting.com
Printed in the USA
BVHW041408280422
635622BV00017B/645